(Ramblings)
About Music
And The Mind

The author lives in Newent, Gloucestershire, UK.
He is a composer and music director of the Newent Orchestra.

Other titles by the same author:

The Final Score
Violin, Instrument of the Devil

(Ramblings)
About Music
And the Mind

Bill Anderton

Dedication

I wrote this book for Annie and Emily
and dedicate it to all my family.

Positive Aspect Books

First published in Great Britain in 2019 by
Positive Aspect Books.
Bill Anderton Music
www.billanderton.uk
Copyright © Bill Anderton, 2019, 2022

The right of Bill Anderton to be identified as the author
of this work has been asserted by him in accordance
with the Copyright, Designs and Patents Act, 1988

A catalogue record for this book is available from the British Library

ISBN 978-1-873763-03-2

All rights reserved. No part of this publication may be reproduced, transmitted, or stored in a retrieval system, in any form or by any means, without permission in writing from the publisher.

CONTENTS

Pre-ramble 6

1. What Is Music? 13

2. From Pythagoras to Dr Who 36

3. Discovering Harmony 63

4. One Man's Music 81

5. A Musical Disaster 100

6. Making Waves 120

7. Myth and Music 137

8. The Musical Cosmos 154

9. Philosophers on Music 173

10. Between the Ears 190

11. The Shape of Music 208

12. Romance and Revolution 225

13. Contemporary Sounds 243

14. Reprise, What Will Music Be? 262

15. The Spirit of Music 271

About Music

PRE-RAMBLE

This book examines many facets of music, its history, its effect on us as individuals, fundamental questions about its existence and its form – how music is put together. The aim is to consider the building blocks and create an understanding of what music is all about, the art and science of music making.

The art is the creative side, composition and performance, while the science is the physics, acoustics, physiology and, ultimately, what happens in our brains when we listen to music. In my role as author, I am in the fortunate position of having experience of all these components - as a composer, a musician and, originally in my career, with an involvement in acoustics and sound reproduction.

It's well documented how music can affect our mood, can be therapeutic, helping stimulate memory and a sense of well-being. Much is also made today of how valuable music is as part of a complete education as it involves team work and cooperation, as well as the need to develop individual skills and knowledge. Involvement in music develops the individual as a well-rounded human being, for music, like language, is an integral part of what it means to be human. It has direct value for the individual as well as being part of our communal cultural heritage.

Each subject that I've covered could be the topic of a book in itself, but I've kept them all concise and to the point, so that together they illuminate how music works its magic on us and how we are affected emotionally and physically.

And it is magic! When those musical sounds travel through the air from instrument to ear, they are no more than pulses of varying pressure waves, but once they have been transmitted to the inner workings of the brain, we experience the full impact and significance of music. So, what is going on? That is the subject of this book and is what I think of as the spirit of music.

Music in the past has meant something quite different than it does today. To discover what the spirit of music is and how it has changed and what it means to listeners, musicians and composers, my quest eventually took on the form of a spirit-of-music journey which goes from the beginnings of the western music tradition in

About Music

classical antiquity to the present day. I was setting off with no illusions about discovering anything new, but putting together different facets of music in new combinations held out the prospect of revealing where the future of music might lie.

The division between the art and the science of music making only became clear in the 18th century's Age of Enlightenment. This project was an opportunity to explore their relationship anew, to walk their borderlands, perhaps even to marry the two together again. To achieve this and as a backdrop to the whole process of gathering and sorting information, I came up with the idea of a series of walks along which there would be an uninterrupted opportunity to speculate and think about music.

These walks took place along Offa's Dyke, saturated with its own history and whose official path runs the entire course of the border between Wales and England. Walking a physical border designed to separate two countries appealed to me as a metaphor for exploring musical borderlands. Along these walks, we talk music and learn about its inner life. Each chapter's musical topic is related to one of the walks and together they make up the whole of the border path. Walking and music, I discovered, go well together.

The first walk, however, was not along Offa's Dyke but was an experimental pre-ramble to see how it all might work. I enticed my friend and musician, Chris, to accompany me, knowing that his own love of music would add much to any discussions. He was keen and we soon arranged to meet up for a trial session, walking through the countryside around our home town of Newent in Gloucestershire.

May Hill, a few miles away from Newent, is a landmark seen for miles around and clearly visible in any direction from which it is approached. From the clump of trees at its summit is a view over the Severn valley towards Bristol and Chepstow where the official Offa's Dyke Path begins. We wanted to look down on that vista and contemplate what the path would represent, so we put on our boots and scarves and began to walk on a chilly but dry day in March.

Our first encounter was with an acquaintance of Chris who greeted him as we were setting off. His friend, Chris explained to me as we walked on, was a propagator of the diminutive wild daffodil. Once, this flower was ubiquitous but there are only three main areas in the country remaining where these tiny heralds of spring are still

About Music

to be found: the Lake District of Wordsworth fame, Farndale in the North Yorkshire moors and the woods and fields around Newent. Mid to late March is the ideal time to see them.

About half a mile out of Newent we can turn off the road, along the back of a gypsy encampment and immediately join a section of renovated canal. Then after this, at Oxenhall, we walk back onto a country lane for a while until turning off into Hay Wood with its mixture of deciduous and evergreen trees.

There are notable similarities between listening to music and walking. Here are some thoughts about walking: you don't need to know anything about walking to appreciate and enjoy it; not all of it has to be enjoyable and this can depend on how you feel at a particular time; the view, the landscape, is infinitely variable; walking in silence is good; walking while chatting is good; you can't go on for too long without a rest; a walk has a beginning and a destination and you might become lost along the way; walking has a rhythm which can become meditative, a mind-cleansing exercise; although you may plan a walk carefully and take maps with you, you never know what will happen along the way or what you will discover – there is always something unexpected; walks can be long, short, quick or slow; usually other walkers have been there before you; occasionally you may discover a new pathway; the same path can appear quite different each time you walk it, depending on weather conditions and time of year; the effort is always worth it.

Almost anything you can say about walking can be said of music, too. For 'walking', substitute 'music'. You get the idea.

We pass a swathe of the tiny wild daffodils at a spot near Dymock woods called Gwen and Vera's Fields and Chris is reminded of an encounter that he had there once before. He recounts looking at the daffodils and commenting to two other walkers that these prolific flowers were a testament to insecticide-free propagation. The two walkers were farmers with no such green credentials and who were less than friendly in response.

One of the similarities between walking and music, 'you don't need to know anything about it to appreciate and enjoy it' does not mean that learning about it is not rewarding. On the contrary, learning about what you are seeing (or hearing) can be satisfying for its own sake. In addition, spotting and knowing that a bird is a

About Music

kestrel, a flower is a toadflax, a particular tree is a larch, can increase your appreciation and ability to spot and distinguish new things. Likewise with music, knowing that a piece is by Bach won't necessarily magnify your enjoyment but it will give you clues about what it is representing and how it is doing this. The way is then opened to a deepening of the experience.

Having a map about music is just as important for travelling along a musical journey as it is for walking without getting lost. That's what this book is – the cartography of music.

As we continue, it occurs to me that the hedgerows are going to be an ever-present feature of our walks. They can be ancient and mark not only the edge of fields and property but the wayside of old paths and trackways. Chris explains to me a rough-and-ready method for working out the age of a hedgerow.

1. Measure out a 30-metre stretch.
2. Count the number of varieties of trees and shrubs present.
3. If there are three species, your hedge may be 300 years old. If there are seven, it could be 700 years old.

This method is not always reliable as some new hedges are planted with many species. Always try to choose a hedge which is away from houses or roads if you use this ready reckoner.

We walk for the next mile or so accompanied by the rhythm and crunch of our footsteps, mindful of our thoughts and aware of the sounds of birdsong and a gentle breeze rustling occasionally in the trees, making wind music. Chris breaks the spell of this meditative, inwardly-focused progress.

"That's a big ask, to explore the spirit of music. How are you going to do it?"

This is the nub of it all – how? The walk helps to clarify my thoughts and ideas and for the first time I feel able to give at least a summary answer. It was this. Without knowing how all the bits would work together, I intended to provide an eclectic mix of topics about the history of music, how music's philosophers and practitioners have used music to express the workings of the universe; how music developed and fits together, its harmony and its form; how the physics of music explains how sound is made and transmitted; how the brain interprets this information and converts it into music; ultimately, why and how music affects us.

This is therefore a melting pot, an alchemical mix about creating, listening and responding to music. The ingredients will be described within a historical context sprinkled with philosophical ideas and the way physics and neuro-science describe what is going on when we perceive music. That's the mix. What the result of blending all these elements will be, I can't say. We'll see.

An image comes to mind while we walk of a musical timeline. A timeline is usually depicted as straight, going from past, to present, to future, but I see it as a circle. If I imagine positioning myself at its centre, I can pick and choose a particular historical time and discover what it has to offer. In this way, all the previous history of music, all the different styles and forms that have developed, can be viewed not as belonging to times gone by, but as ever-present parts of a complete picture built up and surrounding us in the here and now.

With this approach, Beethoven, for example, is as relevant today as in his own time and context. I can be as concerned with Pythagoras's contribution to making music - which was considerable - as with current digital technology. Old and new lie equidistant from the centre of my circular musical timeline.

Each of the walks along the Dyke path is linked with a musical topic and with a chapter of the book. We'll be delving into the overlaps between music theory and creativity, acoustics, mechanics, human biology and their context in social history up to and including the digital age. These are huge subjects in their own right, so it is ridiculous to attempt to encompass them. That is not the intention. What brings the project back into the realms of the possible and the do-able is exploring not the whole of each subject territory but the borderlands between them.

One way in which the art versus science gap may be expressed is between those who know about music, who are versed in its esoteric jargon of cadences, codas, sonata forms and suspensions, and those who love listening to and playing music, know what they love, but don't know why and don't understand the jargon. My work – and this book - has been directed at narrowing this gap and simplifying quite complex topics in music, to make them accessible, understandable and relevant to anyone, in the knowledge that this can be done. Music and maths were once closely associated. For example, the three main areas of university study during the medieval period were music, mathematics and also astronomy; art and science have fruitful areas at their mutual borderline and walking the Dyke has become a symbol for this.

The border lies between objectivity and imaginative 'inner' experience. The imagination plays a significant role in the making and perception of music. The value of the imagination was described by the psychologist C.G. Jung in the early part of the last century with his rigorous study of dreams and the mystical, dream-like symbols recorded by medieval alchemy, full of dragons, weird birds and animals, suns and moons, kings and queens. Surprisingly, the archetypal scientist, Isaac Newton, spent much of his research time looking into this very subject. Newton and Jung respectively worked at the borders of science and the imagination, the results of which went into their own melting pots with amazing results, one exploring and explaining the outer universe, the other revealing the inner. The borderland between these two is where we will be treading.

In writing the manuscript my initial intention was to write a seamless continuity flowing from describing the walk to talking about the music but to ensure that the reader is also prepared a little in advance for what is coming in the text and to overcome any disorienting changes of direction and subject, I took good advice to indicate clearly where these transitions were taking place. Hence, the reader will find a small, hopefully unobtrusive, visual device to indicate the changes from the outer walking journey to the inner musical exploration. This you will discover is suggested by:

 = outer travel   = inner musical journey

We've been walking for nearly two hours and find ourselves back alongside the canal and viewing a glistening small lake, beside the Oxenhall canal. There are Canada geese and a couple of swans floating effortlessly on the calm water. Chris talks to me about his own background and an education in engineering, social studies and popular culture, especially films. He has come to classical music

About Music

relatively late in life but is keen to make progress in learning about it. This is promising as he will be receptive to new ideas and able to let me know when mine don't make sense. He comments aptly that walking tends to bring people out of themselves and to encourage talking openly about thoughts and beliefs tucked away in private recesses of the mind.

Finally, we fall silent. We're walking through woods and onto a road that for the next two or three miles is a steady climb. We walk through the village of Cliffords Mesne and onto May Hill common. This is the steepest part of our journey and we stop a couple of times to catch our breath. There are wild daffodils here too and everywhere the trees and bushes are budding. Wild flowers are dotted around like stars in a green sky. Usually, there is one particular flower that seems to dominate in the spring depending on the weather conditions of the winter before. This year it's the turn of the bright yellow buttercup-style faces of the Lesser Celandine. They are everywhere.

We are out in the open on the last uphill stretch and heading to the trees that mark the summit of May Hill. We arrive and find a bench from which to admire the view and share some food and drink. There it is in front of us – the snaking, shimmering River Severn, its estuary leading in the dim, blue distance to the beginning of the Dyke path from where our quest will begin...

The return walk downhill and into Newent is uneventful, but still full of chatting and intermittent meditative silence. Just before we arrive back, I point out a silver birch tree, not a fully grown specimen but one whose bark is gleaming, bright silver. Silver is the alchemical metal represented by the moon, itself an ancient symbol of the unknown, renewal and rebirth. The birch tree's pagan and old Celtic associations provide an apt moment on which to begin our quest for the spirit of music.

Bill, at home again, stretched out on the sofa

About Music

CHAPTER 1

What Is Music?

In which we make a map and begin a journey

At the precise moment that I begin writing this first chapter, I receive an unsolicited email, '500 Mb of Brand New Samples and Loops – high quality, hand-picked drum loops, audio samples and other noises suitable for electronic music-making.' Imagine a composer from the pre-digital age reading such an advertisement. It wouldn't have made any sense at all, least of all 'noises for music making', a comment which would have evoked a certain sense of vertiginous nausea in any sensitive musical ear.

Everything to do with music has changed in just a few short years, the way it is written, the way it is performed, the way it is reproduced and the way we listen and hear. The rate of change in all areas of life let alone music has become a helter-skelter. This is the inescapable reality in an era of digital technology and post-postmodernism.

Everyone's world is coloured by this unnatural rate of change, is pressured by it. Making time and space to take stock is a necessary antidote for anyone caught up in this maelstrom and the race to go nowhere. My way to achieve peace of mind, to unwind and relax, is to walk.

Close to my early home in North Yorkshire lived the walker and author, John Hillaby. I was inspired by his Land's-End-to-John-o'Groats trek, his reflective books and especially his discovery that walking helped him to deal with a personal life crisis. Walking can cure many ills. So can music. To think, chat and meditate on music and to begin comparing contemporary music making with past eras would, it seemed to me, be a great excuse for spending some quality time rambling through the hills and fields of some spectacularly beautiful countryside.

To our modern way of thinking there is a technical aspect to music making, for example, in the science of acoustics and the way that sound waves are transmitted from instrument to ear. There are many other examples of the science of music which seem to have little to do with its soul and spirit.

It also seems generally accepted that musical creativity is an art form, a means of creative self-expression, whether perpetrated by a composer, a conductor or instrumentalist. It is in the art, not the science, where the soul and spirit of music are supposed to reside. It was not always so. We are setting off now to explore all this, both past and present. The journey began almost immediately to reveal some unexpected insights into the nature of music.

A border is a man-made creation. This is clearly the case when you consider what we mean by the border between the science and the art of music. On one side lies the measurable and technological. On the other is imaginative, creative expression. 'Mand-made' is also a fact of physical borders between areas of land or countries which are drawn up to suit political and economic forces. Different countries lie on each side of a border. A landscape border may be clearly defined and marked by sign posts, dotted lines on maps, customs posts and other various markers.

More often than not the way-markers are widely spaced so that it is possible to stray across a border without any idea that you have done so. One side may look and feel just like the other. So, to travel along a border needs a compass and a route map, the basic tools for finding one's way. A physical border seemed to me to be a great metaphor for exploring such an idea as the borderlands between the art and science of music. This is the reason why this whole 'walking meditation on music' or 'ramblings about music' came into being.

King Offa of Mercia and overlord of much of England constructed a linear earthwork in the late 8th century to mark out the western border of his kingdom. That century is central in the period of Anglo-Saxon rule in Britain and during this century the various Anglo-Saxon kingdoms became the foundation of what we now know as England. In the previous 7th century, the country had been Christianised and Mercia, to the east of Wales, became for a time the greatest of the Anglo-Saxon kingdoms, both in terms of its power and its size. Offa was recognised as the king of the English – recognised by both the Pope and the Emperor Charlemagne, who had united most of Western Europe for the first time since the collapse of

About Music

the Roman Empire. The Anglo-Saxon period ends with the Norman conquests led by William the Conqueror.

Offa's great earthwork is the longest in Britain and forms the backbone of the Offa's Dyke national trail along the Welsh/English border. Much of the dyke has disappeared but surprisingly much also remains, clearly visible as we see along the first musical expedition from Sedbury Cliffs, near Chepstow, to Monmouth. Monmouth's town centre lies about fifteen miles west of my home town and is the closest point of the dyke to home.

The dyke is most peculiar. When viewing this long earthen mound, it seems on the one hand to be quite inconsequential and unobtrusive, but the fact of its existence, its historical significance and its great length soon stir the imagination to the perception that medieval history is preserved and visible in the landscape. The effect on witnessing the earthwork is to have a sense of time travel. One does not visit the dyke, as you would a site of historical interest; one walks along it, an act of pilgrimage that evokes the ghostly sensation of times long past.

The dyke is physical evidence of a border that is at the same time both an idea and a visible functional object. My aim was to walk the full length, about 280 km, in sections, over the summer months. Each walk was to be linked with a particular musical topic and in between each I would record both the musical musings and the experience of the walk itself.

One Sunday morning in early May, my companion, Chris and I were taken by car to about 500 metres from the starting point of the dyke and we nervously covered on foot the remaining stretch– which we would retrace – to its beginning. The view from the starting point takes in the Severn Estuary, engine room of the famous tidal surge, the Severn bore. Visible in the distant reaches of this vista are two suspension bridges, the Severn Bridge and the Severn-Wye Peace Bridge, dedicated to world peace in 1991 by Sri Chinmoy.

The estuary view contrasts dramatically with the initial couple of miles of the walk. These will be nondescript, a stroll through housing estates until we will walk in the clear and away up

About Music

the River Wye valley. The walk to come will be characterised by woodland with occasional exceptions to limited views. In complete contrast is the estuary's panoramic view. Before us, it stretches into the distance as far as the eye can see in Turner-esque pastel early-morning colours.

Turning to face away from the river, we are funnelled into the first few steps of a walk in search of the spirit of music that will take a summer time and more than 270 kilometres to complete.

Unexpected spring sunshine and dry weather today are a relief, so we can relax, get used to each other's walking pace and navigate our way to the path proper. This early stage through the streets of Sedbury needs careful navigation. Once on the way we discover that our map may be useful for confirming particular locations, but the Sedbury to Monmouth walk is clearly signed, gates are well kept and the path maintained, so map reading is minimal.

This all adds up to create the right conditions for talking about music without fear of stumbling or going astray and we are soon doing just that while enjoying the fresh green vegetation and birdsong all around. This first walk is a substantial 28 kilometres end to end, so, walkers beware, take plenty of your favourite picnic food and drink and don't go quickly or you will run out of steam too soon.

I ask Chris what he thinks music is, what makes music music. It's a deceptively simple question and he ponders briefly before tentatively suggesting that for most people a piece of music will have something recognisably rhythmic and melodic. It should make some sense to the listener. In other words, it will have a certain recognisable organisation to it, and have boundaries that define it and hold it all together, rather like a picture frame.

Most music lovers generally don't want to be challenged by their music but want to be pleased, soothed or excited, want to be entertained. Contrasted with this is the fact that contemporary music in particular can be disorganised, even chaotic and may not be designed with audience pleasure in mind. This is potentially where our first musical borderland tension lies and between these two views resides an area which may prove fruitful for us to consider. The borderlands are unclear at this stage so a little exploration of this may be worthwhile.

A couple of weeks previously, as part of the preparation for these ramblings I was on a trip visiting my childhood home in the north east of England. During this visit, I walked through the sprawling industrial town of Middlesbrough and visited their famous transporter bridge.

Along this route, I detoured to see an exhibition at Teesside's modern art gallery, the Middlesbrough Institute of Modern Art, MIMA. The exhibition was called, 'Art and Optimism in 1950s Britain' and featured works by both internationally known and local artists. Everything on view there spoke of the 1950s. Some pieces were descriptive and representational, some were abstract, art produced for its own sake with no particular reference to real events or subjects but clearly rooted firmly in its time. The experience was, for me, informative, nostalgic and thought provoking.

While wandering around looking at the paintings, I mused about the music that was being made in the '50s, post war. The big band era was coming to an end; American rock 'n' roll was being imported into the UK and then home grown. Extreme forms of experimental, abstract music were being created on the continent, which, in contrast with the popular artworks on view at MIMA, had audiences running a mile.

Continuing on my walk that day, I reached a desolate industrial wasteland by the River Tees and the iconic transporter bridge exploited today by Middlesbrough town as its emblem, signifying moving forward into the future. A giant piece of blue Meccano, the bridge stands as a testament more to the past than the future, when Teesside and much of the north east of England were dedicated to the production of iron and steel. Not much room in that landscape for the intellectual niceties of contemporary music, except perhaps the popular styles that could allow an escape from the harsh realities of life.

Further along from the bridge, I stood like one of L.S. Lowry's matchstick men in front of a sculpture almost as big as the football stadium that forms its backdrop. Designed by Anish Kapur and called 'Temenos', which translates from Latin as protected sacred ground, this sweeping structure bends space. It makes the

About Music

observer aware of the cosmic possibilities that lie within something as mundane as metalwork, the same possibilities which inhabit the rarefied realms of music; it depicts the music of the spheres, the sounds that ancient philosophers imagined emanating from the celestial bodies as they swing rhythmically around their orbits, the sound here on earth, frozen in metal. The sculpture suggests melody and rhythm, written and performed in steel.

Nearby, a graffiti poem sprayed on a brick wall, declaims:

Where alchemists were born below Cleveland Hills,
A giant blue dragonfly across the Tees reminds us every night,
We built the world,
Every metropolis came from Ironopolis.

Now, back on our Offa's Dyke trail, I suggest to Chris that a definition of music that would fit his first attempt might be, 'The art of arranging sounds in time to produce a unified composition with melody and rhythm.' This is not original but is a summary from a more complete definition I checked later: 'The art of arranging sounds in time so as to produce a continuous, unified, and evocative composition, as through melody, harmony, rhythm, and timbre.' Put more directly, music can be thought of as sculpting with sound.

Here's another attempt: 'Vocal or instrumental sounds (or both) combined in such a way as to produce beauty of form, harmony, and expression of emotion.' And here is one from mathematician, Leibniz, who lived in the late 17th century at the same time as J.S. Bach: 'The hidden arithmetical exercise of a soul unconscious that it is calculating.' (Wow!) This introduces the idea of a mathematical element in music, that music should contain pattern and process.

Would these definitions cover all the wildly and widely differing forms of music that coexist today? Perhaps in Bach's time they would have sufficed, but not anymore. The 1970s music of Captain Beefheart was certainly rhythmic, but was it the creation of a mathematical brain unconsciously calculating? Anti-music hero Frank Zappa pulled apart any notions of music as beauty of form, harmony and expression of emotion. He also inspired a notorious toilet-themed poster, whose image was on my t-shirt worn for the day. Chris and I were going to have to do better than this in defining music, especially in the light of composer John Cage's famous assertion that all sound can become the basis for music. This is becoming tricky.

It may be helpful here to define what sound and noise are. The Oxford English Dictionary says that sound is a sensation caused by the ear by the vibration of the surrounding air or other medium. That is straightforward enough. Noise, it says, is a sound, especially a loud or unpleasant or undesired one.

Listeners to classical music will know that noise, as defined here, is not a permitted ingredient, but those with an ear for contemporary music will appreciate that unpleasant sounds *can* be used expressively, Noise may be a significant component of such music, if it is a vehicle for expressing, for example, something disturbing or painful.

So far, we have been walking through pleasant woodland, along the side of roads with little traffic and climbing steadily but unconcerned by effort until, unannounced, we arrive at a spectacular view point and see the River Wye far below us, winding itself adder-like into the distance. This is the famous Wintour's Leap, where Sir John Wintour is said to have plunged with his horse over the 200-ft cliffs to escape his pursuers during the Civil War. What a way to go.

We take a breath and remark how brightly green is all the tree and plant foliage. This freshness only lasts for a week or two in the spring around the point when all of nature leaps forth fully armed and budded, ready to career forth into the summer at a pace that will match Wintour's own thundering charge over the cliff top.

The definitions of music we've come up with are outdated and there are some other questions to answer before a better attempt can be made, especially as classical and contemporary music are built on different foundations. Is there something other worldly or mystical about music? Can music create altered states of perception, or the possibility of experiencing these? How is music the language of us all? What is music's place in a rational, scientific culture? What is the value of music? All these deserve some thought before any fresh attempt at defining what music may be...

Chris chats to me about his past. I knew that he had been a keen rower but didn't realise how dedicated and successful, becoming a veteran British then World four-crew champion at his peak. We talk about another of his passions, film and how this medium has played a role in music since its inception. Soundtracks helped to build an audience for contemporary composers, surreptitiously accustoming the listener's ear to new and often atmospheric music, accustoming it to the previously unheard-of concept that music might include noise and the 'unpleasant'. A notable example of exposure via film is the soundtrack music for the 2002 film, *The Hours,* starring Nicole Kidman, Meryl Streep and Julianne Moore. The original score was composed by the most influential of contemporary composers, Philip Glass. Another of the iconic composers of the early 20th century was Arnold Schoenberg, who in the 1920s deconstructed the tonal system of western music but whose own compositions never achieved the luxury of exposure in film.

The inner ear and eye are connected in our imaginations. When listening to music it is easy to close one's eyes and call forth images evoked by the music. Indeed, some programmatic music is written specifically to achieve this. Also, although much contemporary music may seem to be difficult, abstract and disconnected from the listener's experience, a way of finding a way in to appreciating it can be by allowing inner images to unfold in the mind's eye as the music plays.

Today, live performances of both operatic productions and rock concerts make full use of film and the freedom of creativity brought to the medium by digital technology. I mention as we walk a recent production of Mozart's 'Don Giovanni' in which, typically, images are projected onto performers and the stage-set to create illusions of different times and spaces.

The technique enables easy suspension of disbelief and transportation, in this case, to the world of Mozart's 18th-century opera but with all the 21st-century technology and style of this modern production seamlessly enmeshed. In more ways than one, the visual media and music are close to each other.

About Music

In music, as in film, the computer has become a ubiquitous presence. It has influenced and radically altered what music is all about. How has it done this? Without their computers, contemporary composers would not be able to make significant new music with any depth and flexibility. Composition software speeds up the process by automation, for example, in cutting and pasting just like any word processor, while allowing the composer to hear the results instantly.

Using software is a highly flexible and efficient application of the 'old' way of getting music onto paper. The advantages are: speed of note entry, the ability to erase, cut and paste, ease of turning repetitive tasks into single key strokes and instant playback. The process puts at the composer's fingertips the ability to create music scores and, if there are multiple instrument parts, to set these up individually, to extract them and then print ready for performance.

This is still 'writing music' in the old-fashioned sense but now the artist can be not just a composer, but an editor and a publisher, too.

The software can all but write the music and this is a complaint levelled at it. It has the potential to create a dehumanised form of music making, removing the art from the creative process. My experience has been to the contrary. The software gives a freedom to focus on creativity without the distractions and difficulties of getting the notes down 'on paper'.

My music software can apply a selection of instrumental sounds, so I can hear, roughly, what a violin or an oboe would sound like when playing a line of music. I can instantly change instruments or instrumental combinations to hear the effect that this has. One useful little gizmo works when I hold a couple of particular keys down, hovering the cursor, now shown on screen in the form of an ear icon, over any note or chord. I can then hear that note/chord as a continuous sound. This gives the ability to hear a sequence of notes not at the music's set tempo but controlled by the speed that I move the ear-cursor from one note to the next. Composers can thus not only hear their music instantly but can play around with all the variables until achieving the desired sound and effect.

Music can be written using digitally sampled sounds, recordings of different sounds, converted into digital files. This is how the library of instruments that I mentioned is created. Mini digital music files, the sound samples, encompassing all the different timbres that are likely to be required are kept in a library and then joined up by the software to create realistic instrumental sounds. These mini files are also used by the composer to make a piece of music.

This method of composing is something new and was unheard of before my lifetime. It began when tape recording became possible and when 'music concrete' incorporated chunks of what we now call 'found sound' into music, that is, sounds that are not necessarily made by conventional instruments.

It is usual for periods of musical history to be approximately dated and the 1950s is generally accepted as the beginning of what we now call the period of contemporary music. Computerisation and digitisation subsequently took all the laborious time-consuming aspects of sound synthesis out of the equation and put in the hands of the musician and the composer a powerful new tool.

Technicians knew how to analyse timbre-full sound waves into their component parts, into simple sine waves, then put them back together to create the original sound and even create new sounds. This analysis and synthesis of sound waves led to a full understanding of how sound qualities are created and thus how to synthesise the sound of an instrument, or any characteristic sound for that matter. Developing in the 1950s, the sound synthesiser revolutionised music production and music production was never the same again.

'Sequencing' is the term for joining together building bricks made of sound, each sample being akin to an acoustic Lego brick. A composer can today record and feed his own sounds or music fragments into his Digital Work Station (DAW) and manipulate the result exactly as a sound engineer would in a recording studio.

The DAW hasn't superseded the 'old' way of writing down the notes but is the way of music today and into the future. So, with a DAW and some music composition software, all for the price of a couple of weekend rock festival tickets, I can be composer, editor, sound engineer, publisher and even performer with my synthesised sounds.

About Music

The internet and social media have become ways of making, distributing and promoting contemporary music and open up the field for any individual to express themselves and make their mark. Internet-based music production is thus breaking down any elitist barriers that have been keeping classical music production hi-brow and only for the privileged.

To appreciate new music and new types of music, it is necessary to have a certain amount of familiarity. A problem in the early days of contemporary music was that with unappreciative, small audiences and few concerts, there were scant opportunities to hear new music, but the internet, podcasts and streaming are changing this. Contemporary musicians have at last been offered a means to combat the image of their music as obscure and inaccessible.

There are remnants of the dyke visible as we walk. Along this stretch they can easily be missed by the untrained eye, but reveal themselves as soon as looked for. Sometimes the dyke is just a grassy bank, other times it marks field boundaries and has a hedge atop.

The dyke is not the only presence. There are other visible themes emerging along our walk. There is a sea of bluebells surrounding us, their colour a unique and perfect hue. These flowers will be constant companions today, as will be the green-leaf freshness of the trees and undergrowth which glows with an intense inner light. The tiny, spiky, white, wild-garlic flowers have just emerged, too. Their characteristic smell is not yet strong, but there is a hint of it in the air. Neither Chris nor I is yet experiencing any sign of fatigue but we come upon a spot that calls out for us to stay a while and enjoy the view.

A low stone wall next to the path is an ideal place to sit and eat our first picnic and take on board some liquid to replace the sweat lost over the last couple of hours. We are at the Devil's Pulpit and wherever the Devil may be, you can guarantee that close by is his adversary.

Spread out before us is a view over the Wye valley and positioning itself at the focal point of this vista is Tintern Abbey.

About Music

William Wordsworth first visited Tintern in 1793 and returned five years later, when he wrote the poem 'Lines Composed a Few Miles above Tintern Abbey', saying that "no poem of mine was composed under circumstances more pleasant for me to remember than this". Chris and I joke that the view over this area of 'outstanding natural beauty' is extraordinarily, spectacularly, indescribably, exhilaratingly pleasant. Our sandwiches and brownie cakes could be described thus in equal measure.

Tintern Abbey was the second Cistercian foundation in Britain and the first in Wales. The present-day remains are a mixture of building works covering a 400-year period between 1131 and 1536. A major two-year programme of conservation work has been completed on the iconic 13th-century west front, one of the great glories of Gothic architecture in Britain. On September 3, 1536, Abbot Wyche surrendered Tintern Abbey to King Henry VIII's officials and ended a way of life which had lasted 400 years.

The Europe-wide Protestant Reformation, said begun in 1517 with the publication of Martin Luther's work *The Ninety-Five Theses*, wrought its restrictive effects on music which in England suffered badly from Henry VIII's wanton destruction of Catholic institutions, the power houses for much of music's creative endeavours of the period.

The dissolution of the monasteries had a cataclysmic effect on music making as they were places where serious music was taught, written down and performed. In these environments music was not intended as frivolous entertainment but to remind the practitioners of their spirituality and spiritual goals, and to glorify God.

It wasn't only Henry who contributed to this malaise in English music for even before Luther the Cistercians campaigned against anything unnecessary or ornamental that had found its way into the chansons of monkish worship. They criticised shrills, frills and trills, which were dismissed as meaningless, distracting and vain.

In the fourteenth century it is reported that an English Cistercian, John Anglicus, debated the legitimacy of choir monks sucking lozenges to improve their singing of the Divine Office. The lozenges were presumably used to oil the vocal cords and enable hitting the high notes, totally unnecessary musical frivolity in the eyes and ears of John Anglicus. Or maybe it was the sound of sucking that spoilt the mood which he was condemning.

Even after this early stretch of our journey our thoughts have been ranging wide from digital sound synthesis to Cistercian liturgical monkery. We are only just starting on our musical pilgrimage, but already some borderland themes are emerging between the old and the new, between the artistic, spiritual nature of musical expression and some pragmatism.

I take a couple of photos and we pack our bags. This is an important moment. How will our leg muscles respond after allowing them to relax and rest? We need not have worried as we soon resume our pace and rhythmic groove. Lesson number one, E may $= mc^2$ according to Einstein, but for us food + drink = energy.

Just in front of us are two walkers striding side by side with their heavy backpacks, the first packers that we have encountered today. We walk behind them for a while and I am aware that our chatterings might be disturbing their concentration and walking meditations. I suggest to Chris that we overtake them and as we do, he asks if they are walking the whole of the Offa's Dyke path. They are going all the way and are happy to chat for a few moments. The woman is from Cardiff, the man from Bedford and Chris explains that they may well get a glimpse of Cardiff Bay when high on the ridges of the Black Mountains to the south west of Hay on Wye. We wish them well and leave them behind – we can rest tomorrow; they will have another long walk ahead.

Shortly after this, we spontaneously stop for a few moments to admire silently a red admiral butterfly and glimpse a couple of swallows, welcome visitors just returned to us for the summer. Brambles are growing everywhere to the side, but our path is clear.

Music is a route to self-discovery and can be a pathway of personal growth, but the belief that listening to the 'right' music can make you a better person, somehow more intelligent or culturally developed, is at best arguable and at worst counter-productive. Nevertheless, there are elements of self-improvement inherent in music, for example, learning to play as part of a team; learning the discipline of practice and testing one's limits; becoming aware of the cultural heritage that makes us what we are. But from the perspective of making and listening to music, music as self-improving is not the most significant result. The realisation of one's full potential as a multi-dimensional human being is. We discover ourselves through music by giving it meaning and significance. These may prove to be factors in defining what music is.

We chat about contemporary music and the prejudices that have endlessly been levelled against it as discordant and difficult. Much of the history of harmony in music concerns what combinations of notes are acceptable to the ear, what chordal structures and sequences sound well and which do not. In this theory, there are combinations of tones that are defined as unsuitable or dissonant. What constitutes good and bad harmony changes through time and circumstance but what is generally not recognised is that the use of dissonance in music became more and more common in the classical music of the nineteenth century. This was well before Richard Strauss at the end of the nineteenth century and Schoenberg in the early twentieth, who are blamed most for this blow to musical sensibilities.

The storm that hit music in the early twentieth century had been gathering for some considerable time, expressed eventually with greatest force in the Italian art movement called the Futurists. This influential Italian avant-garde art movement of the second and third twentieth-century decades sought to destroy older forms of culture and to demonstrate the beauty of modern life, characterised in their eyes by the beauty of the machine, speed, violence and change. Their attitude of struggle, aggression and destruction was summarised in the manifesto, a 'Music of Noise'. This has tainted our view of contemporary music making ever since.

Any twentieth-century history of western music makes much of racial prejudice and this, too, has unconsciously tainted our view. There was a trend during the *fin de siècle* that music should be kept pure and that certain elements had been creeping in that corrupted this purity. The end-of-the-century literary and artistic climate was of sophistication, escapism, aestheticism, world-weariness, and fashionable despair. Composers, such as Schoenberg, were attempting to stop this decadent rot, but did not foresee a philosophy that opened the way for a racist view that became endemic. How could this happen?

Some musical languages were deemed healthy while others were degenerate. Unacceptable impurity in art was a step away from the notion that racial impurity was to be eradicated. This is too simple a précis but makes the point that we have unwittingly received from that era a sense there might be something impure in contemporary music. There are more straightforward reasons, too, as our ear finds dissonance physically discomfiting.

I describe to Chris some music I recently enjoyed by composer Jonathan Harvey, who died in 2012. The particular pieces were 'Body Mandala' and 'Speakings' both of which seemed to me easily accessible, despite being in the vein of no melody, no clear rhythmic consistency. I can testify that, rather like one's first gulp of whisky, which may have a nauseous taste, with repeated experience an appreciation and desire for more grows.

Chris stops to check the map for we have reached a point where there is a choice of two viable paths. One takes us uphill and through the village of Brockweir. The other descends to the River Wye and follows its course. Even though the latter route is a little longer, we decide to take it. This path will be easier to navigate and our musical thoughts are flowing now and a route uninterrupted by map reading and negotiating the complexities of gated pastureland at this stage will be welcome. We descend to the river and walk along by fields and into woods again, pausing to take another couple of photographs for the record.

We chat more about the relationship between the visual arts and music. Abstract art is a representation of the artist's idea or experience of a subject. The subject can be anything that the artist has in mind, a mood, an emotion, a visual effect, etc. An abstraction is a thing in itself, contrasted with a 'figurative' artwork, which will depict something concrete, such as a scene, a portrait or a still life, etc.

About Music

Music is an abstract art and always has been. There are moments when it tries to be figurative, for example in the expressionist music of Debussy and Schoenberg, or in the tone poems of Richard Strauss, or Beethoven's Pastoral symphony, but unlike art and its representations of nature and the natural, music is in essence purely abstract. It is only able to take on the mantle of figurative when accompanied by a descriptive title or programme note which literally describes to the listener what it is all about.

The seeds of abstract art were sown in the 19th century with the art-movements Romanticism, Impressionism and Expressionism. The departure from being figurative can be slight, partial, or complete. Abstraction exists along a continuum. In the early 20th century, Henri Matisse, with his expressive use of colour and his free and imaginative drawing came close to pure abstraction.

When art that was totally abstract came into being, it was a shock to the viewer and took some getting used to. It was about abandoning the security of map and compass. We may develop personal views about what we like and what we don't like, but generally speaking, modern art galleries are now populated with visitors who have no difficulty with and enjoy the experience of abstract art on which a high value is placed. The risk taken of getting lost proved fruitful.

As listeners have been appreciating the abstraction of music since it first began, there must be something else which they find distressing and makes them run from a Harvey or a Stockhausen but pay homage to, and large sums of money for, a Kandinsky, a Matisse or a Klee.

Modern abstract art has more to do with shapes and patterns than purpose and the same applies to contemporary music. Sound textures and rhythm patterns are made for their own sake yet illuminate something deeper. This suggests a kinship with oriental, spiritual philosophies as Zen and the Tao where an object, the painting, the music, is what it is in itself. It does not represent or point to anything 'other' that might exist already in our world, like the painting of a bowl of fruit.

If the word 'spiritual' means being aware of something outside every-day experience that has relevance to life, then there is a

About Music

Zen-like philosophy at work here such that something that is abstract, like music, points the way and illuminates a spiritual reality.

Abstraction in art does not mean cut off from reality, or cold and unfeeling. The panoramic cut outs of Henri Matisse affect the viewer directly. When you expose yourself to them, you do not choose to respond, you respond as if to a force of gravity which is quite unquestionably there. Likewise with music, to expose oneself and be open to it is all that is required. Abstract art does not refer us to something in the physical world but to a deeper, for want of a better word, spiritual reality. This is music's essence, its gravitational force.

One reason for the relative ease in enjoying and appreciating modern visual art forms could be that abstraction was developed by increasing degrees. Even in the most abstract of Matisse's work, made during the early 1950s at the time represented by the MIMA exhibition, there is still a hint of representation of familiar objects. Music, in contrast, is and always has been a purely abstract art, despite visually evocative titles, such as *The Lark Ascending,* or *The Sea.*

Looking for meaning in music is not the way to listen. There is nothing to get, nothing to understand, nothing to decode. Listening requires not a sharp mind but a receptive one. What is of value in the music must be sought out; it is not self-evident and it is not a thing or an answer. So, again, why is it that contemporary music can be so difficult to listen to – still after all this time?

In classical music composition, a sense of home is created by the key in which a piece is written, particularly in which a piece is begun. The music will then take the listener away from home and by means of introducing new themes and keys give a sense of going somewhere, a journey which usually, classically, ends where it began, back in the recognisable home key, in familiar territory.

Contemporary music is no longer necessarily a journey from A to B and then safely back home to A again. The journey may end up at C; it may even never leave home. Indeed 'home' may not be the starting point or be anywhere to be found. Removing the sense of a familiar home and the sense of journey in a piece of music can turn it into a shifting, restless and textured soundscape. This is unsettling to a listener who likes to know where they are and where they are going. Safety and security are basic human needs. Philip Glass describes music not as a language but as a place to go to.

We arrive at Bigsweir. About four hours have gone by since we set off so we feel that a rest and some refreshment is overdue. We walk amongst the village buildings and Chris points out a Moravian Chapel. The Moravian Church is a protestant denomination, whose foundation began in 1457 in Kunwald, Bohemia. The church places a high premium on Christian unity, personal piety, missions and music.

Bigsweir is a pretty, sleepy village but was once a hive of industry, boat building in particular, with a landing stage that would take 90-tonne vessels at the River Wye's highest tidal point. Ships would dock here and transfer their cargoes to shallow barges which were then hauled up river by teams of men, before distribution throughout the country's canal network. The chapel did its best to moderate heavy drinking amongst the local population. There were once seven inns in Bigsweir. One remains.

We find our way onto the grassy river bank, crack open our rations and admire the iron bridge to our right. Spanning 160 feet, the bridge was built in 1827 as a toll on the road linking Monmouth and Chepstow.

Our next act is to remove our walking boots and let a draft of fresh air circulate around our feet. This feels good but we are soon wondering how much longer we should luxuriate on this patch of the borderlands. Chris reflects on our recent conversation about religious associations and spiritual connections. He quotes from the *Rubaiyat of Omar Kayyam*, a passage that sums up our mutual feelings on the matter:

> Myself when young did eagerly frequent
> Doctor and Saint, and heard great argument
> About it and about: but evermore
> Came out by the same door where in I went.

Neither Chris nor I have particular religious affiliations. We know something of what the main protagonists have to offer, have rejected them but still appreciate that there is something in life which requires

About Music

further investigation and that can't be satisfied by a rational, objective approach, or by the language of religion. Music has connections with this mysterious, unconscious, subjective element, but as soon as you reach out to its dimension and attempt to grasp its nature, to hold it, to own it, it becomes a wil'o'the wisp.

A glance at the map shows we are well over half way now but there are two stages still to go. The first will take us into Redbrook, another Forest of Dean village on the River Wye, where we can expect to encounter Sunday tourists enjoying the river, the sunshine and a break from daily routine. This next section will test our legs, as yet not fully fit for long-distance walking. We pack our bags, being careful to remove any litter and lunch remains, check that nothing has dropped to the floor and walk on through the village and away once more.

There is another companion with us today. Since childhood, I have been the possessor of a rough-hewn wooden walking stick, one of a pair. These have lain as ornaments in my house since that time, the carved faces at their top, staring out with silent, unflinching smiles. Today, I carry one and can sense its delight at being in the open air after all this time. It is light and sturdy, a useful balancing tool and a reminder of my past for it has been in my family some time. The carved head gives it a personality, the nature of a sprite, a mischievous entity. It is music's heritage that concerns us today though, not walking sticks and Chris and I need to focus once more.

About Music

The road winds up and out of the northern side of Bigsweir and after a short distance we dive off to the left into ancient woodland, Wyeseal Woods, through which we will walk all the way to Redbrook. The woods are known to have some of the best lime and oak trees in the country, a fact that we appreciate as we walk through them. Bluebells still mass around us and we walk on with a carpet of blue on either side, our path cutting through like the parting of the waves. These flowers seem pervasive while other flowers are less prolific, meadowsweet and buttercups which also decorate our pathway and add their scents to the air.

Art used to be so straightforward. You could look at a picture, a scene, a portrait and understand what the artist was describing. In modern times it has become as much to do with what goes on in the artist's head as what he or she sees around them. Add to this the emphasis in our culture on indivduality and originality and the result is rootless, 'difficult' art.

There are no general criteria any more on which to judge a specific piece of art. The universal subjects - nature, life, the universe - have become particular and personal, of much more relevance to the artist than the viewer. This applies equally to contemporary music making. Maybe we can think again about the definition of what music is while keeping these ideas about abstraction, paradox, and personal as well as universal themes of expression in mind.

I'm quite sure that our definition and understanding will have changed by the time we reach Prestatyn at the Offa's Dyke trail's end but this is where we are today: if noise is formless, random sound and there is a difference between music and noise (the two seem never to have been closer), then music is not formless or random. In classical music these elements, shape and pattern, were clear and overtly stated. Today, music may encompass shape and pattern as well as admitting noise and random elements. The combination of these blurs the boundaries of what we may define as music.

What also has to be taken into account is that the relationship between music and listener has also been changed beyond recognition by technology. Significant as this is, it is not as big a deal as the changing relationship between listener and composer.

During the 20th century many composers were not interested in compromising their music for the sake of maintaining this relationship. They became less interested in an audience (or so they said) so that what they were writing did not pander to accessibility or popularity. This had a clear disadvantage, forcing the composer into isolation and almost destroyed contemporary music making through lack of interest and funding.

This extreme may well have forced the realisation by composers that popularity and originality were not mutually exclusive. The public success in particular of the style of music called minimalism in reintroducing listenable-to harmony and pattern is a witness to this. The preeminent composers who achieved this and who spring to mind are Philip Glass, Steve Reich, Terry Riley, John Adams and Michael Nyman. There is a host of others following in their footsteps.

Something else changed at the end of the 20th century and this was the new ability of the consumer to listen in solitude at any time and any place, made possible by the internet, portable recording devices and music streaming. Music was being produced for a multitude of audiences of one, and that one person could listen for as long or short a time as he or she liked before abandoning a piece and moving on to the next, like wandering around a sonic art gallery from picture to picture.

The age of recorded music and manipulation of recordings by composers and sound engineers has changed not only how and what the listener hears but how music is perceived. This needs consideration too and encompasses not only the psychology of perception but also an understanding of how the brain functions. Research in this field is still in its infancy but making fast progress.

In terms of our human evolution, I speculate that musicality wasn't originally hard-wired in our brains but became so with the passage of time. This hard-wiring process didn't just stop at the primitive communicative use of musical calls and signalling rhythms but continued to develop over the millennia and is today sophisticated. Maybe even an appreciation of classical music has become hard-wired into our neural systems. No one would argue that

About Music

personal hard-wiring of music takes places as soon as we are born and begin to assimilate children's songs and melodies from our environment. These become part of our personal histories, memory and character. Perhaps our brains also contain the ancestral blueprints of archetypal musical forms that have gone before.

My experience of listening to the classical Mozart, for instance, is to perceive a form so clear in his music that my brain knows precisely where the music is going, can anticipate the next notes and expresses delight when this unconscious prediction is realised. Mozart knew just how to satisfy or indeed also temporarily to withhold the satisfaction and suspend it to create the pleasure of anticipation before satisfaction's final arrival.

We'll be exploring how the brain recognises, interprets and plays with music later. Suffice it to say for this part of the journey that the miraculous experience of music simply does not exist before the brain gets hold of it. Until then, it is mere mechanical vibration, whether of instrument, loudspeaker, air molecules or eardrum.

Our next landmark is Redbrook and we overlook from a height the forested valley through which the River Wye winds. Across the valley we can see the still distant iron railway bridge over the river and over which trains would have trundled and puffed into the last station before Monmouth. The bridge was closed to freight in 1964 but remains a clear reminder of Redbrook's mills that graced the upper section of the town and of its tough industrial and mining past, with its copper and then tin mines.

It takes us a while yet to arrive but eventually our downward path leads us to the riverside at Lower Redbrook and we mix with day trippers and watch the canoeists enjoying a peaceful day on a gently flowing river. This place's atmosphere, created by the forested slopes by the river and the architecture which has moulded itself into the hillsides, speaks now most characteristically of the Forest of Dean with its local inhabitants, their mining history and their buttery, drawling accent.

The penultimate stage is a walk on which we must stay focused as our muscles are in second-wind but tiring and the walk is steadily upwards again. Unexpectedly, though, for my part anyway,

About Music

this section seems relatively easy going, perhaps because our final target is not far away.

Looking over Monmouth from a height we arrive at the Kymin, an 18th century round house and a naval temple folly, built in 1800 and dedicated to some of the greatest admirals and naval victories of the time. The Kymin was once part of the enormous Dukes of Beaufort estates and is still a popular picnic spot. The two-storey round house there was built in 1794 by a group of Monmouth gentlemen. Their Picnic Club was formed for the laudable purpose of dining together while spending the day in a social and friendly manner. No doubt this is sometimes a windy spot and there would have been days when the picnic tables' fayre was blown unceremoniously overboard, along with assorted millinery down the side of the steep hill to tumble into Monmouth. We have had some spectacular views today and this is one of the most memorable.

A short sojourn is all we can afford here before the final walk, downhill all the way. We enter a wood with a high fence around it, presumably to keep deer safe and enclosed. A slip in my concentration leads to a slip on a patch of mud, but I quickly regain balance and walk on unperturbed. Beyond the wood, the path takes us through a couple of hillside smallholdings, one home to some fat and free-ranging pigs, although one seems to be quite grumpy today. These are Tamworths, a lovely chocolaty brown animal described as 'charismatic' by its breeders' club and on the at-risk register of rare breeds. As we pass by, I wonder how pigs respond to music.

We arrive at the pedestrian underpass that takes us below the A40 dual carriageway and into Monmouth town. A walk through the back streets, then down the main shopping road, Monnow Street, leads to the still-intact medieval gate bridge over the River Monnow, part of the old town's defences. The bridge is the starting point for our next walk whose topic will be a ramble on some influential moments in the history of western music, from Pythagoras to Dr Who. Then we can really start exploring those borderlands between countries, both musical and topographical.

Bill, contemplating musical pigs

About Music

CHAPTER 2

From Pythagoras to Dr Who

*In which we work out, musically speaking,
how we arrived here.*

For ramblers, there are some concerns which are ever present. Your feet, for example, are a key concern. Footwear has to be strong, comfortable and waterproof. This is basic and vital as walking on blisters or damp socks is not a pleasant experience. The right gear is required; then you can simply forget about it.

Another constant concern, at least in the days prior to a walk, is the weather forecast. Today, for our second Offa's Dyke path walk, the weather is not looking good. There has been heavy rain during the week and although it is not raining as we set out, the sky is grey and it is wet underfoot. My mobile phone's app tells me that the temperature will be a comfortable 17 degrees Celsius and the wind light. This part of the forecast is good news as high winds and temperatures can be as enervating as a long uphill climb.

Chris and I pose for a photo to mark the beginning of this section of the path which will take us from Monmouth to Pandy as we continue to work our way north along the Welsh-English borderlands. Then we set off from the Monnow Bridge and through the back streets of Monmouth where we admire the picturesque buildings and gardens along aptly named Watery Lane, before embarking into woodland and across fields.

The previous ramble was a valley walk with elevated views down to the River Wye. The stretch today will be through fields, pastures and isolated villages, a lowland trek of about sixteen miles arriving finally in Pandy at the foot of the Black Mountains.

Everywhere is dripping and damp and a bit squelchy. Still, I have my trusty walking stick, plenty to eat and drink and a companion to ramble with. It's not raining when we set off and there

About Music

is even a break in the clouds as we enter the grassy and leafy green pastoral lands of the border country.

We are aiming first for the village of Llanfihangel Ystum Llywern which, Chris's guide book explains, means St Michael's of the Fiery Meteor. We could do with some of the Archangel Michael's fiery spirit to dry our way. We pass through the King's Wood with its birch, oak and beech trees and head steadily west on a clear way-marked path. Chris asks about our musical topic for the day.

I have set this as a ramble through some significant mileposts in the history of our music, starting with the Ancient Greeks, who had an influence that has extended right up to the present day. We'll be avoiding much of the well-trodden history that you will find in any book on the subject but trying to trace some of the borderland events that line the route from then until now. Each sign post will be a step along the way, guiding us to the next historical marker on our musical path. The route commences with Pythagoras and ends with the technological music of today. The task is to work out a line of development leading from an ancient Greek philosopher to Dr Who.

It is commonly and correctly assumed that music and mathematics have a strong relationship. This is not obvious when you listen to a piece of music other than perhaps detecting musical patterns in it. Nor will composers have calculated their music in any mathematical sense. Well, there is bound to be an exception to this in the anything-goes repertoire of contemporary music, but almost universally, composers do not have maths in mind when they compose. So where is this mathematical element and where does it come from? Remember Leibnitz's definition of music as the musical mind at work calculating.

Pythagoras (600 – 550 BC) was the founder of a school of philosophy whose idea was that the universe is based on numbers and these are its basic building blocks. Not only this, but those building blocks are simple, whole numbers. Numbers are the Creator's means of self-expression. The resultant universe is

37

About Music

beautiful because the mathematical laws on which it is constructed are simple, exact and beautiful, too.

Pythagoras discovered more than 2000 years ago that for every right-angled triangle, the square on the hypotenuse is equal in area to the sum of the squares on the other two sides. You probably knew this. What you might not know is that the Pythagorians worked out the notes of our musical scale using whole numbers and they did this by observing what happens when a taut string vibrates.

Their measurements of vibrating strings and their analysis of the ratios between simple whole numbers became the foundation of a theory which, with a truly gigantic leap of imagination, was extrapolated to explain how the planets of our solar system behave. That was an astounding act of genius. The Pythagorians began with their discoveries about simple numbers and developed them through music into a philosophy explaining our universe. The influence of their cosmic musical theories continued for the next two thousand years.

We need to check our Ordnance map which shows that looking down into the valley below we can see the River Trothy and the site of a former Cistercian priory, Grace Dieu. Numbers of these priories were created in the 12th century, particularly in Yorkshire, Scotland and Wales. Some became large and influential, such as the abbey at Tintern, some sparked towns into life by creating money-making markets close by. Most have completely vanished and are just "former sites" such as the one we pass close by today.

There are unavoidable wet patches in the fields where we walk and it is impossible to navigate without sinking into them. After giving that little lecture about having the right equipment, I discover that I will need some new boots to keep the water out. They are leaking and it is a most uncomfortable experience. However, we are soon distracted by our musical ramblings and I forget about my feet for a while. We continue to ponder on and chat about the earliest history of classical music, a world hard to imagine as it is so different and distant from our own.

About Music

Pythagoras observed the properties of vibrating strings by setting up experiments with a single-string instrument called a monochord. The rate at which its string vibrates is measured in cycles per second, or 'Hertz' to use the current unit of measurement (abbreviation, Hz). The man who gave his name to this measurement was Heinrich Hertz who, in the latter half of the 19th century, demonstrated the existence of electromagnetic radiation, or radio waves. Sound waves and radio waves can be analysed in much the same way. With good hearing we can hear sound waves within the range of about 20 Hz (20 vibrations per second) to 20 kHz (20,000 vibrations per second).

If, for example, a string under tension vibrates at 100 Hz, which is within our normal hearing range, it will emit a low tone, a note, which is described as a 'fundamental'. This fundamental can be used as the basis against which to compare and measure other notes and their vibrations. If the string is shortened, by a half (divided by 2) it will vibrate twice as quickly at 200 Hz and the note we hear from it is an octave higher. By dividing the string into simple ratios of 2 (200 Hz), 3 (300 Hz), 4 (400 Hz), etc., we obtain the notes that form our music's harmony and scales.

We'll be coming back to this on our next walk up in the mountains, but for now the main point is that these ratios, between the frequencies of vibration making the notes and the fundamental, are simple, whole numbers. Anything with a regular, periodic motion, from sound waves and electromagnetic waves to swinging pendulums to orbiting planets, can be analysed from this same starting point.

Pythagoras's purpose was to show how the notes of his monochord have a correspondence with the arrangement and movements of the planets. Imagine that the earth is the centre of the universe and is surrounded by a series of concentric spheres, a Russian doll type of arrangement. Each sphere is associated with a particular planet. Each planet travelling around its sphere and on its circular (*sic*) path around the earth does so with a particular orbital time, or frequency of oscillation. Each planet has its own vibrational, oscillating movement and, therefore, the theory went, emits its own tone as it travels.

About Music

From vibrating string to the analysis of planetary movements is a big jump to take. This magnificent mind leap was based partly on the astrological notion that everything that happened on earth had its counterpart in the heavens, everything 'below' is as it is 'above'. This theory of correspondences, inherited by ancient Greek culture from the Babylonian and Chaldean astrologer priests, held sway in all subjects from music to medicine until enlightenment in recent centuries. The Pythagorian view, steeped in this mysticism, held back much future progress in cosmology because philosophers and researchers subsequently and endlessly tried to make the facts fit this compelling theory, even when it was clear that they did not.

Music making in Greece consisted of simple accompaniment to poetry and recitative. It was almost entirely monophonic, that is, a single line of music was played within the narrow range of an octave or so. Instruments included the small harp-like lyre and the more professional *cithera*, as played by the god Apollo and by Orpheus, of underworld fame. Wind instruments included the *syrinx* or pipes of Pan and the *aulos* was a flute created by the goddess Athene.

The problems of harmony in relation to making music were not considered because the instruments were not designed to sustain multiple notes, ensembles were not yet a part of musical culture and, most significantly, making music was considered to be a frivolity in comparison with the mystical musical cosmology described by Pythagoras.

Pythagoras distinguished three sorts of music in his philosophy. Using the nomenclature of a later era: *musica instrumentalis* is the ordinary music made by playing an instrument; *musica humana* is the continuous but unheard music sounded by each person; and *musica mundane* is the music made by the cosmos, which would become known as 'the music of the spheres'.

Musica mundana influenced all subsequent work on understanding the heavens to the extent that the subject of cosmology eventually emerged as a true science in its own right. *Musica humana* was pure Pythagorian mystical theory, but was a starting point for what we are now discovering about the brain and its musical foundations. There are two approaches to this 'inner brain music' today. One is through the physiology of the synaptical functioning of brain matter and the other is through the psychology

About Music

of the unconscious mind, the energy source of all our imaginative creativity.

Musica instrumentalis, from ancient to medieval times the least important of the three, has become in the last couple of centuries or so the most significant, the most written about and the most understood, almost to the exclusion of the other two. It is what we commonly mean by 'classical music', its theory, its form, and its performance.

It is the relationship of all three which forms our musical borderland and in bringing them together may give insights into the secret life of music.

The physical manifestation of the dyke has disappeared and it will be some miles before it resurfaces. The path is now just within the Welsh border in Monmouthshire and will be so for most of this stage. We enter a damp green meadow and off to our right is the River Trothy. It's about two hours since we set off so we feel owed a break and some food. The river is tumbling along quickly but with no sign of the earlier winter floods. A pile of large stones gives the impression of a prehistoric remnant and we lean our backs on it and sip our drinks.

In Greek mythology, Orpheus and his lyre had the power through music to move the stones of the earth. Great stones have had otherworldly associations since prehistoric times and whenever you encounter a sizeable chunk, that feeling seems to emanate from the stone itself.

After a brief rest we press on and straight away meet four purposeful walkers coming in the opposite direction. We chat for a while and learn that they have been walking the whole route from north to south with just a couple of days to go. I admire their walking canes and then realise that mine is not with me – left behind at our last stop. Fortunately, it is only a few minutes away, so I accompany the walkers as I return for it, while Chris takes the opportunity to wait and gather his strength.

We are all three soon reunited and walk on into the village of Llanvihangel. Outside its church is a box pleading poverty and a sign asking for donations to help with its upkeep, an unobtrusive and unremarkable request were it not for the fact of another notice proclaiming the bishop's presence in the church today. There is a luxurious black limo parked incongruously next to the pleading notice. The gangster-style car rather quashed the case for alms.

We find our way round the outside of the church, following our way-marked path into another watery meadow. From a hedge a black butterfly emerges. Its fluttering shows off flashes of an iridescent blue. The Purple Hairstreak is the commonest in the hairstreak family but not often seen as it tends to fly high up in the tree canopy.

We enter a field with a view stretching across lowlands over which we can see the clear direction of our path and in the distance is the grey outline of the Black Mountains. This is our first view of those hills and of perhaps the best known, Skirrid, which is clearly outlined against the sky. Skirrid, Ysgyryd Fawr, is an outlier and marks the easternmost part of the Brecon Beacons National Park. I have a strong feeling of anticipation tinged with excitement as those hills are yet a long way off but we will be walking along their ridges before we know it.

The aim on this pilgrimage is to pinpoint some significant signposts of our own as we travel the musical borderlands. The next is the Greek philosopher Plato (427 – 347 BC) who had some strong opinions about music.

The Greeks developed several different musical scales or 'modes' of which only some survive in modern music making. The most common of these are the major and minor modes and any music student will encounter these at the outset of their studies. Each of the Greek modes, used for tuning the seven-string harp-like lyre, was associated with a human quality or state of being. In the same way that the major mode is today associated with positive feelings of happiness and the minor with a more serious, even mournful atmosphere, each mode was used to evoke a particular effect, from aggression to peace and calm, from healing to enlightenment.

Take a piano keyboard and begin with any white key. Play this and in sequence the next seven white notes to its right (or left) and you will have created the scale of one of the modes.

About Music

Plato became quite upset when music was treated as frivolous for in the hands of a skilled musician, powerful effects can be created, even to the point of moving great stones. Given that by god's hand the universe was making its own music, to employ it for its entertainment value was simply not on. Directing his gaze on those frivolous music makers, he said, "Through foolishness they deceived themselves into thinking that there was no right or wrong way in music, that it was to be judged good or bad by the pleasure it gave."

Plato brings philosophy out of the dream world of mythology and shines the light of reason on understanding maths, music and the universe. In the Middle Ages and the Renaissance, Plato's book, the *Timaeus*, was a widely read work and in it he describes a cosmos based on musical principles.

By the time we reach the Classical (circa 1750) interest had shifted its centre of gravity from the cosmos to the human being and this may be why the *Timaeus* became neglected. By modern standards it is now regarded as highly fanciful.

Most of our walking today has been through fields and meadows, past hedgerows and streams. Then our environment changes and we enter an apple orchard, the path cutting right through the middle of the trees. The blossom is over and the trees are in full green garment. Chris is a keen fan of the cider apple and has run workshops on cider making. He recounts the practice of wassailing at his home and takes pleasure in telling me about the associations of music with this folk and pagan practice.

Singing and playing to the apple trees is a time-honoured means for ensuring an abundant harvest. It is an illogical practice to our modern sensibilities, but there is here the hint of another borderland, a continuous zone that extends between inner human being and the external world, in this case the tree. The link between mind and matter is forged by music.

Chris explains that when autumn harvest time comes, a machine will be brought into the orchard with a strap to fasten around the trunk of each tree. The strap is vibrated by the machine, shakes the tree and the apples fall to the ground. Then a blower

About Music

bundles the apples together and they are thence transferred to conveyer belts to be shipped off for cider making. It's all too prosaic for us and we prefer to dwell on the evocative idea of singing to the trees. Pagan roots are inscribed in our unconscious minds in just the same way that the reality of history is inscribed in the landscape. Both lie not too far below the surface.

Much of the apple harvest from this area will be used for export to Ireland, a market which has developed its taste for amber liquid, despite strong Irish associations with the black stuff.

The next character to sign our musical path and who probably liked a drop of cider himself is the classical Roman author, Cicero (106 – 43 BC), creator of a masterpiece of Latin prose, *Scipio's Dream*, in which he gives a clear account of the music of the spheres.

Scipio's Dream was read throughout subsequent eras and in the 18th century formed the basis of an opera by Mozart. In Cicero's book, the dreamer enquires of the mystical cosmic sounds he hears, "What is that great and pleasing sound that fills my ears?" The reply from his guide, Scipio Africanus, is a clear description: "That is a concord of tones separated by unequal but nevertheless carefully proportioned intervals, caused by the rapid motion of the (planetary) spheres themselves. The high and low tones blended together produce different harmonies..."

It is this image that dwells in the mind of all who subsequently contemplated the heavens and it inspired even the great scientific minds of our own era, Copernicus, Newton, Galileo and Kepler, seeding their imaginations with the means to penetrate the mysteries of the universe. The scene is set, the landscape mapped out ready for the great exploration of this dream.

The history of music as an art form in its own right begins just a couple of hundred years later with a music school set up in Rome by Pope Sylvester (330 AD) for the study of singing. The songs, representations of cosmic melodies on earth, most probably were unisonal (a single melody line) and based on the scales and modes of the Greeks. Scholars suggest that Sylvester was acquainted with antiphonal chanting. Antiphonal music is performed by two

About Music

semi-independent choirs, often singing alternate musical phrases. This style became dominant for some time and formed the basis of later instrumental music during the Baroque period (1600 – 1750) when a soloist, or small group of instruments, the *concertino*, would be set against a larger group, the *ripieno*. Eventually, the *concertino* became the virtuoso soloist performer playing against a background of the full orchestra, the concerto as we know it today.

♪ We are approaching the village of Llantilio Crossenny and making good time. The village has a pre-medieval history that includes events recorded from the sixth century, before our dyke was built but only two centuries after Sylvester established his music school. This part of Monmouthshire was then under threat from the Saxons and through religious devotion and intervention the Saxon invaders were defeated. In gratitude for assistance from the saintly Teilo, a charismatic preacher and traveling companion of St David, the local King Iddon granted land on which the predecessor of today's church was built.

Unsurprisingly for a Sunday afternoon, the village is deserted apart from a couple of dog walkers. This was to be the place of our mid-walk break but we feel the urge to press on to the White Castle, one of the impressive Norman castles that have been built along this part of the border.

Half an hour later and things are starting to get heavy and I don't mean the musical conversation but the mud on our boots. We have entered a potato field, freshly prepared and planted and the path takes us straight through the middle of it, between the lines of planting. This is literally heavy going and our boots frequently sink to the ankles.

Potatoes need a lot of moisture to grow well, so these are ideal conditions for the farmer but not for us. Any conversation stops as we concentrate on picking our way through and glance up every now and again to check that the other side of the field really is getting closer.

We make it across. There are signs of intensive farming here as these weed-stripped fields have clearly been chemically conditioned. Later, after our walk, I find that the mud on my jeans has carried a chemical that transferred with the damp onto the skin beneath and has caused a rash. Next time I'll wear gaiters to protect the bottom part of the leg from damp. We are, to be frank, a little cheesed off at this stage of our journey when it begins to drizzle.

Chris talks to me about his fascination for improvisation and how jazz has brought this art to the fore, particularly with its crossing and syncopated rhythms that are so mesmerising.

The art of improvisation has largely been lost by classical musicians who would be at sea without the security of a detailed, music score firmly placed in front of them. Composers from the classical period onwards became more and more prescriptive in their performance instructions. In contrast, if you look at an earlier Baroque music score, one of its features is that there are few indications to the performer, if any, as to how it is to be performed. Dynamics, tempos and the overall feeling of expression are left to the imagination and interpretation of the instrumentalist.

Improvisation was an integral part of musicianship at that time. The keyboard, 'continuo' accompaniment might be provided with a single written bass line to play and in addition some numberings called 'figured bass', a code to suggest the outlines of the chords to be constructed by the player.

Every village we encounter along our path has its own church and it was always the main religious centres that had the most influence on what and how music was to be played. The writings of the Christian theologian, Augustine of Hippo (354 – 430 AD) were influential in the early history of Christianity. In his *Confessions* he says that there will always be a place for music in the church but he is also undecided about different forms of music and whether they lead to or away from God. In other words, as far as the church was concerned, there was a much-discussed right and a wrong way to make music.

Born in Rome, the best of the medieval writers on music was Boethius (480 – 524). Through him, the basic vocabulary of music theory was transmitted to the late Middle Ages and the Renaissance. His textbook, *Principles of Music* was a prestigious and widely read music theory. The 'quadrivium', of academic essentials is so called

About Music

for the first time: arithmetic, geometry, astronomy and music the vital areas of study for anyone seeking a rounded education. Boethius also makes a critical distinction between *musici*, important theorists of pure music, and *cantores*, mere singers and instrumentalists. Boethius further expressed the distinctions between the three Pythagorian types of music: music of the spheres, inner mind music and ordinary music making.

The Christian churches have had a profound influence on our music and one of its household names is attached to a style of religious incantation called Gregorian Chant. It was during the pontificate of Pope Gregory the Great (590 – 604) that the earlier Greek modes or scales of music were further developed and Gregorian chants, called also 'plainsong' or 'plainchant', were sung antiphonally between priest and choir when a crude notation was first employed.

Gregorian chants are a form of monophonic, unaccompanied sacred song. They were not sung in a key – the key system came later - but made use of the classical Greek modes. It was sung by choirs of men and boys in churches, or by women and men of religious orders in their chapels. It is the music of the Roman Rite, performed in the Mass and the monastic Office.

The first notation was created in European monasteries in the 9th century, probably at the time our dyke was being constructed. It was developed specifically for the recording of Gregorian chant. At last, there was a way of writing down music. The notation was based

Remove from me all scorn and contempt, for I have kept your commandments; for your law is the object of my meditations.

About Music

around symbols called 'neumes'. These represent the notes which are chanted on a single syllable. They were written on a four-line staff, which eventually became the five we use today.

At first glance the system seems to be too crude to be of great help, but a closer consideration reveals it to be quite sufficient for recording and reproducing this music. There are some of its symbols quite clearly still represented in today's modern notation, such as the use of a dot after a note to show that it is to be lengthened. The names of some of the notations are quite delicious, too, such as the '*Scandicus liquescens*' and the '*Quilisma*'.

The next significant development was again church inspired and stemmed from a series of monastic changes known as the 'Cluniac Reforms'. Founded at Cluny in France in 910, these monastic reforms spread into England and encouraged the use of multi-voice elaborations of Gregorian chant, called 'organum'. This was the early stage in the development of Western polyphony, the simultaneous reproduction of several different lines of music.

Polyphonic music consists of several rhythmically independent voices which combine in a harmonically satisfying way. The new technique coincided with developments in the pipe organ, itself capable of polyphonic music and therefore of supporting and encouraging this style of composition. The key factor for the organ was that it could sustain and harmonise several notes at the same time.

Polyphony was a momentous development but brought with it two problems. The first was that the system of notation that had developed so far was insufficient to encompass the new complexities. Cometh the moment, cometh the man and in this instant came Guido of Arezzo (992 – 1033), inventor of modern music notation.

From his revolution has stemmed our ability to write down complex music. Guido sold his ideas to Pope John XIX and it was thereafter adopted throughout Christendom.

The second difficulty was one that had been known about for some considerable time but largely ignored. It was only when polyphony and more particularly the widespread use of harmony took its hold that a niggling little problem became a niggling large one. Pythagoras's maths didn't quite add up. It was approximate

About Music

enough for several hundred years but it was becoming apparent that the discrepancies needed to be dealt with. In order to maintain the harmony between notes, as music became more complex, the tuning system would have to be slightly altered, or tempered. Those beautiful whole numbers would need some adjustment.

Meanwhile, the most influential scholastic philosopher of all time, Thomas Aquinas (1225 – 1274) signalled that beauty of expression in art and music required three attributes: clarity, order and proportion, emphasising the Pythagorian truths that the universe is created to be simple, exact and beautiful. These were the criteria on which a piece of music would be judged; these are what God appreciated most.

The fact that Pythagoras's lovely whole number system needed tweaking caused some controversy which to this day has not been completely resolved. One of the earliest discussions about temperament, the tweaking process, took place and was recorded a couple of hundred years after Pythagoras's time, so 'the problem' has a history almost as long as the history of western music itself.

♪ When you walk, conditions vary considerably but even when they are quite adverse the experience can be enjoyable. If the view, the weather, our feelings were always the same, like a piece of music, it would soon become boring. Today our mood and feelings are being tempered by the grey skies, damp air and feet, but this does not quash our enthusiasm for the walk or our conversation as we ramble on.

We arrive at the White Castle, the sturdy remnants of a Norman fortress built overlooking the sloping meadows around it and signalling to the Welsh beware and go no further across this border. The castle stands on a low hill about two miles from the village of Llantilio Crossenny. It was once covered in a white rendering, remnants of which are still visible, that would have gleamed out against the landscape as a menacing sign of Norman power.

We are greeted by a lady in a kiosk and pay our entrance fee. She grumbles that the weather has ruined her trade, keeping visitors at bay perhaps more effectively than any Norman battalion. She

About Music

smiles knowingly and asks if we encountered 'the potato field'. We grimace and she nods sympathetically but with a poorly disguised hint of Schadenfreude. She tells us that there are tales of walkers getting stuck in that field and never making it out again.

A rather bedraggled re-enactment group is encamped within the castle walls and we stop to talk and take photographs of them. Their costumes are mixed, some early medieval, some Renaissance, some Tudor, giving an air of time without rules. They are ordinary folk enjoying both dressing up and making history live again. They succeed, for even this small contingent imaginatively creates the possibility of time without barriers and I sense the presence of ghosts.

Chris and I take refuge in one of the dingy main gate towers and, to the rhythmic, echoing, background accompaniment of dripping water, try to make ourselves comfortable on the unevenly worn stone steps where we eat our sandwiches. It is drizzling outside. The tower has no roof and for the first time on this trip we dig out waterproofs.

There are three Norman castles along this section of the border, Skenfrith, Grosmont and White. All three were royal castles in the late 12th century, and in 1201 were granted to Lord Hubert de Burgh by King John. The White Castle is the best preserved and, unlike the other two, was not intended as a lordly residence but for military purposes alone. The buildings included a hall, a chapel and a kitchen.

There are parents with small children trying to make the best of their outing to the castle as we leave and re-enter our borderland walking world. The castle has created the impression that the borderland we traverse is not just between Wales and England any more but is between past and present, between worlds.

The White Castle's heydays coincide with the beginnings of a great cultural movement in Italy. Continuing for about 300 years from the 14th to the 17th century, the Renaissance is considered to be the bridge between the Middle Ages and modern history. The Renaissance, literally the time of rebirth, is a period marked by intense human endeavours of discovery in art and science that took inspiration from classicism, prior to Christianity. During the

About Music

Renaissance, cracks begin to show for the first time in the ubiquitous music theories of Pythagoras.

There were two main types of Renaissance music: sacred music and non-church or secular music which was the province of the rich and courtly. There was folk music too, but that was for common people, so no one bothered to write it down and the tradition continued only by passing the music from person to person. Most was simply forgotten.

Chris talks to me about how important music is for everyone, whatever their background, their wealth or their education. The church used to have 'the best' music, but now it is the province of 'us folk'. In our home town, the local secondary school recently decided to drop music studies from its curriculum and the outcry was so instant and so forceful that the decision was quickly reversed. Music may be pursued as a solitary activity as never before but in equal measure it is part of the fabric of what makes the wholeness of a community.

No one wrote down early folk music and the value of such music was only recognised as late as the 19th and 20th centuries when collections of music were made and became part of national identities and a resource for the inspiration of composers.

The Renaissance was a time of scientific as well as artistic activity. Its scientific endeavours were not yet fully formed and were still part of a mystical tradition. If the 20th century has been characterised by an endless search for, and a high premium placed on, anything new – newness and progress as the gold standard - then the Renaissance was all about rediscovery of the wisdom of the ancients and anything old had immediate and inherent currency value. For example, the ancient, spiritual, philosophical and magical tradition of alchemy permeated science, this being superficially a search for the means of transmuting base substances into gold but, at its heart, was a means for delving into the secrets of life.

About Music

In England during the early years of the Renaissance, Henry V (1386 – 1422) was reinvigorating the 100 Years War with France, culminating in victory at the Battle of Agincourt. Henry loved music and supported composers of his time such as John Dunstable (1390 – 1453), who was to become lauded as the father of English contrapuntalists. Counterpoint is the relationship between voices that are interdependent harmonically - polyphony - and yet are also independent in rhythm and contour.

Counterpoint is another great leap forward in the development of music where its vertical properties, the harmony, and its horizontal, the melody, are of equal importance but are independent. The art of the composer was, henceforth, to combine these two dimensions with, as Aquinas dictated, clarity, order and proportion. A considerable quantity of Dunstable's compositions has been unearthed in cathedral libraries making it clear he was regarded as the greatest composer in Europe. His personal influences were not only religious but secular, too, and the influence of folk music can be clearly discerned in his writings.

John Dunstable will be found in any music history but a name that may not is that of Marcilio Ficino (1433-99), one of the most influential humanist philosophers of the early Italian Renaissance. An ardent believer in sympathetic magic, a type of magic based on sympathy or correspondence, Ficino was especially

About Music

drawn to its musical aspects. His astrological music was indebted to Boethius's description of the correspondence between the cosmic music of the spheres, the human organism's inner music and ordinary music making. Ficino's way of invoking the cosmic spirit was through music. This theme has not entirely vanished from the modern repertoire as witnessed by the continuing popularity of Holst's great 'Planet Suite', inspired by the same awareness and desire to penetrate heavenly secrets by musical means. Holst was by no means the only subsequent composer to pursue this but is the best known.

Ficino's life work was an attempt to reconcile Christianity with the pagan classics, including the *Corpus Hermeticum* of Hermes Trismegistus, alchemy's fundamental treatise, its bible, thought for some time to be a much more ancient text than it turned out to be.

We pause in our ramblings to absorb and admire the beauty of the meadows through which we are walking. The white, yellow and occasional red, blue and purple flowers are tiny stars in a sky-floor of green. After the last of the ewes and lambs are taken out of the meadows in early May, the grass is allowed to grow. Later in the season, it will be mown to make hay to feed livestock over the winter.

The ewes and lambs have already eaten the first flush of spring grass and leave the meadows cropped short so that sunlight reaches right down to the surface of the ground. This encourages the wild clovers which naturally add to the fertility of the soil. It also checks the grasses, and gives a precious advantage to colourful flowering wild plants. Above us, there are blue patches in the sky and walking prospects are improving.

Our way is being marked by a series of music's personalities who have made their mark on its development, guiding our way along a historical path. We come to talk next about one of the greatest musical luminaries, Thomas Tallis.

Tallis (1505-85) lived through Protestant and Catholic monarchies. Considered to be one of England's greatest composers, he was at work during a difficult period in the conflict between Catholicism and Protestantism and his music encompasses this turmoil. Tallis perfected the art of creating counterpoint between layers of unaccompanied voices set to liturgical subjects. He composed the unique motet 'Spem in alium' written for eight five-voice choirs. In later life he eschewed the complexities of composition espoused by the famous English composer, William Byrd, in favour of the virtues of simplicity.

Thomas Tallis lived a long life by sixteenth-century standards. He was 80 when he died, having served at the Chapel Royal under four monarchs, beginning with Henry VIII, himself respected as a musician and composer and ending with Elizabeth I. Elizabeth was said to dance "six or seven galliards in a morning" as part of her "ordinarie exercise", so she can assuradlie be credited as the inventor of the dancercise workout.

The sixteenth century was an unfortunate time to be a church musician in England. The country shuddered with political and religious upheaval as Henry VIII, then Edward VI, then Mary and finally Elizabeth attempted to establish their own religious reforms. Heretics were sent to the stake, traitors executed in the Tower. Music was one of the battlegrounds, with significant risks attached for its practitioners.

Composers delicately negotiated the move from the elaborate and large-scale Catholic works of the early sixteenth century to a plainer style under Edward. This was promptly reversed just a few years later, when Mary came to the throne, but she herself didn't reign for long and, in the end, it was Elizabeth who found the compromise between the needs of the Catholics at one end of the religious spectrum and the Puritans at the other.

Tallis worked at the hub of English church music, the Chapel Royal, for forty years. And through it all he turned out piece after piece of glorious music, seemingly unperturbed when all the rules changed and changed again. As Peter Phillips of the Tallis Scholars put it, "What it took in terms of stamina and personality to survive and excel as Tallis did, in the times he did, has something of a miracle about it."

It is not just a history of music that is developing as we ramble but the overlap between some of music's facets, marked by

About Music

diverse personalities and events, suggesting a particular path for us to take. This is becoming clearer as we walk between the opposites of the personal and the cosmic, the art and the science, the inner and the outer worlds of experience. In classical times and before there was no such clear separation; division began to take place in the Renaissance, particularly as science came of age and defined the boundaries. There are prominent figures in this process and two in particular are Francis Bacon and René Descartes.

Bacon (1561-1626) was called the father of empiricism, which means that he is credited with introducing a proper scientific method into the development of knowledge. The relationship between science and music was becoming fundamentally changed with the rise of scientific method and rationalism.

With Descartes (1596-1650) begins modern philosophy and his method was to go back to first principles, take nothing as fundamentally true, except for the fact of his own existence, and recreate all knowledge from that starting point. He has lent his name to the idea of 'cartesian dualism', that mind and the material world are two separate and independent realities. Rationalism and science were spelling out the end of the universe as a cosmic musical instrument that was in a holistic relationship with the inner musical man. Somewhat academic you might say, but something momentous was again happening in music as a direct result of this sort of thinking.

The following period in musical history known as 'Baroque' is generally defined as occurring between 1600-1750 and during this time music reached new heights of complexity. This was the time when experiment in musical forms reached its peak only to be exceeded in the 20th century. There was a wild sense of freedom of expression. Instrumental music developed quickly, while the use of harmony became, on the one hand, more and more outrageous and on the other, clearly bound by rules defining how new sounds and ideas were to be incorporated.

Real music, as opposed to the trifling music of songsters and instrumentalists had been an expression of how the universe worked and music was an homage to this. The revolutionary astronomers of the time, Copernicus, Galileo and Kepler made great advances in our understanding of the planetary system and of these Kepler in particular is worth more than just a mention. His planetary laws of motion, which opened the modern era of cosmic science and thence to space exploration, were inspired by his study of Pythagorian harmony and its application to the music of the spheres. His achievement – and the achievement of others of that time – was to break the stranglehold that false assumptions had held on their science for two thousand years. Theories about music and harmony played a central role in this process.

We have reached a point along this historical route where scientists, influencing the entire outlook of the enlightened western world, played a critical role in how music continued to evolve. Isaac Newton (1643-1727) is known today as the original archetypal scientist but even his great mind and its inner workings were indebted to the mystical machinations of alchemy. It is not generally advertised that he spent much of his time on his alchemical experiments and the library of books that he possessed were on this very subject. While Newton was at work in his alchemical laboratory, Stradivarius was at work in his workshop, in his own way turning base materials into gold by creating some of the greatest stringed instruments to have been brought into this world.

In their time, the emphasis was still on music as an expression not of the composer's or the musician's feelings but as an expression of god's miracle, our universe. The greatest stringed instruments and scientific discoveries were being born while some of the greatest composers were, too: Henry Purcell and the exact contemporaries Friedrich Handel and Johann Sebastian Bach brought music to a peak of beauty and form, prior to another revolution wrought by Beethoven.

Histories of music divide the periods of its development into neat time slots. When we talk of the music of Handel and Bach, they fall into the category and time of Baroque music. Kepler, Newton and Stradivarius were all at work during the Baroque period. Before Baroque music was Renaissance music and before that the time of the early medieval period. After the Baroque era, from 1750 to 1850 is the classical period, characterised by the music of Haydn, then Mozart and then Beethoven who takes the classical into the period of the Romantic composers from 1850 to 1900.

About Music

This does not give anything like a clear picture of the processes at work in society that drove the changes. It is a convenient way of categorising and simplifying what was a gradual complex process and which by no means took place in an orderly step by step manner. For example, we tend to think of only a handful of composers as significant, citing always the cream of the crop, Bach, Mozart, Beethoven, but there was a myriad more, many composers entirely forgotten, some not worthy of mention but many who made influential contributions to a continuing, long process of musical evolution.

One of many threads that runs through the musical genre of each era, was that of harmony, the combination of notes sounding together. Its evolution goes a little like this: first there was a single line of music; then others were added to support it; next the individual parts began to be rhythmically independent of each other but still with satisfying harmonic progression. This is polyphony and a fundamental characteristic of Renaissance music and then the Baroque. By the classical period the horizontal component of music (the melody) had equal importance with the vertical component (the harmony and harmonic progression). New combinations of notes making up chordal sequences were heard, at first being thought of as outlandish and controversial, then, with familiarity, being accepted into the composer's harmonic vocabulary and into the audience's ear.

Another thread was spun by the evolution of musical instruments and music for different groups of musicians, first to support vocal lines, then for playing in small ensembles. These became bigger until music for the concert hall was common. There are other threads, religious, social and philosophical, that can all be traced as influencing the evolution of music.

Each period in history is characterised by its own music, each clearly distinct in flavour, each quite different from what came before and what came after, each woven from a multitude of different influences. Any neat characterisation of the end result hides the true process, which may have had its defining moments but was, by and large, a gradual one of trial and error, of chance as much as design.

With the classical period, the familiar big three arrived, first Haydn, then Mozart, then Beethoven and music was never again the same. These highly influential musical geniuses did not just simply appear out of nowhere. They were all of their time and place, made rather than born. Take a step back, say, to the astronomer, Galileo's father, Galileo Galilei (1564-1642), a contemporary of Francis Bacon. His writings about music were influential, expressing strong views on the nature and value of music. He was a reactionary who advocated a return to Greek classicism and simplicity in order to reaffirm the essence of music as a force for cosmic understanding. These views laid the foundation for what we now call classical music and paved the way for Haydn, Mozart and Beethoven.

The form of the music did indeed become simplified and refined by the classical composers, reaching its own perfection with what became known as 'sonata form' and the symphony. However, the seismic shift was not so much to do with these developments, part of a natural progression, but was more to do with the change in how the world was viewed, how reality was perceived.

No longer was the universe centred on the Earth, Copernicus and Galileo had seen to that; no longer was the universe inhabited by God, Newton had dispensed with Him in creating his clockwork cosmos. With this, the focal point of creation was drawn away from the heavens and focused on the individual, on man, the measure of all things, according to the classical Greek philosopher, Protagoras.

Music became a means of expressing individual feelings and philosophies and the greatest exponent of this was Beethoven. One could speculate that Beethoven was the originator of the musical selfie. Although what you can hear in his music has universal significance, the music is self-expressive, an expression of the man, of Beethoven.

The classical and romantic periods have been described by contemporary composer Steve Reich as the greatest distraction in music, taking us away from its purpose of penetrating and expressing the workings of the universe, focusing it instead on the mutual feelings of human beings. From this viewpoint, classical music has been an aberration which has almost obliterated the true significance – the spirit – of music, its ability to make sense of our place in the cosmic scheme of things. Wow!

Music was no less metaphysical after Beethoven but its search for transcendence was forced to shift from focusing on the

About Music

external universe to one of an inner journey. The cosmos could now only be understood and described by ever more complex mathematical and scientific theories. Music's role was usurped.

♪ Chris and I have been walking steadily through the meadows, focusing on forging this musical pathway and now we realise we have been making good time and are approaching Llangattock Lingoed. We are tired and hungry again and are grateful to arrive at the village's cool stone church, St Cadoc, only a little over two miles away from our destination today in Pandy.

The building has a barrel-vaulted roof and a beam across the front of the altar which is the remains of a 15th-century rood screen, intricately carved with interweaving vines. The vine was a significant symbol in ancient Greece, being a representative of the god Dionysius and his cult of divine intoxication. A large festival in ancient Athens was held in honour of Dionysius and involved performances of dramatic tragedies, no doubt accompanied by music.

The church atmosphere proclaims peace, calm and reverence, even if the carvings are a reminder of the connections that can be made with pagan revelry. The rood screen itself is a common feature in late medieval church architecture and is typically an ornate partition between the chancel, the space around the altar, and nave, where the congregation sits.

Chris is resting outside on a bench in the church's porch and calls out to me. When I join him I find that he is looking closely at a bat which is lying panting next to him on the bench. The creature was asleep but perhaps unwell and we leave it in peace. I return inside the church and find a description of the Lesser Horseshoe bat colony that lives in the church's rafters. Bats are in some cultures symbols of death or trickery. They are also used as symbols of the underworld where people live in the shadows of darkness.

There are always two sides to a story and in Chinese culture they are bringers of good luck. This little church is clearly full of ancient lore and sympathetic magic. We munch casually on the last of our food supply, drink water and then embark on the last stage of our journey today.

About Music

The 1700s were the 'Age of Enlightenment' when scientific experiment realised new discoveries in all fields of human endeavour. The Enlightenment's purpose was to reform society through reason, to challenge unquestioned ideas grounded in tradition and faith and to advance knowledge through the scientific method, opposing the dogmas of superstition and intolerance. In a rational, scientific world, music became not the means for describing the universe but an antidote to the science that did.

Contemporary with Ludwig van Beethoven was the French mathematician and physicist, Joseph Fourier, best known for initiating investigation of the mathematical analysis of waveforms, the Fourier series, and its applications to problems of heat transfer and - vibrations. Fourier analysis shows how a complex vibrating sound wave can be analysed into its simple wave components. An unintended result was the opening of a way to create new sounds, for synthesising them. The electronic sound synthesiser was probably not something that Beethoven could have possibly considered as a means for making music but its gestation was taking place while he lived and composed.

Our path now begins to slope steadily downwards as we pick our way by hedgerows and through yet more fields. We can see clearly the outline of the Black Mountains whose summit ridges we will walk on our next ramble. Seeing this impressive view makes me feel like a hobbit, about to leave the familiar countryside of the Shire and embark on a great adventure which will lead through unknown, alien territory. The hills await.

Chris tells me that exploring unknown territory always reminds him of the cowboy films that used to capture his imagination as a boy. We talk about the exodus of Jewish composers from Europe to America before the mid-20th century at the time when persecution drove them away from their homes to cross the Atlantic. It was the entertainment and music industries which gave them a platform for their work. The film genre of the American Western was largely a Jewish creation.

About Music

Our mind travel today reaches a climax a little earlier than this at the end of the 19th century when music is being propelled into an age of technology and experiment. Reverence for the old transforms into worship of the new and of the great god science. Just before the new century, one man was making inroads into our understanding about acoustics and the relationship of sound with the inner workings of the brain. Hermann von Helmholtz (1821-94) was a German physician and physicist who made significant contributions to several widely varied areas of modern science. His contributions to music included work on acoustics, the analysis of sound waves and the perception of sound.

His discoveries would influence not only our understanding of the perception of music but, together with the discoveries of Fourier, the way that music can be created. Their work would lead in the next era to electronically synthesised sounds and an understanding of how the brain responds to music.

There is an almost unimaginable chasm between Pythagoras and his Monochord and the BBC's Radiophonic Workshop which created the synthesised and infamous Dr Who theme. How we got from there to here has, like the life of Thomas Tallis, a little of the miracle about it.

At the turn of the 20th century, composers attempted to throw off the shackles of the preceding age and free music from what they saw as the constraints of classical and romantic forms, which were dominating the whole realm of music. Richard Strauss's opera, Salomé, was even more controversial at its premiere in 1905 than Stravinsky's infamous *Rite of Spring* just eight years later. It was not just the link between a biblical theme and the shocking erotica involving the severed head of John the Baptist, but, even more difficult to take, its chordal dissonance was a shock to sensitive ears.

Music had turned inwards for its inspiration and what came out, although highly expressive, was not necessarily easy or pleasant to listen to. There followed the breaking down of all its traditions and sense of music as a journey that would conclude safely back home, a process in music that had fulfilled a human need for security. Serialism, music concrete, Futurism, neo-classicism, minimalism, ambient music, are just some of the genres that were in this

About Music

whirlpool of new ideas and we'll be making them the subject of a later walk.

In the 21st century, composers are adapting digital technology for their own needs and working on space-age projects that Dr Who would have felt proud of. Perhaps as a reaction to rampant technology and complexity, there has been a move towards regaining the clarity of early music and that music's qualities that are able to illuminate reality. This time round, that reality is more to do with the microcosm of the composer's inner universe than with the outer cosmos. It is the deep oceans of the unconscious and musical functioning of the human brain which comprise an, as yet, largely uncharted territory.

Almost without warning we arrive at a main road. The noise of traffic, unheard all day until now, jolts us out of our reveries and musings. We are in Pandy, at the foot of the mountains, close to a rather tempting public house.

Bill, feeling a little cosmic

About Music

CHAPTER 3

How Harmony Was Discovered

In which we traverse mountains and do some musical sums

The weather is better this early morning in mid-June, warm, cloudy, some occasional sunshine and a light breeze. I have new comfortable boots and another seventeen-miler to look forward to. This walk will take us up into the Black Mountains and along a ridgeway until later this afternoon we will descend into the town of Hay-on-Wye.

The Black Mountains form the eastern boundary of the Brecon Beacons National Park. These hills are less well known than their westerly counterparts but are equally wild and beautiful. Our path will take us precisely along the Welsh-English border and for much of it we'll be able to look down into both countries from an elevated vantage point, Wales to the left, England to the right as we head north.

The start, in Pandy, is represented by an unremarkable stile, signed 'Offa's Dyke Path'. It is just a few yards away from the public house, the Lancaster Arms (now closed), on the A465 Hereford to Abergavenny road, where we finished our previous walk. After the usual photo to mark the occasion, we hop over the stile into a field and are on our way again with fresh legs and a confident step.

The path leads us through a field, across a stream, the Afon Honddu, over a railway line and then climbs steadily upwards. On our left we pass a farm and on one of the farm buildings, clearly visible to walkers on this path, is a graffiti extract from a poem, 'The Lofty Sky' by Anglo-Welsh Dymock poet, Edward Thomas:

> Today I want the sky,
> The tops of the high hills,
> Above the last man's house,
> His hedges, and his cows,
> Where, if I will, I look

About Music

Down even on sheep and rook,
And of all things that move
See buzzards only above –

Past all trees, past furze
And thorn, where nought deters
The desire of the eye
For sky, nothing but sky.

  Thomas, a soldier in the First World War, was killed by the concussive blast wave from one of the last shells fired after a battle while he stood to light his pipe. There is a terrible irony here but, for us, even this could not dampen the life-affirming sentiment held in the poet's words which fuelled our feelings for the journey ahead.

  We are walking steadily upwards, glancing back at the patchwork view that expands into the valley below. This is a long climb, which we take in silence, reserving our breath for the effort. The path dips a little, skirts an ancient hill fort then continues upwards.

  We arrive on the top of Hatterall Hill at the south end of the Hatterall Ridge. The remarkable feature about this route through the Black Mountains is that from here to Hay Bluff, the northern end of the ridge and about four miles this side of Hay, is an uninterrupted elevated stretch of about eleven miles. From this point on we will still be climbing up to a height of about 700 metres, but it will be a gentle slope as we walk steadily along the border with views on either side into Herefordshire on one side and Powys on the other.

  Ahead, the path is clear. It twists and turns but a little as it arrows towards Hay Bluff. On either side is peaty moorland and I have been warned that it may be boggy in parts. There are occasional burnt patches in the heather revealing where it is being managed – burning the heather in one season ensures healthy growth in the next. The heather is spotted with dots of cotton grass, each white tip made by some biocosmic marker pen.

  There is no noise, but there is music, for tumbling down upon us as we walk is the song of skylarks. We can hear several at once and see them every few seconds soaring up from their nests to take our attention away from their vulnerable nests. As we walk, we

About Music

leave one set of larks behind then others take over. All the while along this path, for the next five hours, we are accompanied by song.

The Dyke is non-existent for this stretch, presumably because the mountains provide the natural barrier which would have been the Dyke's function. We pass a group of Welsh ponies grazing unconcernedly and there are occasional other birds, too. We see ravens flying, carrying with them a suggestion of the folkloric blackness and bleakness of mortality.

Any personal reveries on ravens and time are shattered by the shuddering appearance of three cyclists – cyclists up here? We step aside as they rip through the air and jolt past us. They come and vanish in a trice then the sense of wilderness immediately returns to remove the fact of their momentary existence.

I say to Chris that our music discussion is to be about the origins of harmony. This, I have learnt, is a tricky topic as it can become quickly labyrinthine in complexity without much effort. My intention is to pull all the necessary historical bits together and work them into a clear, easy to understand essay. As this involves a little mathematics, I suggest that we wait until our first picnic stop and then I'll work through the explanation to see if he can follow it step by step. This suits him fine so we can stay focused on the walk for the time being.

We come across the first of three triangulation pillars or 'trig' points marking our height above sea level, this one at 464 metres. These concrete blocks were erected throughout the country, the first in 1935, the last in the 1960s. When they were all in place it was possible to see from any one at least two others. The idea was to map the angles between line-of-sight points and from this construct a series of triangles. Once this had been done, the triangles were referenced to a single line and it became possible to create a highly accurate mapping of the whole country.

The trig points are concrete icebergs in the sense that much of their construction is below the surface of the earth in which they sit to give them stability. Since the advent of geostationary satellites and the Global Positioning System, they have become redundant and many have been vandalised or fallen into disrepair. Measurements taken from the network of trig pillars were accurate to 20 metres over the entire length of Great Britain. Today, the receivers that make up the Ordnance Survey Net are coordinated to an accuracy of just 3 mm.

When the Ordnance Survey announced the demise of trig points back in the 1990s, an unpredicted backlash caused them to think outside the triangle. OS decided to offer adoption to those who cared about them, the walking public. Questions were raised in parliament and a code of practice drawn up.

These pillars are invaluable for walkers who use them as points to aim for, to define the tops of hills and to rest their backs against. And, let's be honest, by far the most important function is as a back rest.

The next marker we encounter is a left turn sign onto a path leading down the Welsh side of the hill into Llanthony. The Augustinian priory there was founded in the 12th century and during the eventual dissolution of the monasteries inevitably fell into decay. The ruins still remain.

A detour to the priory at Llanthony would regretfully take up too much time, so we carry on along our ridge way. We pass a second trig point at 552 metres. Then a few minutes later, we decide to sink into the heather to recharge our batteries, to have some food, some drink and a music lesson.

Below us we can see the vale where Llanthony Priory lies. Chris takes off his boots to air his feet and asks me if I've heard about extreme walking. This, he informs me, is an activity conducted with bare feet. I can imagine it quite possible when the soles have become hardened but I can feel my own cringing at the thought of nakedly walking this stony path.

I dig out a couple of typed sheets on which I've prepared some notes about the discovery of the classical music scale and how harmony came to be. We discuss it while taking refreshment and satisfying the desire of our eyes for the view. Chris looks at the maths and says that it's a pity many people are put off by even the most basic sums and so miss much that is of interest.

Then, as if his bootless feet and the mention of sums has made a spell, we are joined by a strange companion.

"Good day, fair gentlemen. How goes your journey? May I join you and ease my limbs?" He sits beside us and we both stare at him in surprise. He is bare footed, a strong, brown-skinned man,

About Music

fully bearded and wearing a light linen tunic and a wide brimmed hat. He looks at us with amusement. We regard him with amazement. Not wishing to appear rude or unwelcoming, we quash our surprise and warmly invite him to sit with us.

"I am Pythagoras. May I know the names of my companions?" We stutter our replies.

"We Greeks like to walk and think", he continues. "We are the great walkers and thinkers. I would profess that walking is the source of the greatest of ideas. When you walk, your mind clears of all its worldly dross and the view it then has into the realm of numbers is without veil."

He is smiling all the time, but then becomes quite serious. "Make the most of my presence for I will be gone soon." I gather my thoughts and ask him about music. Chris is still looking at our companion's large, brown, leathery feet.

The man sees this. "My race is not fond of shoes," he responds, "They are only for occasions of importance and when conducting business". Chris nods and then both he and I quieten as Pythagoras explains about his music to us.

I make a record of his words and this is his explanation. I have begun with background information first about musical notes and intervals, so that his theories make sense to our modern ears.

There are eight notes in a scale which starts and ends on the same note, the top note being an octave above the start, for example, A, B, C, D, E, F, G, A.

An 'interval' is the distance between any two notes and is worked out by counting the number of notes in between plus the first and last notes. For example, the interval from C to D is called a 2nd; the interval from C to E (that is, C to D to E) is a 3rd, and so on. C to F is a 4th; C to G is a 5th.

Here are a couple of examples using different starting notes: G to D is a 5th; D to A is a 5th. Just check this last one: the interval goes from D to E to F to G to A. There are five notes counting from D to A, therefore the interval is called a 5th.

Pythagoras tells us that he created his scale by piling fifth intervals on top of one another. This is a bemusing suggestion.

About Music

"My philosophy won't be clear in your minds yet, so give me just a little time to converse and explain", he urges.

Pythagoras then revealed to us how he found the notes of a scale. He explains that the interval of the fifth is used to find the notes and make the scale because this interval embodies the simplest ratio after the octave. Hold up. What, you may ask, is a 'ratio'?

Imagine a string under tension, fixed at both ends and under tension. Place your finger exactly half way along. This is called 'stopping the string'. The string length has effectively been *divided* by 2. When the string is plucked, the rate the string vibrates, its frequency of vibration, is double that of the vibration of the full-length string; when the string length has been *divided* by 2, the frequency of vibration has been *multiplied* by 2.

If the sound vibration frequency of the open (unstopped) string was 100 cycles per second (100 Hz, to use the standard unit of measurement), it is now vibrating at 200 Hz and the frequency *ratio*, obtained by comparing the two notes, is 2:1 or 2/1 (and, yes, ratios and fractions are two ways of saying exactly the same thing).

The string length is halved (length ratio 1:2); the frequency is doubled (frequency ratio 2:1). The fractions are inverted, turned upside down, when converting length ratio to frequency ratio. This particular frequency ratio, 2:1, represents a note an octave above the starting reference note, sometimes referred to as the 'fundamental'.

If at this point, dear reader, you are remembering that you are allergic to even the mention of the word mathematics, rest assured that the following should be quite easy to follow, but if daunted and thinking that life is just too short for such machinations and you have an important appointment to go to, **just skim through and absorb what you can.** You'll come out the other side quite unscathed and can read and walk on with us.

Pythagoras explains that the string on his own single-string instrument, the monochord, did not function in the same way as the string on a modern violin but the end result was the same. On a violin, or any instrument in that family, the bridge over which the strings are stretched is in a fixed position and the violinist makes different notes by stopping the string with his or her fingertips in different positions. On Pythagoras's monochord, the bridge is

About Music

moveable. The string length and therefore the pitch of any note played on it are altered by moving the bridge.

Now imagine that instead of stopping the string at the half-way point you stop the string exactly one third along. This is the simplest whole number division after 2:1. The string has now been divided into two unequal parts, the longer section of string is 2/3 of the whole length; the shorter is 1/3. The longer section, with a length ratio of 2:3 (short bit compared with long bit), will vibrate at 3/2 times the original note's frequency. This creates the interval that we now call a fifth.

That's the difficult part over with. All you need to know in addition (and just take my word for this unless you are familiar with the maths) is that adding intervals together is the same as multiplying their frequency ratios. So, to add two 5th intervals, you multiply 3/2 by 3/2 and the resultant new interval has a frequency ratio of 9/4. Got it? Now we are ready for Pythagoras's experiment, to pile up the 5ths, adding them on top of one another to see what happens:

Beginning on an open string note (it could be any note, but let's use C as the starting reference point, 1/1), the note which is a 5th interval above this is G (1/1 x 3/2):

G = 3/2
Next 5th interval up is D (3/2 x 3/2)
D = 9/4

Pythagoras pauses, thinks, then speaks again, "There is a slight problem". And explains, "9/4 is greater than 2/1, which means we have a note higher than the octave above our original note, C. To keep the results within the range of a single octave, you must simply divide it by 2."

The result is still the same note, D, but an octave lower. 9/4 divided by 2 is 9/8. Come on – remember your basics about fractions.

D = 9/8   Next 5th interval up is A (9/8 x 3/2)
A = 27/16   Next 5th interval up is E (27/16 x 3/2)
E = 81/32   Again, (27/16 x 3/2) is greater than

About Music

2/1, so divide by 2 = 81/64
E = 81/64   Next 5th interval up is B (81/64 x 3/2),
B = 243/128

The next 5th interval up is F (243/128 x 3/2) = 2.85. Divide this by 2 = 1.43, but this is getting too complicated.

Using Pythagoras's method, we now have the notes C, D, E, G, A, and B.

One note from our scale is missing – F and this needs special treatment. We might have found the F by adding on another 5th to B, but it can more conveniently be found by employing the next simplest ratio after 2/3 which is 3/4, made by stopping the string in a ratio of 3:4, thus neatly filling the gap between E and G.

If we slot this into the series and also add the C an octave higher than the original C, this creates the Pythagorean scale:

C	D	E	F	G	A	B	C
1	9/8	81/64	4/3	3/2	27/16	243/128	2
	9/8	9/8	256/243	9/8	9/8	9/8	256/243

The first line of numbers under the notes shows the frequency ratios *compared with the starting note*, C. The lower line shows the ratios by *comparing successive notes*.

You'll see that there is a rather obscure fraction between B and the upper octave C, but at least it's the same as between E and F. These two intervals, B-C and E-F are half tones. The rest are whole tones. In this scale they are called the 'Pythagorean Tone' and the 'Pythagorian Semitone', or 'hemitone'. The maths shows that the Pythagorian tone is (unfortunately!) just a little greater than two semitones.

Pythagoras's description concludes with this. He looks at us quizzically, trying to work out if we have understood or if his time has been wasted.

"I have a feeling this may be too much for your minds that lack the art of philosophy, but really it is all quite simple. You may not have known about my experiments with vibrations, but perhaps you have heard of my work with triangles?"

About Music

I think of the trig points and the mapping of the country using triangulation and reflect that this man has had immeasurable influence, touching us today, reaching out from those ancient classical times to be here, now. Pythagoras casts us his final thought.

"My friends, remember that life is a quest and that harmony is what we are striving for. In this, consider the role that discord may play. To create harmony, we must understand discord. In music, both are vital for a sense of progress, of travelling along our journey, of achievement. But discord should not last long."

With that thought, he rises, adjusts his tunic, tilts his hat, shakes our hands and walks away. As we pack our bags and prepare to continue the journey, Chris whispers audibly, "What a remarkable man."

*****

This represents the beginning of music as science and art. The method used to create the Pythagorian scale is straightforward but the resulting ratios are quite clumsy. Some intervals, the major third intervals (C to E, F to A, B to D) were just too complicated and not pleasing to the ear. This didn't bother the Greeks because their music was essentially only melody. Harmony was more a mathematical exercise than a musical pleasure for them. However, it prevented musicians for centuries from making anything but music with simple textures.

Something momentous then happened to solve this problem and propelled music into modern times. Since its occurrence, music has been built from a fundamental and strong sense of key and, even more significantly, built on the use of chordal harmonies called 'triads'. In music, 'key' and the 'triads' are equivalent to geographical trig points in that they provide the means for knowing where you are in a musical landscape.

A triad is the simplest of chords which consists of a root note, the note an interval of a third above this and a note another third above.

Musicians discovered that if the major third intervals had their ratios reduced, 'tempered', by 80/81, a fraction called the

About Music

'diatonic comma', or 'comma of Didymus', it resulted in much simpler ratios of 5/4, in keeping with the principle that simple maths embodied beauty and divinity. The result was much more satisfying, both mathematically and musically.

Didymus the Musician, incidentally, was a music theorist who lived in Rome at the end of the end of the 1st century BC or beginning of the 1st century AD, at the time of the emperor, Nero, of Rome-fiddling fame.

A simpler scale resulted giving more harmonious sounds when notes are played at the same time.

C	D	E	F	G	A	B	C
1	9/8	5/4	4/3	3/2	5/3	15/8	2
	9/8	10/9	16/15	9/8	10/9	9/8	16/15

The difficulty with the new scale, which was called the 'just' or 'pure' scale, is that there are two different values, 9/8 and 10/9, for the size of the whole tones which were called major and minor tones (not to be confused with major and minor intervals). After the Middle Ages, the problem becomes more significant when compelled to consider music which was more complex and extended.

The development of music theory after the pure scale stage is one of finding a cure for an illness and discovering that the cure creates an unwanted side effect needing further treatment. Our next consideration will be about these musical side effects and the ultimate cure for the scale.

♪ There are occasional other walkers on the path today and there is other human activity, too. We gaze upwards in awe, our attention caught be the gossamer image of a paraglider, almost imperceptibly floating through the air, supported only by a sliver of fragile half chute. The peace of this scene proves to be just as fragile, shattered by a squadron of angry-engined microlites which fly as mechanical mosquitos over our heads, crossing the border from one country to the other. Peace soon envelops us again, defined by the enduring skylark song.

About Music

We walk on. In places the path becomes quite civilised and there has been some construction work to make it easier going, particularly over the boggy bits. The pathway is laid down before us and there are bags of building materials to either side, dropped by helicopter and awaiting further renovations. Then, just as quickly, the path becomes peat and stone again, so we pick our way carefully.

A third trig point at 610 m is passed with views to Herefordshire's Black Hill Ridge. In a short step further, we come to another peak and as we do so a walker comes into view carrying packs both on his front and back. We chat with him awhile and he tells us these are his parachutes for paragliding and that they will soon be needed. We wish him well and then take the opportunity to rest again.

Chris tells me that the celebrity gardener and farmer, Monty Don, has a farm close by and I mention another farm building marked on our map called 'The Vision'. This was the setting for a novel and a film made about Welsh twin boys brought up there during the time before and during the First World War and their lives thereafter. We discuss the hard times that hillside farmers had when surviving the harsh mountain winters, the wet, cold weather and the snows. I remember the poem that launched our walk. The boys' father was set against their education, regarding it as a criminal waste of time, given the more pressing needs and labours of farm life on the hill.

There are occasional side paths marked on either side of the ridge, leading down into the valleys but we ignore them and continue straight on.

The next resting place is determined by a large flat stone positioned temptingly bench-like just to the side of the path and overlooking the continuing spectacular vista. We sit and turn our heads to glance ahead along the path to where the Black Mountain reaches its peak.

Twyn Llech, the Black Mountain, 48 kilometres to the west in the Brecon Beacons is a mountain not to be confused with the Black Hill just 2 km to our east. The Black Hill is the only so-called 'Marilyn' to fall exactly on the Welsh-English border, straddling Powys and Herefordshire. It is the highest point on the Hatterrall Ridge at 703 m.

About Music

A Marilyn is a mountain or hill which must have a drop on all sides of at least 150 metres, regardless of height above sea level. The name was coined as a 'hats off' rhyming slang to the designation Munro, referring to a Scottish mountain with a drop height of more than 914.4 m. While we sit, I talk more about harmony.

In the 15th and 16th Renaissance centuries, pieces of music became longer and more complex. Musicians moved to the new principle of tonality which made the triad a central feature of harmony.

Variety was achieved during the course of a piece of music by moving the bottom note of a scale, called the tonic, onto a different note and building a new scale on that. The shifting of the tonic note or key was called 'modulation' to a new key.

By the 17th century, Baroque composers had limited the use of the modes to mainly just two: the Lydian mode, which we now call the major key and the Aeolian, which we call the minor.

In most pieces of music, the first modulation to take place is up by a fifth, the tonic moving, for example, from C to G. This is where – and why – the just scale's problem becomes apparent. The effect of its slightly different size whole tones means that we can see immediately A is not in the right place; instead of being 9/8 above G, it is 10/9. So, a new note is required in this scale, slightly sharper (higher in frequency) than A. The sharpening required is 81/80, the comma of Didymus.

With this modification, the scale is correct up to and including E. But now there is a greater problem. The next two intervals of our major mode are in the wrong order. We have a semitone followed by a tone, but need a tone followed by a semitone. F must be replaced by a completely new note a semitone higher. The new note is called F sharp (F#).

Every key will require both adjusted, tempered notes and additional new notes.

For keyboard players a compromise had to be found to avoid having an unwieldy number of keys in front of them. This was achieved by mistuning the intervals to give a compromise between true intervals and the freedom to modulate away from the opening

About Music

key. 'Mistuning' and 'tempering', if you hadn't realised it by now, are pretty much the same thing. The result of finding a compromise solution evolved into the modern piano keyboard which also has black keys to provide the necessary extra notes for playing in different keys. An added bonus of these extra notes meant that richer harmonies could be included in the composer's armoury.

The historical process in music, leading from ancient Greece to the grand piano, bequeaths to us in modern times the phenomenon of the concert pianist. As an aside, for a musician, his or her instrument has become not only a means of music making but also as an instrument of self-development. The relationship of a player with his instrument is always unique and personal. The effect that an instrument has on its player can be life changing.

The performance pressures on these people may be too great to bear and always affects their development as individuals. Chris tells me about a young Canadian pianist, Marika Bournaki, a prodigy and teenage musical brat but who has become an educative and supportive musician of others. She has gone from self-centred to selfless through the medium of music and her piano keyboard.

Drifting up from the fields below and on our right hand, we hear music and see cars, vans and caravans parked in a field. The summer festivals have begun, music always their main feature and the focal draw that brings people together for a good time. Later this year, I'll be making my own annual pilgrimage to Reading, marking, for me, the pinnacle of the summer months and a secular celebration that has at its core all the qualities of a spiritual experience.

We are approaching Hay Bluff, the high point at the end of the ridge-walk and our path skirts around it. The sky seems to open up even more to the satisfied delight of our eyes. We encounter some more walkers, youngsters chatting away happily on their day out.

There are other systems of tuning a keyboard instrument, but the one called Equal Temperament (ET) has become the accepted norm since the time of Bach in the early 18th century. In ET, all distinctions between major and minor tones and between the various semitone sizes are rejected in favour of making all the tones the same size and all the semitones the same size. The octave can therefore be divided into twelve equal semitones. What effect does this have on the triad intervals of the fifth and the major third on which the whole of our western harmony is built?

In equal temperament, all the semitones are equal distances apart; some of the 'pure' intervals become squashed a little, others become wider. The fifths become squashed to make them fit. The necessity of this can be mathematically demonstrated: twelve fifths piled on top of one another $(3/2^{12})$ should equal seven octaves $(2/1^7)$. It doesn't; the piled-up 5ths overshoot. You can check the maths:

$$(3/2)^{12} = 129.746 \qquad (2/1)^7 = 128.000$$

The effect on major thirds is where ET really falls down. ET major thirds are made wide, about one-seventh of a semitone wider than acoustically pure fifths. Nobody comments, but it's a noticeable discrepancy away from the pure harmony.

Our final stop is just beyond the Bluff and from where we sit, we can see our day's destination nestling in the blue haze below, roughly four miles away. At the foot of the Bluff is a minor road, the Gospel Pass, and car park with an ice-cream van. Our map shows that these are close to a prehistoric stone circle. Chris looks thoughtful and asks perceptively, "So was harmony discovered or invented?"

So far, we've been considering the musical scale and harmony as something that was defined using vibrating strings and some maths. There is more, because the intervals in the pure scale are all to be found as the building blocks for sound itself, whether sound made by a musical instrument or something else – anything else which can create the audible sensation of pitch.

Harmony in the European music tradition evolved from a naturally occurring arrangement of notes known as the harmonic series, discovered by Pythagoras and subsequently analysed properly by mathematicians in the 17th and 18th centuries. The first of these

About Music

is Marin Mersenne (1588-1648), a French theologian, philosopher, mathematician, and music theorist. Some sources say he discovered these harmonics, which he called *sons extraordinaire*, but in fact he defined the harmonics that Pythagoras had already recognised and used to build his scale.

Also attributed with defining harmonics is Jean-Philippe Rameau (1683-1764), a brilliant French composer and music theorist. Rameau understood harmonics in relation to harmonies and dissonances, the intervals between notes that sound good or that clash when the notes are sounded together.

The 'good' harmonies are intervals between notes of the octave, the third, the sixth, and, to a lesser degree, the fourth and the fifth. The 'bad' intervals, the discords, are the second and the seventh. One particular interval was even banned from use for a while by church authorities. This was called the 'Devil's Interval' and in musical parlance is described as an augmented fourth or diminished fifth, which are essentially the same thing.

This particularly devilish interval is used commonly today. It still creates a disturbing effect in the music, but our modern ears will detect little hint of Beelzebub in its acoustic effect.

If you go back and look again at how the Pythagorian scale was constructed, you will see that the 'F' which was slotted in to the scale last of all was not made by adding a fifth interval to 'B' and this was a consequence of the interval being that devilish diminished fifth. Oh, no!

Rameau's paper, *Treatise on Harmony*, published in the 1720s, was a theory of harmony based on his ability to hear several different notes, the harmonics, sounding simultaneously when an individual note was played on an instrument, on a harpsichord, a violin or a wind instrument such as a flute.

A pitched sound with a fundamental frequency of, say, 100 Hz, will stimulate resonating sympathetic vibrations in the medium carrying and transmitting the sound waves, for example, in a piano frame. It does so in the simplest of ratios compared to the fundamental 100 Hz, namely 200 Hz, 300 Hz, 400 Hz, 500 Hz, etc. This is, literally, the simplest mathematical progression.

Conversely, there are no vibrations at frequencies between the tones of this series. The harmonic series, unlike the Pythagorian scale with which we started this section, is a property of the natural world, pure and simple.

The combined effect of the harmonics in this series is the main feature which gives a sound its particular 'timbre' or quality. The timbre depends on the relative loudness of the harmonics. The relative loudness or 'amplitudes' of these is infinitely variable and therefore gives rise to the potential existence of an infinite range of different sounds when these different combinations of harmonic amplitudes are combined into a single sound. This is what makes a violin sound different from a piano, or a siren sound different from a whistle.

Conversely, a sound wave that consists of the fundamental frequency only, with no harmonics, will sound highly uninteresting, a little bit like a tuning fork, for example, or, for any engineers out there, a simple sine wave generator. We have a walk coming up later that is about acoustics, so there will be more on this later.

Starting with the fundamental and analysing a sound into its harmonics, the sequence of successive intervals as you go up in frequency is always octave (2/1), fifth (3/2), fourth (4/3), major third (5/4), minor third (6/5), and then progressively smaller intervals, *ad infinitum*. The prevalence of the octave, fifth, fourth and major and minor thirds at the beginning of the harmonic series provided the foundation for our appreciation of musical harmony.

We have taken something fundamental to the physics of nature, i.e., existing in nature, and altered, or tempered it, to suit our ears.

Here is a graphic representation of what the harmonic series looks like:

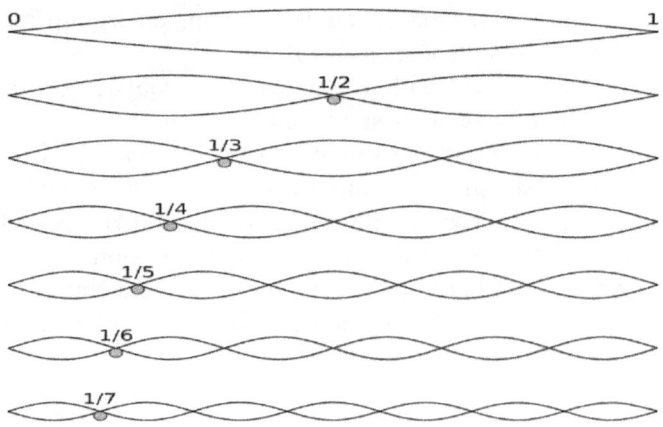

About Music

Our path heads downwards all the way. We walk along the Gospel Pass road for a while and then head off to the left across a grassy common, making for the corner of the common and a wood that lies ahead. This is the only time on our journey that the designated path has disappeared but we are confident of our compass direction and will pick the path up again at the place where common and wood converge at the common's far corner.

There are orchids in the grass.

We have learnt how the basis of key and harmony was first a mathematical idea and then was supported by the discovery of the harmonic series, a naturally occurring phenomenon. But considerations about the creation of musical harmony are not only based on maths and physics, for harmony has a physiological basis, too. Helmholtz's *On the Sensations of Tone* describes how when two notes are sounded together the ear perceives the difference in frequency between them as a third vibration of 'beats'. Some of these can distress the ear.

Fred Lerdahl, a modern theorist, says, "When a periodic signal reaches the inner ear, an area of the basilar membrane is stimulated, the peak of which fires rapidly to the auditory cortex, causing the perception of a single pitch. If two periodic signals simultaneously stimulate overlapping areas, the perturbation causes a sensation of 'roughness'."

The worst of these are the semitone and the interval of the seventh, its 'inversion' - if two intervals add up to make an octave, then they are called 'inversions' of one another. For example, inversions are the fifth and the fourth; the third and the sixth; the second and the seventh; the unison and the octave.

Don't fret if you don't know what the 'basilar membrane' or the 'auditory cortex' are, as part of our later route's exploration will be into an understanding of the role that the brain plays when it responds to sound vibrations and to music. All that matters for now is this reveals that the uncomfortable sensation of dissonance has a physical basis in the ear and the ear's relationship with the brain.

About Music

We are finally making our way through fields on the outskirts of Hay-on-Wye and then by houses and their gardens. Chris spots a sign outside a building advertising an oak furniture maker and he recognises the maker's name, a traditional craftsman.

One last field and we arrive in the car park by the tourist information office. Somehow our legs know just where to go and take us gratefully to the nearest pub.

Bill, in a harmonious temper

About Music

CHAPTER 4

One Man and His Music

*In which we meet some sheep and the
Count of Counterpoint*

It is the late Middle Ages and Henry V is on the throne. He is vigorously pursuing a military campaign in France, having revived the Hundred Years War. The wars drain the royal purse, but the economy is booming as, thanks in part to the plague, the problem of overpopulation has been temporarily solved.

Henry likes to make war and likes to listen to music. He has a particular interest in liturgical music and gives pensions to well-known composers. A hymn of praise to God, which he ordered sung after the battle of Agincourt in 1415, still exists today. This battle crippled France. The greatest composer of the time is an Englishman called John Dunstable.

Imagine what it would be like to go for a walk in the countryside along these borderlands in the times of Henry and Dunstable. What roads that exist are muddy in the wet, dusty when dry, inhabited by trundling carts and packhorses, with groups of pedestrians walking together for safety. An occasional messenger gallops by. From an elevated vantage point on the dyke, we would see massive irregularly shaped fields. These are huge, up to 1,200 acres, with no fences or hedges.

In these fields are individual strips of about an acre each which are managed by their tenants. They are to our eyes the greatest set of allotments we have ever seen.

Groups of the strips are left fallow every second or third year, others planted with wheat, oats and barley. Around these huge areas and bounded by ditches and earth walls is woodland and grassland for sheep.

Surprisingly, woodland is no more plentiful than it is today. It is, however, extremely well managed for it is the main source of building materials and firewood. Every last twig is valued and accounted for. There are few evergreen trees. The only common one is holly. The squirrels are red.

Wide low-lying meadows are used for hay making. Any walls and ditches are sparse and disorganised so both humans and, more annoyingly, animals can stray onto the cultivated strips and cause damage. This is a source of agitation and argument amongst the tenants.

As we walk in those times, we are aware that the most dangerous wild animal is the marauding robber and his gang.

Contemporary imagination clings to the idea that the countryside is eternal and unchanging. This is a fallacy. It is in constant flux, not least so in the Middle Ages when the factor affecting the landscape most is disease. Waves of plague strike, decimating the population.

As we walk through a village, we make some startling discoveries. Property owners have no time for making their dwellings and gardens pretty. All they are concerned with is whether or not something has practical use. This gives an impression of disorderly untidiness to us, but to the villager anything without a practical use is a waste of time and space.

Buildings are often left to rot when empty. The plague, rents and taxes empty the houses. This means that labour is in short supply but despite appearances the rural economy is booming.

Now, today, in early July, we are going to imagine that it is into this historical world that our walk takes us with the intention of experiencing what it might have been like for a musician and composer in those days who ventured into the rural landscape. The route begins in the Herefordshire town of Hay-on-Wye, known in modern times for its second-hand book shops, will continue north along the Offa's Dyke Path for about fourteen miles and conclude in Kington, a pretty village in Shropshire.

For this stretch and the remainder of the Offa's Dyke path I will be walking alone, apart from, of course, those I may meet on the way, accompanied only by my back pack and impish wand, my walking stick. The way is now too far from home for my companion, Chris, to stay with me.

Despite heavy rain the previous night, the sky is clearing and it is, once more, dry underfoot. I begin at the Wye Bridge in Hay and spend a moment or two admiring the view from the bridge over this wide stretch of the river with its flecks of white as the water bumps over stones and boulders. I walk into a wood and then emerge onto the river bank, walk a while along it and then veer off to the left into farmland.

I am being careful not to lose my way at this early stage of today's walk and can see from the map that the path skirts fields and farm buildings, doglegging as it does so. My confidence increases as I encounter the familiar acorn symbol on gates and finger posts signifying that I am on the dyke's designated path.

Crops are starting to ripen but are not yet fully grown. The bracken is well up and the foxgloves nearly over. It is the beginning of summer proper and the natural world has a relaxed atmosphere, a sense of calm. I consult my compass and the map again and look back at the view over Hay-on-Wye before turning to the northwest and marching on.

As I enter a field, I see striding towards me another walker. It is a young woman. She is sturdily built, is carrying a huge backpack and her two walking poles are topped with flags, one heralding King Offa, the other has the red Welsh dragon on a green background. I am invisible to her as she passes without a glance. Perhaps she has been told not to talk to strangers.

I pass alongside a wood called Bettws Dingle. It is delightful how the onomatopoeia pours from the Welsh language. Appending the word 'dingle' adds rhythm. It's a great name for a wood. 'Bettws' means a place of prayer.

The dyke path hits a road not much more than a track, but it is easy walking. Such tracks were used by the animal drovers.

Drovers' journeys have been made for hundreds, if not thousands of years, but particularly since the 11th century until the advent of the railways. 'Drove' as a place name can be traced to the early 13th century and there are records of cattle driven from Wales to London in the early 14th. There is increasing evidence for large-scale cattle rearing in Bronze-Age and Iron-Age Britain.

Imagine we are in John Dunstable's time. Imagine a huge, slow procession of hundreds of animals being herded along this remote track by men on sturdy ponies and on foot. The procession is about half a mile long from beginning to end and there are small black cattle with wide horns, sheep, pigs and even geese, all walking in line. Small, short-legged Welsh corgi dogs are snapping at the heels of the cattle to keep them moving at a steady pace and men with sticks are walking alongside to keep the animals from straying from the track.

The cattle and sheep have been entrusted to the drovers for herding all the way to the distant markets. We are delighted to come across a procession like this as joining it means we will be relatively safe while in its company. When the drovers reach their final destination, a market town many miles away, they will send the corgis back home on their own. The dogs will find their way and will know to stop at certain friendly houses and hostelries where their board and lodging has been paid for already by the drovers.

The surrounding hillside fields are full of freshly shorn sheep. They are all munching or lazing around giving the impression of happy contentment. The relief of not carrying all that weighty wool, especially when it gets wet, must be bliss for them.

I am walking along Red Lane when I am joined by John Dunstable himself. He is wearing the livery of his household, that of the Duke of Bedford. The colours are red, blue, gold and white with labels of not only English lions, but of Brittany and France, too. His French label is blue with gold fleur-de-lis. His jacket is silk and edged in silver giving the clear impression of a man of some colour, wealth and status.

"Good day, sir. How well goes your walking today?" I thank him for his enquiry and reply, "I hope you can walk with me for a least a little of the way?"

"It is my pleasure for the next while as there are certain things that I would wish to pass to you regarding my music and which may assist your quest."

I can tell from his demeanour that he is an educated man. In his time, matriculation would have been to one of two universities, Oxford or Cambridge, while most other education was in the hands of the religious institutions. Dunstable would have studied the Trivium of grammar, logic and rhetoric, and the Quadrivium, arithmetic, astronomy, geometry – and music. We have already discovered the association of music with these other subjects as highly significant.

About Music

From the trained musicians of the great households to the humble ranks of society, music in that time is integral with the fabric of life. This man, John Dunstable, is widely given credit for changing the face of music between the Middle Ages and the Renaissance by introducing new, sweeter harmonies. In addition, he was probably the first English composer to have a substantial influence upon continental European music.

"We must talk a while," he insists and suggests that we sit on a grass bank to refresh ourselves. I share my water bottle with him and we can see Newchurch from our vantage point, the next village on our route.

"My times are cruel," he tells me, "We do constant battle with the French, although that campaign goes well. I travel to French lands frequently with my master and have seen the terrible wounds inflicted on our soldiers. I know of the vile things they do to the French, even hacking their women and children to bits." He pauses and grimaces.

"This is not my true life for it lies in music and it is this that I want to tell you about in the desire that its secrets will live in your own times.

"I do my master's work when I must and God's work when I can, for it is the true spirit that drives the music and makes it live and breathe. In every note I write is the awakening to a greater life, a hidden life, one which surrounds us in every stone and blade of grass. This life glistens and shines in my eye and I make it real through music for anyone who will listen.

"The way that I do this is through harmony. Before me, certain harmonies were shunned. The one reason for this was a binding by the past and the worship of tradition. I knew this is as a fettering chain and have found the key to release its padlock. In my freedom, I make harmonies that hum and buzz in the ear and make honey for the soul."

I cannot hide my admiration for this man who comes from an era of barbaric cruelty and hardship. He is clearly a privileged man of means but even so he is worldly wise and has seen the worst. Yet, his music, I know, is elevated, otherworldly and beautiful. He is the representative of making music eternal on earth.

About Music

In our own time we worship the new and are ever striving to make our way into a better future. In his world, the past is revered and traditions upheld through endless patterns of ritual. Dunstable has broken this enthralment and is moving on. We need to pause our pointless progress and look back to meet him coming towards us.

Listen to Dunstable's 'Sanctum' if you would like to hear a sample of his music. Here is a little background about him. Nothing is known about his early life. His earliest works are from around 1410, so he may have been born around 1390. As I surmised, he must have received an impressive education as he became not only a composer but a mathematician and astronomer. Many composers of his day made their living as members of the clergy, but no one knows if this is true of Dunstable. His music is liturgical in character.

As he made a record of ownership in a book, we can tell he was a musician to John, Duke of Bedford and, circumstantially, the town of Dunstable was part of the territory of the Duke of Bedford. A more substantial connection is that Dunstable was, in 1437, given land in Normandy that had earlier belonged to Bedford.

With the death of the king in 1422, Henry V's nine-month-old son inherited the throne, becoming Henry VI. Bedford was appointed regent of England and France, the latter meaning that he was in charge of the ongoing Hundred Years War. Bedford visited France frequently between 1422 and 1432 and may well have taken Dunstable with him.

A French poet, Le Franc claimed that Dunstable's French contemporaries, the composers Guillaume du Fay and Gilles Binchois, "Took of the English manner and followed Dunstable, whereby wondrous pleasure makes their music joyous and famous."

I smile to myself and wonder how Dunstable would take to the current incumbent of Woburn Abbey, the 15th Duke of Bedford.

Dunstable may have left the Duke of Bedford's retinue in 1427, when he first appears in the pay records of the dowager, Queen Joan. He served her until at least 1436, earning the largest salary of any of her retainers. It is probable that he continued in Queen Joan's service until 1437, when she died. After that, he found a position

About Music

with the Duke of Bedford's younger brother, Humphrey, Duke of Gloucester.

We walk now. He talks. I listen.

"Your music has lost its sense of purpose and direction. I know that it expresses human emotion and feelings well and that you have what you call abstract music, which expresses nothing at all, but what I mean is the ability to express that which lies beyond the human. By this I discover that which is truly human.

"Beyond our world are other worlds, in just the same way that beyond our little orb lie greater orbs. You travel outwardly, I go in and through. How do I do this? I travel by the most sublime vehicle," he concludes.

Dunstable and I are approaching the village of Newchurch. There are small pale orange butterflies flitting in the hedgerows amongst the dog roses and I spy witches' broom there, too.

If you have ever looked up into a tree and seen a cluster or ball of twigs, you've seen a parasitic witches' broom. This happens when many small twigs start growing in the same spot. The medieval mind was full of superstition and outrageous mythical beings. The witch was in her greatest power. Its symbols were everywhere.

We both stop and stare at our feet. Crossing the road in front of us are dozens of tiny frogs. At first, because they are so small, I think they are insects but a closer inspection reveals that each is a perfectly formed frog. We pick our way carefully, avoiding their miniature hops and jumps and walk into the village. Here is how John Dunstable saw it.

He approaches the town on foot. The year is 1440 and it is a hot summer's day. The first thing that assails him is the stink as we pass across a bridge - over Shitbrook - as he nears the great wooden entrance gates. There he espies the severed heads and limbs of traitors on display. Then he is further pressed by the beggar boys who come out of the town to meet visitors, such as any person might who travels long distances to buy at the market.

Inside the town gates, Dunstable and I are faced with some of the finest houses and inns but then encounter narrow lanes of poorly built and dilapidated dwellings. Yet further in, the streets

About Music

become a little wider again and much noisier, nothing like the gentle country sounds of birds and breeze. We hear street music and enter the quarter where all the trades people live and work. Dunstable explains to me that he has written people's music copied from the merry tunes that we hear and indeed, he says, the tunes he writes in his maturity are mightily indebted to them.

Dunstable tells me, "However, it is the Lord's music that I am bidden to write both by my employer and by the Creator Himself. I have studied the Quadrivium. I am said to be knowledgeable about the stars and planets but it is music that I know and love best. Soon I am to travel abroad with my Duke of Bedford. On these trips I learn much about music in other countries and I can tell you that we in England are making quick progress.

"I myself have made it clear to those who will listen that harmony in several lines can be made better to the ear if the repeating of octaves and fifths is sore limited and the thirds and sixths used to the full. Also, I make it easy on the voice with smaller leaps than before. This means that the purity of the music can be fully expressed and my Lord and Maker pleased to the full."

We watch a cruel prank being played on an old man who has his hat stolen and is tripped by the beggars. They run off while everyone who sees laughs openly and long at the poor bewildered fellow.

This is a cruel age, one in which laughter is made from misfortune. A knight will weep on encountering the beauty of a flower but would straight away spill his enemy's guts with no qualm. Dunstable ponders on and explains to me how badly this age's women are treated, too. "But that suits me, as most men", he explains, "For we have our clothes cleaned, our meals cooked and our sexual appetites sated so that we can concentrate on God's work and making money."

Here is how I saw it back in the here and now. I walk through the quiet village of Newchurch with its picturesque cottages, their gardens kept well and orderly. All is at peace. The passage of drovers coming over the hills from Painscastle and heading for Kington would have kicked up a dust and a huge fuss as they came through here, but perhaps the greatest but long-gone disturbance was a visit by Charles II who came this way at the head of an army.

Cottages are grouped around the church, rebuilt in 1856 but which contains a font that may be pre-Norman. There is a house close to the church, the Great House, originating from around 1490, a restored timber-framed building, housing the widest domestic cruck in Wales.

A cruck is a curved timber; usually the curve is natural. It is also called a crook frame and is the origin of the word crooked. This naturally bent timber is combined with another and a cross-beam to form an 'A' shape, pairs of which are then erected vertically to support the walls and roof of a building. It's a simple idea and works well. These ancient oak beams inside buildings are much prized today for their aesthetic value as much as their architectural history.

John is, I imagine, in the church seeking further inspiration and I leave him to his prayers, walk out of the village up a steep hill and continue my walk along the dyke path.

As I walk, I reflect further on Dunstable's times. In many parts of England, lords turned from grain production to a business that was both less labour intensive and more lucrative - wool. This is the time of the first enclosures, when the formerly ploughed fields of nearly empty villages were fenced in to be used for sheep runs.

The progress made by the peasantry in this period was not permanent. Unfree peasants had enjoyed security of tenure. When fifteenth-century tenants became free men, however, they lost that security. A few of the most fortunate converted their property into freehold land that they rented perpetually. These fortunate peasant families had gained security that was comparable to the security of a knight's family.

Most peasants only had a leasehold or copyhold on their land. Like a modern lease, it ended at a certain time and the landlord could renew, change, or just take back the land. Leaseholders had no security at that point.

Henry V was king from 1413 until he died on the last day of August, 1422. An unintended consequence of his revival of the Hundred Years War was that 'the language of England' was now spoken by all the king's subjects. A Church council in 1414 declared, "Whether a nation be understood as a people marked off from others

About Music

by blood relationships and habit of unity, or by peculiarities of language... England is a real nation". The nation of England was, henceforth, self-evident.

Henry's child son was not crowned as Henry VI until 1429. Three brothers supervised the early years of the infant king. They were the main protagonists in the era of the Wars of the Roses. In 1431, Henry VI was taken to France and crowned in the cathedral of Notre Dame in Paris. At the age of ten, he was the only male monarch ever to be king both of England and France. The year before, Joan of Arc emerged as the symbol of hope for the French army; *plus ça change*.

I'm awoken from my reverie by the sound of tapping. At first, I cannot tell either from where this comes, or what is making it. Regular percussive noises have no place here. I turn to the side and spy a thrush with a snail in its beak, striking it on a stone by the side of my path. It makes a few hits then checks to see if anything has happened, then continues to pummel away until it can eat the juicy morsel within. This is the first thrush that I have seen for some time. It is clear that they have been in decline, making this, for me, a moment of magic.

Music of the two Henrys' time can be divided into two general categories, sacred and secular. Christianity was a dominant part of medieval culture and an entire musical style developed to support it. Sacred music was set to the text of the Bible or at least inspired by it. This meant it was necessary for composers of sacred music to have some sort of education, a rare commodity in those days. For those who did not have the musical training and Biblical literacy needed for composing sacred music, there was the less-sophisticated but equally important realm of secular music.

The goals of sacred and secular early medieval composers were different. The sacred composers sought to bring a more mystical atmosphere to church than could be obtained by simply reading the Bible out loud. It was composed to pay homage to God. Secular music, on the other hand, was composed solely for its entertainment value, for dance or to express love.

About Music

At least in the early medieval times, sacred composers were formally trained in music and secular composers were usually not. Not only did the two forms of music serve different purposes, they also represented a musical separation in society between the formally trained and the untrained, between rich and poor.

This division still exists between the untrained commoners who listen to folk, pop, rock and country music and those who are formally classically trained. The difference is that today the division between the trained and untrained is not delineated by religion and secular wealth.

Medieval secular music was usually passed along orally and rarely written down so little has survived. Further, medieval musicians and composers didn't feel the need to stamp what works they did write down with their names.

Secular music in the Middle Ages was represented by the wandering troubadors, trouveres, and Minnesingers. Troubadors were found in England, southern France and northern Italy, trouveres in central and northern France, and Minnesingers in Germany. They were primarily poets and the music was most likely accompaniment, a tradition that reminds us of the same practice in ancient Greece. As secular music's purpose was entertainment, there was little drive to develop its style. It was from sacred music that medieval music evolved, where the inspiration to please God was present.

With the birth of Christianity came the mass. At first, it was customary simply to read excerpts from the Bible. However, in the tradition of the Jewish culture, many parts of the mass were chanted. Picture a large group of people in an acoustically resonant structure such as monks in a large church or cathedral reciting a prayer or a passage from the Bible. They start to hold their voices over some syllables. Maybe they let the pitch of their voices rise or fall over that syllable for added effect.

It is easy to see that this might have spurred plainchant, or Gregorian chant, into existence. Few pitches and rhythmic variations were used and plainchant therefore has a unique monotonous sound; it was simply one note at a time being sung by one person or a group of people. Plainchant is a melody line with little variation and with no harmony.

About Music

In the 12th century, particularly at the cathedral of Notre Dame in Paris, sacred composers became restless with plainchant and started experimenting. They started by adding the same note an octave higher or lower to notes of the plainchant. This doesn't really change the harmony, but it adds a richer texture to it.

Then, they started adding an additional voice to the plainchant at the interval of a perfect fifth or fourth instead of just at the octave. Hence came the birth of 'organum', the first form of polyphony. Once the effect of adding other notes to a plainchant was realised, there was no stopping the possibilities that the newly discovered concept of harmony would allow. The idea of harmony quickly spread to secular music and composers began creating both sacred and secular works using the new technique.

Dunstable's influence on the continent's musical vocabulary was enormous, particularly considering the relative paucity of the works we know to be his. He was recognised by the famous and influential Burgundian School for possessing something never heard before in music. The 'Burgundian School' refers to the style of music written by a group of composers active in the late 14th and 15th centuries around the Burgundian court. This style was described as *la contenance angloise*, the English countenance, a term used by the poet Martin le Franc in his 24,000-verse composition, *Le Champion des Dames,* dating from 1440 or 1442. Le Franc added that the style influenced the chief Burgundian composers, Dufay and Binchois, high praise indeed. Burgundy was the area surrounding the deltas of the Rhine, Scheldt, and Meuse rivers which now includes part of northern France, western Germany, Belgium, Luxembourg and the Netherlands.

The Burgundian court moved from place to place throughout the 15th century and the composers connected to it came primarily from the Low Countries. Typically starting as singers in the court they then became known for their compositions. Many of them travelled extensively across Europe, taking the Burgundian style of music as far as Italy.

Different inventive styles and ideas were developing and compositions included new musical genres: Mass, motet, chanson, ballad, virelai, madrigal, frottola, villancico, canzona, ricercare and rondeau.

About Music

Writing in about 1476, the Flemish composer and music theorist, Tinctoris, reaffirmed the powerful influence Dunstable had, stressing the "new art" that Dunstable had inspired. Tinctoris hailed Dunstable as the *fons et origo* of the style, its 'wellspring and origin'.

The *contenance angloise*, while not defined by Martin le Franc, was probably a reference to Dunstable's stylistic trait of using full triadic harmony, along with a liking for the interval of the third.

Cast your mind back to our previous walk along the Hatterall Ridge to remind yourself about intervals. The interval of the third (say from C to E) and its inversion, the sixth (from E to C) are the sweetest. Triadic harmony, if you remember, is built from chords of three notes, the intervals between them being placed at thirds apart, for example, C-E-G.

Travelling on the continent with the Duke of Bedford, Dunstable would have been introduced to French *fauxbourdon*. This compositional technique employs three voices, the upper and lower voices progressing an octave or a sixth apart, while the middle voice extemporaneously doubles the upper part at a fourth below. Borrowing some of these sonorities, he created elegant harmonies in his own music using thirds and sixths.

Taken together, these are the defining characteristics of early Renaissance music, and both Le Franc's and Tinctoris's comments suggest that many of these traits may have originated in England, taking root in the Burgundian School around the middle of the century.

I am half a mile or so from the village of Gladestry and as I come over a ridge, pass by a disused quarry and veer in direction from NNE to NW. The view opens out and I can see for the first time the panoramic sight that includes Hergest Ridge. This elevated feature lies just beyond Gladestry and for me walking along it will be the highlight of this section. The ridge has an apocryphal association, as I remember, with the vinyl album of Mike Oldfield following on in the '70s from his magical *Tubular Bells*, called, simply, *Hergest Ridge*.

About Music

The musical output of medieval England was prodigious, yet almost all music manuscripts were destroyed during the English Reformation, particularly as a consequence of the Dissolution of the Monasteries between 1536-40. As a result, most of Dunstable's work has had to be recovered from continental sources, predominantly those from northern Italy and the southern Alps. Because numerous copies of his works have been found in Italian and German manuscripts, his fame must have been widespread. Of the works attributed to him only about fifty survive.

Dunstable was one of the first to compose masses using a single melody as *cantus firmus*. This is a preformed melody line to which are added additional contrapuntal parts. A good example of this technique is his *Missa Rex seculorum*.

From here we are only a step away from the times which spawned the 'art music we listen to today, the music of Bach and the Baroque, Mozart and the Classical and Beethoven of the Romantic eras which seem so much closer and familiar to us. The medieval world is another universe but it is enmeshed musically with our own.

Both polyphony and counterpoint mean that the music is written with voices which are independent but coherent and which sound well together, which harmonise. In addition, counterpoint, or contrapuntal music, has its voices both melodically *and* rhythmically independent. Instead of the voices moving together from one chord to the next, they move independently and create new chords and new sonorities. The music is becoming complex.

One effect of this, when one voice may move before another, is to create a temporary discord. The discord will then become harmonious again with the next move. In musical terminology this process is called suspension and resolution and creates the experience of tension followed by release in the music. It was used to great effect by the later Baroque composers.

To cope with the complexity that was becoming apparent, composition rules developed that are with us today.

When I was learning music theory, we were told not to allow intervals of the octave or the fifth to follow one another consecutively, so called parallel fifths and octaves. This was said to be poor practice and has been, by most students, unquestioned

About Music

wisdom since the 15th century. I never asked at the time of my education the obvious question, "Why is this so?" and am sure many other students never did, either.

I came across an explanation one day which satisfied my curiosity. It is of some interest because, seemingly contrary to what is taught, parallel octaves are ubiquitous in ensemble and piano music. Even worse, it would seem, we have discovered on our own journey that parallel fifths were the norm in organum, early forms of polyphonic Gregorian chant.

It is at the point in history when polyphony developed that this particular question arose. Of all the intervals, when the two notes of a fifth are sounded it can be difficult to hear the individual notes. One seems to hide behind the other. This is still true but perhaps to a lesser degree of the octave interval. This means that when two or more voices are singing simultaneously, that is, in polyphony, the independence of the melody lines becomes unclear at the point where these particular intervals between the voices occur. Hence, resting on and repeating this interval consecutively muddies the effect of having two independent melody lines and makes them sound like only one again, as in the earlier forms of chant.

Composers of the classical era worked out some highly elaborate ways of constructing contrapuntal music so that it avoided parallel octaves and fifths. The tricks they used eventually blossomed into our modern discipline of classical counterpoint and harmonic theory.

I arrive in Gladestry where the church of St Mary's boasts a flying dragon on its weather vane. I suck gratefully on my water bottle for the weather is warm and sunny and the sweat on my back tells me that I have been using up my body's supply of liquid at a rate of knots. I chat with a local who enquires where I have come from and where I am going. He makes me even keener to see the ridge as he tells me the view in this clear weather will be spectacular.

Fleeting, friendly encounters such as this with their titbits of information make me realise how valuable our simple human contacts with one another are. In times past, in remote places, they would have been a requirement for survival and sanity.

About Music

Dunstable is believed to have written secular music, but no songs in the vernacular can be attributed to him with any degree of certainty. Because so much of the surviving 15th-century repertoire of English carols is anonymous, and he is known to have written many, most scholars consider it highly likely that some of the anonymous carols from this time are his.

Dunstable was probably the most influential English composer of all time, yet he remains an enigma. His complete works were not published until the quincentenary of his death in 1953, but even since then works have been added and subtracted from his oeuvre.

We know very little of his life and nothing of his undoubted learning. We can only make an educated guess at most of the chronology of the small amount of music that has come down to us and we understand little of his style – why he wrote as he did, what artistic or technical principles guided his composing, how his music was performed, or why it was so influential. Even so, we are left with the glaring facts of his genius and influence on music thereafter.

My exit from the village involves a steep climb up Yewtree Bank and my thoughts become still as I focus on the effort required. My eyes are cast down as I walk uphill, not too steep a climb but a steady one that makes me sweat and breathe hard. I know that if I stop and look back, the view will be opening out into a wide panorama but I continue to climb, reserving this treat for a few more minutes hence.

The slope levels out and I then turn to see swathes of bright green bracken leading the eye to the curved horizon. Above are cotton wool clouds in a bright blue sky. From here on the path is easy. It is wide and grassy, short grass nibbled by sheep, a causeway that runs along Hergest Ridge and then will drop me down into Kington.

It is easy to imagine the drovers along here, perhaps enjoying as I do the fresh air and the sky. I know there will be times of dense mists, wet and cold that chill to the bone, but I choose not to

About Music

allow this thought to penetrate the sight and atmospherics of summer at its best.

As the years pass, the countryside kaleidoscopes its shifting patterns but the old track ways remain constant. I am walking a path that has been trodden for hundreds, perhaps thousands of years. No wonder these old straight tracks have been endowed with properties of the mysterious and the mystical. It is along them that the doorway into other worlds is easily opened.

Is that doorway in the landscape or in my mind? It matters not. All I know today is that I feel a sense of belonging in this territory. Walking here makes my body and mind feel good and part of something which goes beyond the surface appearance of the sky and the land. The door is open.

Through it is the land that Dunstable and other musicians were seeking to illuminate and express. Listen to the music and it is clear that they were succeeding. How were they doing this? With just a few simple lines of music that interwove harmony and rhythm they were expressing the cosmic nature of the universe. Music has the ability to do this but since that time, particularly in our own, it has veered off this course and found different routes to take.

I am mindful of Mike Oldfield's music which, although in the pop/rock genre was revisiting what those medieval musicians did, namely playing with lines of music and letting them combine to become multidimensional. The effect, using the tools of the recording studio, is like listening again to the mesmerising chant of counterpoint in action.

To my left I see a large glacial boulder, the Whet Stone. Like the tracks, these ancient stones surround themselves in otherworldly atmosphere and many have been the focal point for pagan activities. The Whet Stone is alleged to have served as a trading point during the plagues of the 14th century. Farmers left wheat here for the quarantined townsfolk. There is a legend attached to the stone whereby it leaves the hill at dawn to drink from a stream.

To my right is the more prosaic site of the abandoned Kington Racecourse, with its curved tracks still quite clear. Horses roam this ridge, often drinking at the ponds which I pass and riders may occasionally appear, as this is one of the few bridleways that occur along our path.

About Music

Today we think of music as an art form in its own right. During Dunstable's times, music and science were still one. The Quadrivium places music alongside arithmetic, geometry and astronomy, but from then on advances take place in all the academic subjects, the consequence of which is that a gradual separation of science and music takes place.

This reaches a culmination in the Romantic era of the 19th century when the arts celebrated everything that was human and individual, while science was busy dissecting, measuring and categorising. This was the era of the famous, of the celebrity scientist and musician. In Dunstable's time it was rare even for a piece of music to bear a signature.

Today, there is another seismic change in music taking place as the emphasis shifts back again from the personal to the cosmic. This time the route lies inwards into the universe of the collective unconscious and the quantum universe. The gods of old may no longer live 'out there' but they surely may lie within.

This is why the music of the past is of such great importance to our modern times for it was making a similar exploration. The difference is that today we can – hopefully – distinguish the true from the imaginary. The medieval mind was full of the ghosts, ghouls and witches that were projected from inside to out with little awareness of the process which lay behind this. Science and particularly psychology have given us the means to explore this 'universe beyond' but from a perspective that keeps a foothold on reality.

Old music is not so old; it is music from another point of view. Old music is as relevant today as it was when first created. You only have to listen and you can hear this to be true. Music created in the same spirit as Dunstable's and those following in his footsteps is now not a means for exploring the universe as it was then, but is for discovering the hidden dimensions and the potential facets of who we are and what we can become in the future.

About Music

The green ridge track dips down and I can see the buildings of Kington waiting in front of me. As I walk easily down the hill, happily swinging my stick, I can hear voices singing John's music, gently evoking, celebrating and worshipping its own being. A few minutes later, I walk along Church Road and into the centre of Kington.

Bill, wondering who he'll meet next

About Music

CHAPTER 5

A Musical Disaster

In which we float gravity free, break musical eggs and prepare to leave the Middle Ages

Johann Sebastian Bach was born in 1685.

For students of classical music, its history might be divided into two parts, Before Bach (BB) and After Bach (AB). Before his time and judged with our modern sensibilities, music had an aura of anachronism; after, music became serious, worthy, self-improving. AB seems relatively close to our own world, familiar if different, whereas BB is distant, has associations with primitive agriculture and dark ages rather than industry, empire and cultural enlightenment.

BB we may picture the music of the troubadour and his love songs or the monastic, chanting monk. AB we can visualise courtly scenes, then superstar composers and lavish musical extravaganzas, both religious and operatic.

However, it is before Bach when we find the most significant aspects of music in terms of its wholeness as an art and a science and when the spirit of music is clearest. AB, music increasingly fragments into genres, styles and personalities. It becomes a means more of entertainment and self-expression than a vehicle for approaching spiritual enlightenment.

At this point in our ramblings, we are approaching a half-way point. Today's walk runs from Kington to Knighton in Shropshire and arrival in Knighton will mark the fact that we are about half way. In terms of the number of walks, there will still be another ten to go beyond this fifth one. In the development of music this neatly reflects the increasing speed of change and the corresponding increase in material that we will need to consider.

So, before setting off, let's picture for a moment what the musical world looks like in its run-up to this half-way point.

If you explore texts about the history of western music, some may well ignore much of the context within which its development takes place. But context is of paramount importance, for music, like human beings, does not operate in isolation from the societal mix within which and out of which it is created. Music has intimate connections with philosophy, art and science, as well as social occasion and fashion.

So, what did our world look like in 1685, at the time that Bach was born? The 17th century is the Early Modern period of European history. By the end of the century, Europeans were aware of logarithms, electricity, the telescope and microscope, calculus, universal gravitation, Newton's Laws of Motion, air pressure and calculating machines, all due to the work of the first scientists of the Scientific Revolution. They included Galileo Galilei, Johannes Kepler, René Descartes, Pierre Fermat, Blaise Pascal, Robert Boyle, Christian Huygens, Robert Hooke, Isaac Newton and Gottfried Leibniz.

In 1685, the Edict of Fontainebleu outlawed Protestantism in France and King Charles II died in London. Previously, Charles I had been executed at Whitehall on 30 January 1649 at the climax of the English Civil War. Although the Parliament of Scotland then proclaimed Charles II King of Great Britain and Ireland in Edinburgh on 6 February 1649, the English Parliament passed a statute that made any such proclamation unlawful. England entered the period known as the English Interregnum or the English Commonwealth and the country was a *de facto* republic, led by the puritan, Oliver Cromwell

Two years after Bach's birth, Isaac Newton published *Philosophiae Naturalis Principia Mathematica* and four years later John Locke published his first 'Letter Concerning Toleration'. Locke was known as the Father of Classical Liberalism and was one of the first of the British empiricists following the tradition of Francis Bacon. Empiricism was the philosophy which emphasised experience and evidence as the basis for knowledge. It is the philosophy of modern science.

Turning the clock back a little for a run-up to Bach's birth, what did the universe look like in the previous 16th C? In Europe, the Protestant Reformation dealt a major blow to the authority of the papacy and the Roman Catholic Church. European politics became dominated by religious conflicts, paving the way for the Thirty

Years' War, which laid waste to and bankrupted European countries in the following century.

In 1503, Leonardo da Vinci began painting the Mona Lisa and completed this three or four years later. Yet another seismic cultural event, just before his death in 1543, was the publication of Copernicus' book, *On the Revolutions of the Celestial Spheres*, considered a major event in the history of science. It began the Copernican Revolution and contributed to the scientific revolution. At the end of the century, in 1600, Giordano Bruno was burned at the stake in Rome for heresy. Bruno was an Italian Dominican friar, philosopher, mathematician, poet, and astrologer. He is celebrated for his cosmological theories, which went even further than the then novel Copernican model.

While supporting heliocentricity, Bruno also correctly proposed that the Sun was just another star moving in space and claimed as well that the universe contained an infinite number of inhabited worlds, identified as planets orbiting other stars. We're still working on that one.

Beginning in 1593, Bruno was tried for heresy by the Roman Inquisition on charges including denial of several core Catholic doctrines. The Inquisition found him guilty and he was burned in Rome's Campo de' Fiori. He has become regarded as a martyr for the cause of science, although there is some dispute about whether or not his scientific views were the cause of his demise.

All of these events contributed to fuelling the process by which the previously held view of the universe, the Pythagorian and Platonic system of concentric spheres and its 'Music of the Spheres', was at long last being debunked. The shift of the centre of the solar system from the Earth to the Sun, itself now only one star many, was psychologically disturbing. Man's sense of himself as the focal point of God's purpose and activities was uprooted.

The religious authorities held to the traditional view represented by the wisdom of the ancients, while the new scientific, empirical approach took no received knowledge for granted. While Rome had such power, had its earth-centred view and its dogma, no scientist was safe.

During the 16th century, Spain and Portugal explored the world's seas and opened world-wide oceanic trade routes. Large parts

About Music

of the New World became Spanish and Portuguese colonies. While the Portuguese became the masters of Asia's and Africa's Indian Ocean trade, the Spanish opened trade across the Pacific Ocean, linking the Americas with Asia. It is regarded by historians as the century in which the rise of the West occurred.

Even this brief background to considerations for our walking, musical speculations of today gives a flavour of the huge revolutions that were taking place in all human endeavours.

The walk begins at the War Memorial in the centre of Kington, an old market town in the northwestern tip of Herefordshire. Hergest, a mile to the southwest was the home of the Vaughans, a well-known Welsh family. Thomas Vaughan in 1460 was charged by Lancastrian Henry VI with seizing for the king some of the border estates of the Duke of York and the Earl of Warwick. Later he would change his allegiances and subsequently die at the Battle of Banbury, fighting for the Yorkists in 1469.

I walk through back streets and in just five minutes am on the outskirts of Kington, ready to cross the A44 and begin the walk proper. Yesterday, the conclusion was a descent off Hergest Ridge; today, I begin to climb again up through fields and by farm buildings. The route twists and turns, so I keep a continual lookout for the acorn signs which guide the walker along this route.

The weather is warm and sunny. There have been showers predicted for later in the day but I feel confident that they will not interrupt a walk which promises glorious views and may have perhaps a few surprises in store. The route goes over common land on Bradnor Hill, heading for the heights of Rushock Hill.

The common is owned by the National Trust and accommodates – the first surprise of the day – a golf course, said to be the highest in Europe. Lofty courses are not uncommon in this part of the country, but this particular one must provide some challenging winds to combat while keeping the score card to a minimum.

It is turning into a perfect summer's day. Crops are ripening and the bracken is high. The vegetation seems to absorb and then re-emit the sun's heat together with a mix of scents, creating a flower-shop hit of fragrance.

Heading directly up the side of Rushock Hill, over a couple of styles, thence over the top of the hill brings a joyful encounter, the second great surprise. I was expecting to meet the dyke again on this walk but not in quite such a spectacular fashion. The dyke hasn't been seen since leaving it in Highbury Wood near Lower Redbrook, some 55 miles back. Its course in the intervening miles has been fragmented but now it is with me again.

I arrive at the dyke where it runs across my path as a T-junction and the route map indicates that I should turn left and walk along its top. The surprise is not so much in my renewed relationship with the dyke but in the length of the stretch that lies before me, a bank of earth snaking for miles across largely open countryside. For the first time, heading along it in this northerly direction the walker can truly appreciate the magnitude of construction involved in building this earthen wall.

The dyke gives me a sense of freedom. It was intended as a barrier, but here, in this particular place, the path along its top leading into the distance, the view to the horizon in each direction, the sky and the solitude, all conspire to create a feeling that, I imagine, is like drifting in a gravity free environment. The physical and mental chains of daily life have no grip in this world. All things are possible here. I float, rather than walk along the dyke.

In the fifteenth century, we are coming to the end of a significant time span. Politically, we've reached 1485, the conventional end of the medieval period. In the pre-Reformation English church, most clergy did their jobs reasonably well if in an uninspired fashion. But the clergy had lost its leadership position in society and English clergy were no longer part of an international class. They had also lost their dominant position in the economy, together with their monopoly of learning and piety. The only thing left to lose was the privileged legal separation from the rest of society. One can begin to see, if very dimly, the shape of the national Church of England that will eventually come into being.

About Music

Greater lay participation in religious life did not mean active revolt against the clergy, but it is clear that some of the older institutions of the church were losing their relevance for the English. This is particularly evident in regard to the monasteries, of which there were many.

A few strict houses, especially those connected with the Carthusian order, attracted lay interest and patronage, but most of the monasteries were increasingly irrelevant to religious life. The separation of religious life from the life of the world that they symbolised left people cold, especially since the religion of the 15th century monasteries, though not necessarily corrupt, was somewhat diluted.

The growth of lay literacy, especially literacy in English, had for a long time now made it possible for people to live a rich spiritual life without the need for clergy. From the middle of the 14th century lay mystics began to appear.

Mystics were people who lived an interior life that an earlier century would have thought appropriate only for monks (a notable female exception was the visionary Benedictine abbess, Hildegard of Bingen, who was, amongst other things, a notable composer). Through prayer, asceticism, and contemplation, these lay mystics sought to make direct contact with God. They did so without any formal ties to an established religious order and without any ambition to found a new one.

Reading was part of their life. The classics of Latin devotional literature were increasingly translated into the common language. Furthermore, mystics and other pious people wrote down their experiences and thoughts for others to read. All of this activity had been monopolised by the clergy before the fourteenth century. Now it was available to the laity.

Two factors conspired to accelerate the spread of this culture after 1450: growing economic prosperity and the printing press. By 1452, with the aid of borrowed money, Gutenberg began his famous Bible project. Two hundred copies of the two-volume Gutenberg Bible were printed, a small number of which were printed on vellum. These expensive and beautiful Bibles were completed and sold at the 1455 Frankfurt Book Fair, an event which is still an annual pilgrimage for international book publishers today. The vellum

About Music

Gutenberg Bibles cost the equivalent of three years' pay for the average clerk. Expensive, yes, but mass production and dissemination were underway.

By 1473, some technical problems were overcome and the first fully printed music appeared in the 'Constance Gradual', printed probably in 1473 in Germany. In 1476, Ulrich Hahn printed the *Missale secundum consuetudinem curie romane* and claimed to be the first to print music. Hahn's methods were copied and soon missals for the celebration of the mass and graduals, chants in the liturgical celebrations of the Eucharist, were sprouting up all over Europe and later, by 1500, in England. The breakthrough was the development of woodcut printing.

This method, a precursor of letterpress, allowed printers to create complex images such as music notation which required variable spatial placement of images and symbols. A woodcut is a carved block of wood where the inked characters to be printed are left higher than the surrounding wood. Though simple in concept, the skills required for a quality woodcut are far from basic. It requires an artist's and craftsman's skills and the ability to imagine everything backwards as the block must be a mirror image of the printed page.

Distribution of music was made possible on a wide scale by these innovations in printing. Demand for music as entertainment and as an activity for educated amateurs increased with the emergence of a bourgeois class. Dissemination of chansons, motets, and masses throughout Europe coincided with the unification of polyphonic practice into a fluid style. This culminated in the second half of the sixteenth century in the works of composers such as Palestrina, Thomas Tallis and William Byrd. We are being thrown with considerable force into a new musical universe.

♩ I catch up with two walkers, a couple. The man is Finnish and the woman is German. The dyke attracts walkers from many different countries and this couple is clearly well organised, armed with maps and a detailed itinerary. My walking pace is a little faster than theirs but I walk with them for a while and chat about our mutual experiences.

About Music

I leave them soon but just a little further on more walkers come towards me and one stops and greets me, asking how much further is their walk into Kington. I tell him it is about six miles. He is flushed and a little breathless. Clearly the ups and downs of the dyke path and the heat of the day are having their effect. I wish them well and walk on, feeling good, for in comparison I feel fresh with plenty of energy in my legs.

The path crosses a couple of minor roads, goes through wooded plantations and from these always emerges to more views. I am still walking on top of the dyke which in places is up to several metres high. A good path has been made along its top to reduce erosion by walkers.

I remember a quote by George Borrow in his *Wild Wales* to the effect that, if caught on the wrong side of the dyke, Welshmen may lose their ears, Englishmen, their lives. I am careful not to put either ears or life at risk.

Just south of a minor road, there is a gap in the dyke with inturned banks. The suggestion is that points like these were used for traffic control through the dyke, check points which look quite different from the usual crude farming cut-throughs. A hamlet just to the east is called Bwlch, which means 'a pass', giving credence to the idea.

There are some more fine views along the valley. To the west lies Radnor Forest, while forward beyond the valley of the River Lugg is Furrow Hill, the next significant climb. Despite the reference to forest, Radnor Forest is only partly wooded and provides good walking with a succession of hills over 600 metres high.

In the 16th century, the whole of Europe was thrown into a period of religious unrest as the Protestant Reformation gained ground. The English Reformation was driven by Henry VIII's desire for an annulment of his first marriage to Kathryn of Aragon, mother of Mary I, so that he could marry Ann Boleyn. Ann would become the mother of Elizabeth, later to be crowned Elizabeth I, the last of the Tudor dynasty. English Reformation at the outset was more a political affair than a theological dispute.

About Music

Ruling from 1509 until his death in 1547, Henry VIII's interest in music was apparent from an early age. One of the reasons the teenage monarch cut such an impressive and popular figure at the beginning of his reign was his devotion to the art. He had received a thorough musical education and was accomplished on the lute, organ, and virginals; he could also sing well. The royal court included musicians from the Netherlands and Italy as well as England. One of Henry's favourite activities was sight-reading songs with his courtiers.

Henry certainly recognised the importance of government support of the arts. Edward IV had employed only five musicians; his grandson increased the total to fifty-eight. Benefiting from these increases, the Chapel Royal, a body of priests and singers serving the spiritual needs of the Sovereign, flourished. Emerging as a distinct body in the late 13th century and dating from 1483 as presently constituted, the Chapel Royal has become associated with a number of chapel buildings used by monarchs for worship and ceremony. The Chapel's choir, known as the 'Children of the Chapel Royal', achieved its greatest eminence during the reign of Elizabeth I when William Byrd and Thomas Tallis were joint organists. Today, the two main Chapels Royal are located at St James's Palace in London.

In January, 1535, the newly appointed Vicar-General of the English Church, Thomas Cromwell, sent out his agents to conduct a commission of enquiry into the character and value of all ecclesiastical property in the kingdom. Overtly, they were reformers exercising the new powers accorded to the Crown by the Act of Supremacy: "from time to time to visit, repress, redress, reform, order, correct, restrain and amend all such errors, heresies, abuses, offences, contempts and enormities... which ought or may be lawfully reformed."

The tough-minded officials chosen for the job had no doubt what the Crown expected of them. It took them only six months to submit for Cromwell's scrutiny an accurate and detailed tax-book, the *Valor Ecclesiasticus*. Along with it came evidence of corruption and scandalous immorality in England's monasteries.

Such evidence was not hard to find, for by the 16th century many of the religious houses had long since lost their sense of purpose. Some, as landlords, oppressed the local population with exorbitant rents. Heavy debts encumbered others that had been poorly managed. For a thousand years communities of English monks had pursued God's work in what Alfred the Great had once called a marvellous freedom from the tumult of the world, but their number had been declining steadily after the Black Death.

During Henry VIII's reign, this ancient tradition came to an abrupt and sometimes violent end. Within five years, Cromwell's agents had closed down every religious house. With them were shut down the libraries and musical culture that they supported.

Cromwell's agents had next turned their attentions to the universities where the humanist principles central to Renaissance learning were instituted and the doctrines of the medieval scholastics abandoned.

Just at the very time that the dissolution was completed, the composer William Byrd was born and the Renaissance was about to take root in Britain. Musical history in Britain had been going a different way from continental trends. Isolated composers drew on their own native traditions with its polyphony in free flow. In England, the most gifted composer among many was said to be John Tavener (1490-1545). His six-part masses represent the epitome of this polyphonic tradition, just before it was silenced by the uncertainties created by religious reform.

In 1517, a German theologian and monk, Martin Luther, sparked the Protestant Reformation. His ideas spread quickly, thanks in part to the printing press, arriving in England just as Henry was looking for excuses to elevate himself above papal influence. Luther challenged the power of the Pope and the Church, and asserted the authority of individual conscience. At the same time, it was increasingly possible for people to read the Bible in the languages that they spoke.

This created a problem for composers, as the Protestant Reformation meant strict rules of conformity. How much damage may this have done to the creative freedom of musicians? Settings to Latin words, for example, were forbidden. The music was to be a clear and uncluttered exposition of religious faith.

In some ways, the music escaped heavy censorship even when differences were being expressed in burnings and torture. Protestant music differed only in that it was simpler in style and set

About Music

texts in the language of the congregation. Elements of musical style were maintained throughout the switches of ecclesiastical authority: Catholic and Latin under Henry VIII; aggressively Protestant under Edward VI; Catholic and Roman again under Mary I; Protestant once more under Elizabeth I.

Composers were able to encompass both multitudinous polyphonic voices and the more simple and homophonic styles, that is, having all the parts moving together in chords. New ways were being learnt from secular song which had the ability to work on the listener's interior self with immediacy. Available now to composers was a fully coherent harmonic style against which troubadourian dissonance could create the intensity of a bodily wound or ache. This is exactly what was required of Protestant music which had to appeal directly to the emotional life of the listener's inner ear.

In the corner of my eye, I glimpse a fluttering of pink feathers, so immediately stand completely still to determine what it is I am seeing. It is a linnet chirping at me and flitting amongst some low-lying branches. As I stand in this meditative state, I hear for the first time this summer the massed sound of crickets. These sights and sounds hold me locked in stillness with all thoughts of history banished, replaced by awareness only of the present moment's insistence.

The official Offa's Dyke Path has now temporarily left the line of the dyke, although traces can be seen on the map. Its course is re-joined on Furrow Hill. Before this though, there now begins a long descent into the Lugg valley. Stirring from my focused reverie, I continue along the way.

If there was one century in the past that saw dynamic, radical changes in established ways of thinking comparable to the 20th and 21st centuries, it would be the 16th. It is during this period that the Scientific Revolution began and observation replaced religious doctrine as the source of our understanding of the universe and our place in it. This is where we came in at the beginning of today's walk.

About Music

At mid-century, Copernicus suggested that the sun was at the centre of the solar system, not the earth. This was by no means a new idea but its effect from that time on was radically to reposition human beings and call into question our centrality in the scheme that God had made.

Britain was late in responding to the Renaissance, but eventually it too was exposed to the new ways of thinking that were gripping the continent, encouraged in part by the English Reformation and Cromwell's agents. The Renaissance had begun in Italy and the rapid developments and changes that were taking place in music were not without their Italian detractors.

One Vincenzo Galilei (1520-91) held strong views on the nature and value of music. He was a reactionary who advocated a return to Greek classicism and simplicity in order to reaffirm the essence of music as a force for cosmic understanding. Vincenzo was the father of the famous astronomer, Galileo Galilei, whose telescope caused such religious controversy.

Vincenzo, lute player, composer and music theorist, was one of a group of musically minded philosophers and musicians who formed a society known as the Florentine Camerata. This was a group of humanists, musicians, poets and intellectuals in late Renaissance Florence who gathered under the patronage of Count Giovanni de' Bardi to discuss and guide trends in the arts, especially music and drama.

Vincenzo's work on string tension and pitch developed further Pythagoras's work, placing it on a firm and now correct mathematical foundation. Although far less has been written about him than his illustrious son, he holds a pivotal place in the development of western music. Like John Dunstable, his significance and contributions are underestimated.

Before him, it had always been accepted that the *musici*, the theorists, were the true musicians. Performers were no more worthy than clowns or idiots. He clearly outlined and articulated for the first time a new scientific music theory that led to the rise in stature of profane musical composition and performance.

Vincenzo articulated and explained the use of dissonance in certain circumstances. He had a modern conception, allowing passing dissonance, "if the voices flow smoothly" as well as on-the-beat dissonance, such as suspensions, which he called 'essential dissonance'. This describes what came to be a ubiquitous Baroque practice, especially as he defines rules for resolution of suspensions by a preliminary leap away from, followed by a return to the expected harmonious note of resolution. This sounds somewhat specialised stuff but is a vital compositional technique that has been used extensively ever since. Without it, music would lose much of its expressive ability. Without it we would perceive music to be somewhat superficial, static and directionless.

In keeping with the paradoxical nature of the Renaissance, that is, leaping forward while elevating classicism, Vincenzo's musical philosophy was geared to a return to the simple, straightforward music of classical Greece. His argument was that the polyphony of his day was incapable of working the marvels that the great figures of antiquity were able to accomplish with their simpler music making. From Vincenzo, a direct timeline can be drawn on which soon appears the subsequent rise of secular operatic performance and what we now think of as 'classical' music.

In operatic works, when you hear accompanied recitative interspacing the arias and vocal ensembles, you can detect the monody of ancient Greece surrounded by new forms of music that were shaped in the Renaissance. Ironically, the Camerata's intention of reviving classical monody was eclipsed by the practicalities of making contemporary music attractive to the modern audiences of the time, which naturally involved the extensive use of polyphony. So, far from being simple music, opera developed into the most sophisticated art form of all.

What has happened to the Music of the Spheres in all this? The new emerging models of the universe, heralded by Bruno, Copernicus, Galileo, Kepler and Newton, all paid homage to it. The sound of the spheres eventually died away, but the harmonic theories of Pythagoras were looked at anew and developed into a model that not only worked but could, literally, be *seen* to work through Galileo's telescope, culminating in Kepler's three laws of harmonic planetary motion.

About Music

My walk is taking me through shady woodland and then to the banks of the River Lugg. I cross the river via a footbridge and then walk alongside for a few metres before finding an idyllic spot to stop, to rest and to meditate. The Lugg is known in this area as a habitat for otters and dippers, little birds that might nest behind a waterfall or weir, flying fast up and down the river just above its surface. They are also able to walk on the river bottom, completely submerged while looking for food. The shallow, sparkling river is, today, flowing gently and making the most relaxing river noises that you can imagine.

I have brought with me a hand-held recorder just for moments such as this. I set it up by balancing it in the fork of a branch of a low-lying river-bank tree and press the recording button. It is in situations such as this that you become aware of ambient intrusive noise, for even in the depths of the countryside it is almost impossible to escape the distant drone of an aeroplane, tractor or other combustion engine. In addition, even a slight breeze can sound like a hurricane on the final recording.

The ear will filter out continuous or irrelevant noises and focus its attention on those that are interesting, useful or surprising. A microphone knows no such discrimination but absorbs all vibration that it senses and records all with no favouritism. The end result may not correspond with what the listener at the same spot hears. This physiological fact about the ear and its relationship with the filtering censorship of the brain has interesting consequences when listening to music. I'm looking forward to exploring this further when a later walk will be linked with the brain and music.

Today, the acoustic situation is blessed and I relax with my picnic while the recorder silently mops up the sound scene around it: gurgling, gently splashing water flow, the buzz and hum of insects, the occasional rustling leaf and ever-present birdsong.

After a few minutes, a gate on the path about 50 yards away creaks open as a walker arrives. He has a dog, a golden retriever. I can tell immediately that the dog has somehow detected my microphone and comes up panting heavily and swishing his tail. He straight away finds the microphone and sniffs it loudly. I smile, knowing what the recorded effect will be and later I laugh aloud

About Music

when I listen to the snuffling end result. The walker gives me a friendly greeting, calls to his dog and continues on his way.

Elizabeth I, the last Tudor monarch, was born at Greenwich on 7 September, 1533, the daughter of Henry VIII and his second wife, Anne Boleyn. Elizabeth was queen of England and Ireland from 17th November, 1558, until her death in 1603. One of her first acts as Queen was the establishment of an English Protestant church, of which she became the Supreme Governor.

Her early life was full of uncertainties, and her chances of succeeding to the throne seemed slight once her half-brother Edward was born in 1537. She was then third in line behind her Roman Catholic half-sister, Princess Mary. Indeed, Roman Catholics always considered Elizabeth illegitimate and she only narrowly escaped execution in the wake of a failed rebellion against Queen Mary in 1554.

Elizabeth succeeded to the throne on her half-sister's death. She was well-educated, fluent in six languages, and had inherited intelligence, determination and shrewdness from both parents.

Her 45-year reign is generally considered one of the most glorious in English history. During her reign, a secure Church of England was established. Its doctrines were laid down in the Thirty-Nine Articles of 1563, a compromise between Roman Catholicism and Protestantism.

The arts flourished during Elizabeth's reign. Country houses such as Longleat, now a safari and adventure park in Wiltshire, and Hardwick Hall in Derbyshire were built. Miniature painting reached its high point with Nicholas Hilliard, known for his portrait miniatures of members of the courts of Elizabeth and James I. Theatres thrived, the Queen attending the first performance of Shakespeare's 'A Midsummer Night's Dream', while composers such as William Byrd and Thomas Tallis worked in Elizabeth's court and at the Chapel Royal, St James's Palace.

Building on the progress made in music during the medieval era, Elizabethan music was comparatively more refined and sophisticated. Influenced by the development of theatre, music in this period became more expressive, echoing many types of moods and emotions. The court of Elizabeth and the homes of the nobility featured much musical entertainment. Commoners also listened to music in church, in their communities, on the street, and at home.

The Elizabethan era featured a number of new instruments and there was widespread evolution of the instruments already in existence. New instruments included the bowed, fretted viol, an early precursor of the fretless violin. Viols appeared first in Spain in the mid to late 15th century. When it was introduced, the viol was played sitting with the instrument upright on the lap or between the legs. The viol is also called a 'viola da gamba', viol of the leg. There was a whole family of different sized viols.

Another new instrument was the hautboy, a precursor to the oboe. A number of tempered keyboard instruments were introduced. These created sound with plectrums that were attached to the instrument's key mechanism and which plucked strings rather than struck them, as in the modern piano. These keyboard instruments included the spinet, a small compact upright; the harpsichord, similar to the spinet with a more metallic sound; and the virginals, which was similar to the harpsichord but small enough to sit on top of a table.

One remnant from the medieval era was the lute, which was the most popular instrument of Elizabethan times and favoured by courtiers. Variations of the lute emerged, including the chitarrone, which had an extra peg box for more strings and longer neck which could be several feet in length.

Other popular instruments used in this era included the harp; the rebec, another early precursor of the violin; the cittern, which was similar to a contemporary guitar; the trumpet; the crumhorn, a curved horn; and percussion instruments which included the drum, cymbal, triangle, and tambourine.

When Elizabethan composers wrote music, they did not dictate what instruments should be used but left that decision to those who played the composition. Musicians of the era experimented by with different ensemble combinations. One of the best-known combinations that emerged came to be known as the English consort, which consisted of a violin, flute, lute, and viol.

During the Elizabethan era, a number of musical forms were developed and new ones introduced. These included two types of songs for voice, the madrigal, a musical arrangement consisting of several vocal parts with no instrumental accompaniment, and the ayre, which had only one vocal part but was accompanied by many instruments. The well-known song 'Greensleeves' is an example of an ayre.

Anthems, which were church songs, and choral works also became popular. Masques, elaborately staged combinations of dance, music, and theatre, were created by royalty to mark special occasions such as coronations and visits from dignitaries.

There was a wide variety of uses of music in the Elizabethan era. It was essential at court as the Queen was a patron of composers and musicians, playing the lute and virginals herself. She employed approximately 70 musicians and singers over the course of her reign.

At court, many forms of music were played, including traditional English ballads, church music, dance music, and madrigals. Elizabeth danced regularly and dancing was accompanied by the court musicians. They plied their trade from the minstrels' gallery, an elevated structure that overlooked the great halls of many castles and palaces. The ways of the court were imitated by the nobility, who had their own musicians to play during dinner and other events and middle-class families usually had one servant who could play an instrument.

While music had been used to accompany poems in medieval times, music began to accompany plays as they became more fashionable. In the theatre, music was used to heighten the mood and plot, emphasise the drama and sometimes provide special sound effects. The most prominent Elizabethan playwright, William Shakespeare, made hundreds of references to music in his plays and poems. 'As You Like It' and 'Twelfth Night' each include six songs.

Because travelling minstrels and troubadours fell out of favour and travel was limited during the Elizabethan era after the ravages of the plague, street and tavern musicians became more common. These musicians did not travel but played locally at the fairs, festivals, and feasts which were often related to religious events.

They typically played traditional songs on portable instruments such as fiddles, lutes, recorders and small percussion instruments. Larger towns had their official musicians known as

About Music

'waits'. The waits emerged during the earlier medieval era when they were part of the town watch and alerted residents to danger. By Elizabethan times, the waits simply provided free music and concerts for residents and were expected to compose for major events and ceremonies.

The sixteenth century is considered a high point in the English liturgical style and many of the hymns written at that time are still played today. Church music of the era also included madrigals and canzonets, light songs which were simpler than madrigals, in addition to sacred songs and full services.

The best-known composer of the Elizabethan era is William Byrd, who served as an organist and chorister of the Chapel Royal. The most prolific and versatile English composer of the era, Byrd wrote hundreds of pieces over six decades, including masses, motets (songs for multiple voices without instruments), liturgical music, secular songs for solo voice and small vocal ensembles, pieces for keyboard and for strings, and instrumental fantasias.

Byrd was a student of Thomas Tallis who was particularly known for his church music and served as an organist at the Chapel Royal and chorister at St Paul's Cathedral in London. Like Byrd, Tallis was favoured by the Queen, and in 1575 she gave the two composers what was essentially a twenty-one-year monopoly on the printing and sale of music. Among Tallis's best-known works are the motet *Spem in alium*, various church services, and his 'Lamentations'.

This walk began with the premise to explore the disaster that hit music during the English Reformation and the Dissolution of the Monasteries. During that time, music may well have suffered by its containment within certain restrictive liturgical requirements, but by and beyond Elizabeth's time it is clear that music flourished and continued to grow with the creation of different forms, instruments and ensembles and, of course, through the genius of composers like Byrd and Tallis. They adapted themselves brilliantly within the dictatorial constraints imposed by church politics, much as Shostakovich was compelled to, under the iron thumb of Stalin's communist Russia in the 20th century.

About Music

My walk continues along the top of the dyke. There is a fence on my right and I see two wheatears flying just ahead of me. They sit on a fence post and let me approach and then when I am a few metres away, shoot off along the fence showing me their trademark rear white feathers when they fly. Their old name of white arse is well-founded. After a while they give up and disappear, presumably having made sure I am not going near their nest. For a few minutes, the breeze picks up; there are one or two threateningly dark clouds in the sky and there is a hint of drizzle. I've been expecting this but am fooled again as it comes to nothing and the sunshine returns.

There is a view from here towards the distant Malvern Hills to the southeast and the Brecon Beacons in the southwest, over 30 miles away in each direction. This is a particularly prominent part of the dyke, wooded along the bank's sides and with a clear path along the top.

Two walkers approach me and one, rather surprisingly asks me where is the best place to see the dyke, as if he had no idea that it was beneath his feet, rather like standing under Big Ben and asking for the time.

Further along, I see an obelisk in a field to my right. It bears the inscription, "To perpetuate the memory of Sir Richard Green Price, 1st baronet, born 1803, died 1887, for services to the county of Radnor." Price is credited with constructing the first railway lines to Knighton, Llandrindod, Presteigne and Radnor. The memorial may at first sight appear to be an homage to the great man, but many such monuments were erected by these noblemen themselves, or their families!

I wonder where I would find monuments to Thomas Tallis and William Byrd. One 'monument' to Byrd is included in Peter Ackroyd's novel, *English Music*. In this he puts words into Byrd's mouth, as an old man, "My voice is quite gone now. I am like to an old crow still wheeling around the sky. But the spirit of music is still strong within me. The spirit is not broken, no, nor yet even touched by time. Remember the herb basil, which the more it is crushed the sooner it spring forth, or the poppy, which flourishes when it is trodden with the feet."

About Music

Later will come the last of the great early English composers, Henry Purcell, who, like Byrd was able to look back as well as forward in making his musical creations. After him, musical culture was so influenced by, so mixed up with continental styles that in effect English music died. It ceased to contribute to the development of western music. Fashions were for the French, Italian or German styles and to facilitate these, teachers were imported from those countries and naturally taught, not as Byrd would have done, to absorb the air and country around, but how to copy their foreign betters. The world was preparing to receive J.S. Bach.

The wooded hills beyond Knighton come into view and a brief stretch of level walking provides views to Shropshire's Titterstone Clee and Brown Clee. Then it is a descent for about half an hour or so all the way into Knighton and eventually I pass under the arch of the Norton Arms and into the town. That evening, I write a little poem:

> I walk, the horizon curves.
> I walk, the earth holds.
> I walk, not knowing what may happen.
> Nothing extraordinary for dull eyes.
>
> Walking is music.
> It has words like a song,
> Rhythm like a drum
> Melody like the birds
> Harmony like friendship.
> Occasional discord.
>
> May walking never end.
> Unfortunately, probabilities are against this,
> So, as with all cards dealt,
> Make of it the best.

Bill, feeling poetic

About Music

CHAPTER SIX

Making Waves

In which we see music

Today could be the hottest of the year and I will be walking a section of the dyke that has some demanding stretches. This makes me a little nervous but I do know that my body responds well to heat, so as long as I have plenty of water in my bottle, then all should be well.

Something else is making me feel uncertain. It is a trepidation that the previous walks have been so spectacularly beautiful and inspiring that this next might be a let-down in comparison. Time will tell, but whatever happens today, I am sure that walking is changing me. The countryside along the border is not exactly wilderness and so a feeling of solitary isolation is to overstate the experience, but what does arise when you walk for hours with perhaps only an occasional, momentary human contact and with little mechanically generated ambient noise, is a sense of wholeness, of becoming part of the landscape.

Our British countryside as a panoramic quilt of fields and pastures, stretching through valleys and plains, then up the sides of hills and mountains, is readily appreciated as a man-made sculpted surface. Its kaleidoscopic pattern of features has been gradually shifting over long centuries, sometimes imperceptibly, sometimes dynamically, creating a sense of one's own restless history. This can flourish into a spiritual sensation as you walk. An appreciation grows of why this countryside is so valuable, economically and for the soul.

Today's walk is from Knighton to Clun, both Shropshire towns. Clun in particular is a picturesque place, with its River Clun, olde worlde pubs and village shops. The walk starts in Knighton by the Offa's Dyke Centre which exhibits a history of the dyke's official path, opened in 1971. I walk round the outside of the centre and through the wooded area behind it, stopping for a moment to place my feet either side of a line that has been drawn in the earth to show the exact position of the England-Wales border. Then the path comes out into the open by the side of the River Teme. It continues along

About Music

the riverside for a few hundred metres then I cross a railway track and begin a steep walk out of the valley and up towards Llanfair Hill.

This section's musical theme is about the physical facts of making music, what happens when a string vibrates or an air-column makes sound waves; what happens when these waves then pass from instrument or loudspeaker to the ear. I began this project by writing about art and what abstraction meant, to get a feel for how this might apply to music. My thoughts return first today to this theme as I press on up the hillside and my breathing becomes deeper and rhythmic.

There has been an evolving process in the way we respond to art, to images and to music, designed by their creators to take our perceptions beyond surface appearances. At first the images of art were symbolic, depicting what the artist imagined to be the reality of the worlds beyond our physical senses; then they became figurative, depicting different ways of seeing surface reality, making us aware of the light itself. Then came abstraction whereby, instead of an image representing something particular, it did not and we should simply allow ourselves to respond viscerally to it. The individual's response becomes part of the artwork itself. In music, we similarly bring our own responses and discover in ourselves qualities of beauty, ugliness, passion, fear, bravery, joy, loss and so on. All that abstract art asks, is that we look. Music asks that we listen.

The complexity of the music is irrelevant; it might need to be complex to achieve its formal artistic end but equally, simplicity can work, too. The complaint that 'a child could have done that' when you view a piece of abstract art whose construction is simple is to miss the point. Yes, a child might have created it, but there would have been no intention to illuminate our human condition, to make the perceiver aware of their own responses and humanity.

Like any 'thing' that is made, there is a physical aspect to the making of music as of any art form. It has a tangible, concrete reality that we perceive via our senses, so I should include now as part of the mix the physical realities of music-making, vital for its creation and perception. The physics of vibration is interwoven with music's ability to communicate with and stir our inner being.

About Music

The path winds up a hillside to a triangulation point on Cwm-sanaham Hill. From here to Llanfair Hill is one of the best sections of the dyke, continuing to make its presence known and snake along the heights. I am familiar enough with the dyke almost to sense its presence with my eyes closed, as if it emits some sort of vibration. This sensation is equally strong whether the mound is low or high.

There are long stretches when the dyke is just a simple mound of earth, but equally there are times when trees both small and tall grace its top and sides. Hawthorn in particular may have been common and at one time may have increased the difficulty in crossing from one side to the other but equally may have provided cover for any illegal crossings.

I hear the groan and then roar of a motorbike and as I pass over a track and by Garbutt Hall a scrambler stops to open a gate and then wizzes off up the dyke path. He comes and goes quickly leaving diminishing ripples of sound in the atmosphere, the sky and earth easily absorbing this acoustic intrusion. A short while later I stop for refreshment and find that close by me the motorcyclist has stopped too.

I am at about 430 m above sea level and can see at eye level the top of Llanfair Hill to come, the dyke stretching between. The motorcyclist leaves me again with another roar followed by another emptiness.

Any sound, any music, is, before it reaches the brain, a vibration. A motorbike engine makes a rapid series of explosive sounds, a musical instrument causes a vibration when plucked, blown or struck and those vibrations are transmitted to the ear as waves of varying air pressure. The molecules of air in the space between instrument and ear vibrate in sympathy with the instrument's mechanical efforts, the molecules pushing and shoving against each other to cause variations in pressure. The ear drum picks up the vibrating pressure waves and transmits them to the inner ear.

A musician causes vibration; the brain transforms this acoustic energy into music. Essentially, you hear not the instrument but what is going on in your head in response.

About Music

What is in some pressure waves that can make the brain respond so beautifully? What is in others, like the motorbike's music, which makes us wince? The Pythagorians were not interested in finding out by analysing vibrations other than some considerations of the lengths of vibrating strings. That's not good enough for discovering what is going on here, for we need to consider the physiology and the responses of the brain.

The vibrations of a string are too small and quick to see with the naked eye and analyse in any detail. The air itself is invisible. If we were able to see the vibrations, it might be a revealing help.

One way to 'see' sound is by creating graphical waveforms. Any vibration can be represented visually by a waveform defined by two properties: its frequency, which is how fast the vibration repeats its cycle, the higher the frequency, the higher the pitch; and the amplitude, which is a measure of its energy. The higher the energy, the louder is the sound. Sounds have two other properties which are revealed in a waveform, namely how quickly the sound builds up and how quickly it dies away.

Percussive sounds will tend to have a rapid build-up and decay of energy. Violins and flutes will tend to be described more by their smoother continuous waveform patterns. The smoothness may vary allowing the timbre of a single instrument to change. For example, a violin will sound different to the expert musical ear depending on how the bow is drawn across the violin string. This is a simplification but illustrates the fact that waveforms have few parameters to consider in their construction. That is reassuring if you are worried by the prospect of complex theories about waves.

The heat is beginning to tell while a bunch of grasshoppers is making its own acoustic point. Grasshoppers are generally larger than crickets but with shorter antennae. They have a row of pegs along the inside of the hind leg which acts as a file, or rasp. The grasshopper rubs this against a thickened forewing, causing a vibration and thus a sound in a process called stridulation. Grasshoppers have ears in their backsides.

In comparison, the chirping sound of crickets, which tend to come out at dusk, is created when the top of one wing runs along the teeth at the bottom of the other wing. As the male cricket does this, he also holds his wings up and open so that the wing sails can act as an acoustic membrane, like a loudspeaker. Crickets chirp at different rates depending on their species and the temperature of their environment. Most species stridulate at higher rates the higher the temperature is. Crickets' ears are on their front legs.

Natural sounds, such as those made by grasshoppers and crickets, do not operate in isolation; they are part of an acoustic environment. Work on analysing sound recordings made in acoustically rich environments, such as a rain forest, shows that the sound each creature makes inhabits a particular bandwidth of frequencies. This situation may have evolved so that a species and its sound type do not compete with others. Sounds rub shoulders and blend with one another but each can be clearly heard in its own right.

This is similar to an orchestra, where each group of instruments has not only its characteristic timbre but its particular frequency range, too. These overlap but in general violins and flutes are higher than bassoons and cellos. Violins and flutes with their similar frequency ranges don't compete because they have very different sound qualities, as do cellos and bassoons. The skill of an orchestrator is to write music sometimes combining and sometimes separating out all the different instrumental timbres at will.

The natural environment has its own orchestra which can span sounds from the lowest bass frog to the highest treble bird tweet and whose sounds quite happily inhabit their acoustic spaces together. Unfortunately, diminishing natural environments and diminishing species means diminishing soundscape diversity, too.

At this point, I would like to describe the simplest type of waveform. The reason for this is not because this is a starting point before building up the complexity. No, for as we shall conclude shortly, it is an incredible fact that all sounds are a sum of simple waves, nothing more and nothing less. Each individual sound has its own unique combination of simple wave forms. Hence, it is worth looking closely at the simplest of them for these are the building blocks of sound, its fundamental particles, so to speak.

A tuning fork is a two-pronged instrument which can create a pure simple sound wave. It makes a rather uninteresting sound but the fork offers a demonstration of what is happening to make the wave when its two prongs vibrate.

About Music

Each prong is moving backwards and forwards with 'harmonic motion'. This is the same type of movement that a pendulum makes as it swings backwards and forwards, or a weight on a vertical spring when bouncing up and down. The pendulum, the weight, or the fork tips all behave in the same way when in motion. They move most rapidly when they travel through their middle position, slow up, reverse and accelerate to a maximum speed as they pass through their middle position in the opposite direction, slow up, reverse, accelerate and repeat the cycle.

In the case of our tuning fork, as the pair of prongs vibrates, their regular cycle of movement alternates between moving towards each other, reducing the local air pressure on one side and then moving away from each other, increasing the local air pressure and pushing the vibrating pressure wave out into the surrounding air, thus generating its sound.

The oscillating pendulum, spring bob or tuning fork's movement can be plotted as a graph which has its horizontal axis representing time elapsed and its vertical axis representing the distance travelled. Each tuning-fork tip oscillates between its position of rest, zero on the graph, and its maximum displacements. The resulting sound wave can be represented by a graph which would look like this:

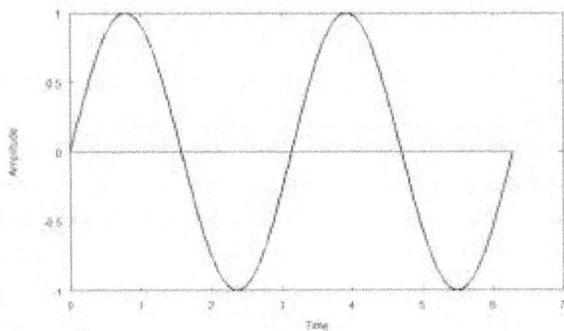

If the sound created was louder or quieter, the height of the wave would increase or decrease; if it was higher or lower in pitch, the wave would look more spread out or bunched up tighter.

About Music

If you cast your mind back to an early algebra lesson at school, you may remember that graphs can be represented by an equation involving x, the horizontal axis, and y, the vertical axis. A simple straight line, for example, might be represented by $y = ax$ where a is the slope or gradient of the line.

Our oscillating wave must have an equation of its own. The simple wave is called a 'sine wave' and this gives a clue about its equation. Again, casting your mind back to early maths lessons, the term 'sine', you may remember, is used commonly in the subject of trigonometry.

What on earth has this to do with music? Trigonometry is a study of the relationships between the angles and sides of triangles and this can – stay with me here - be used to understand and see the motion of a wave.

The angles and side lengths of right-angled triangles are related to one another and are expressed in terms of 'cosines', 'sines' and 'tangents', which, hopefully, you came across at school but then, probably, forgot all about.

However, they reappear again as soon as you look into how waves behave and indeed our simplest graphical representation of a pure tone, a wave caused by an object vibrating at a single frequency, is, to reiterate, a 'sine wave'.

It is a fact that if you plot a curve of the graph $y = \sin x$, the resulting shape is our simple wave. This in itself may not seem earth shattering but it opens a doorway to understanding how waves operate and how the mathematical basis behind them is described by trigonometry.

In case this whets your appetite to delve further in this mathematical direction, you may remember that sines, cosines and tangents are ratios of side lengths in a right-angled triangle from the point of view of one of the triangle's angles, θ (Greek letter, theta). The opposite/adjacent is the tangent; the opposite/hypotenuse is the sine and adjacent/hypotenuse is the cosine. Pythagoras is looking over us here and feeling quite proud. We are making connections between triangles and music!

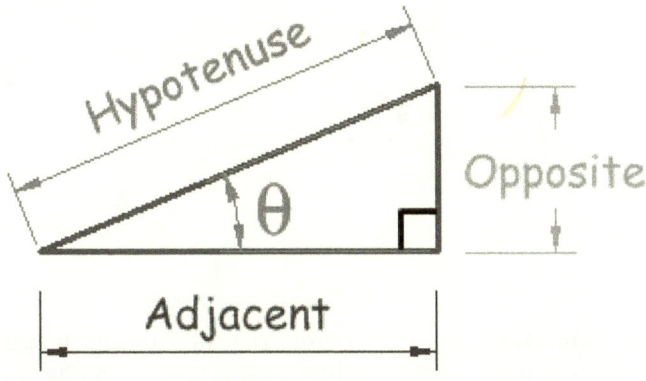

The exact law of motion is made clear by looking at the motion of a point P' projected on the diameter of a circle by a point P on the circle's circumference. If P is moving at constant speed, P' will oscillate to and fro on the diameter with the type of harmonic motion that I've described.

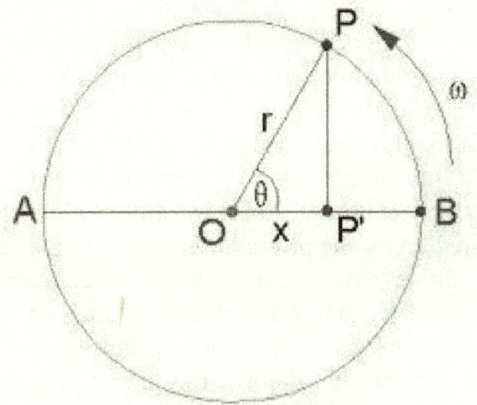

The next diagram shows how this motion can be visualised and drawn as a wave.

About Music

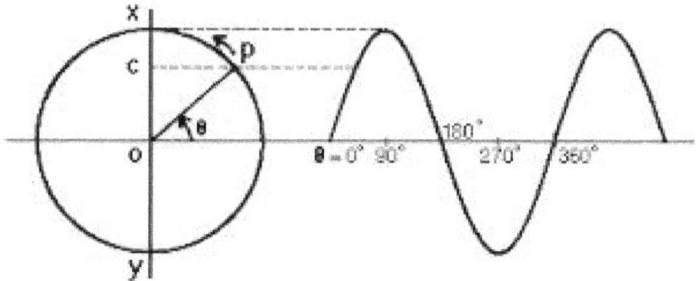

One final point before the risk of pushing the maths too far kicks in is that the vertical height of the point P can be defined as the sine of the angle θ. For example, if you make the radius = 1, then sine θ = P/1 = P. Hence, we've arrived at the equation of the wave as sine θ – it's a sine wave!

I guess the main point that I want to make here is that trigonometry is the basis for working out the laws of wave motion, the waves that make music.

My attention is caught by an old rusting plough attachment that was clearly abandoned on the dyke many years ago. Its wheels are half buried in the soil as if the earth has risen to claim it like a praying mantis grasping a metal fly. Conditions up here are harsh for farming and this old plough is a testament to that.

Early steel ploughs used for thousands of years were walking ploughs, directed by the ploughman walking behind and holding onto handles on either side. Steel ploughs were relatively easy to draw through the soil as the constant adjustments of a wooden blade to react to roots or clods were no longer necessary. The metal plough could easily cut through them. Consequently, it was not long before the first horse-drawn ploughs appeared with the seated ploughman.

My plough would have been drawn by an early tractor. The earliest of these were steam powered at the end of the 19th century, but by the early 20th century came the internal combustion engine and the tractor as we know it today. What a racket they would have made.

About Music

I began by saying that any sound is made up of simple waves added together. In fact, it was the converse of this that was discovered first, that is, any sound can be broken up into its constituent simple waves. The scientist who discovered that any complex sound wave can be broken up into a set of simple sine waves was a French mathematician and physicist, Joseph Fourier (1768-1830). Fourier's discovery is important in the development of our understanding of acoustics. Indeed, his way of analysing waveforms can be applied to any wave, whether acoustic or electromagnetic, which means his work has become vital in other areas of science too, such as in the transmission of radio waves.

Its basis is quite straightforward. Any complex waveform, for example, the sound made by a musical instrument, can be analysed into a series of simple waves, each wave vibrating at a particular frequency and amplitude. Combine these back again and you reconstruct the original sound.

Fourier was renowned initially for showing how the conduction of heat in solid bodies takes place and how this conduction could be analysed as a mathematical series of simple waves, today referred to as the Fourier Series.

Fourier's theory was the first accurate one on heat diffusion. Originally trained for the priesthood, fate had something completely different in store for this great man. A close comrade of Napoleon, Fourier played an important role in Napoleon's Egyptian expeditions. He is also credited with the discovery of the greenhouse effect.

If it were not for greenhouse gases trapping heat in the atmosphere, the earth would be an unbearably cold place. During the day, the earth heats up; at night, it loses some of this heat in the form of radiation. Gases in the atmosphere prevent the loss of this heat into the depths of space and keep the earth warm enough for life to continue. The most notorious of the atmosphere's greenhouse gases are methane and carbon dioxide. Environmentalists are well aware that today there is too much of these gases in our atmosphere, exacerbating the greenhouse effect.

Where Fourier comes into our story about music is in the type of heat energy transmission which is involved in the greenhouse effect. The heat energy is carried by infrared waves which are a form of electromagnetic radiation and therefore subject to analysis by Fourier's mathematical technique, the Fourier Series, in just the way that any form of wave transmission would be.

However, it is the application to acoustics that interests us here. To analyse sound waves into pure tones, sine waves, and then be able to reconstruct them means that new synthesised sounds can be made and this leads directly in the 20th century to the development of the electronic synthesiser.

The earliest seeds of modern electronic synthesisers began in the twilight years of the 19th century about a century after Fourier. In 1896-97, an American inventor named Thaddeus Cahill applied for a patent to protect the principle behind a musical instrument known as the Telharmonium or Dynamophone. Weighing in at a staggering 200 tons, this mammoth electronic instrument was driven by twelve steam-powered electromagnetic wave generators.

This behemoth was played in real time using velocity-sensitive keys and, amazingly, was able to generate several different sounds simultaneously. The Telharmonium was presented to the public in a series of concerts held in 1906. Christened *Telharmony*, this music was piped into the public telephone network because no amplifiers and loudspeakers, no public address systems, were available at the time to reproduce it.

In 1919, Russian inventor Leon Theremin took a markedly different approach to synthesising sounds. Named after the man who masterminded it, the monophonic Theremin was played without touching the instrument. It gauged the proximity of the player's hands as they were waved about in an electrostatic field between two antennae and used this information to generate sounds of variable pitch. This unorthodox technique made the Theremin difficult to play but its eerie, spine-tingling, unvarying timbre made it a favourite on countless horror movie soundtracks. Robert Moog, whose synthesizers would later garner worldwide fame, began to build Theremins at the tender age of nineteen.

In Europe, in 1928, the Frenchman Maurice Martenot devised the monophonic Ondes Martenot. The sound generation method of this instrument was akin to that of the Theremin but in its earliest incarnation it was played by pulling a wire back and forth.

About Music

At the end of 1963, American innovator Bob Moog met the composer Herbert Deutsch, who inspired him to combine a voltage-controlled waveform generator and amplifier module with a keyboard, thus creating the first prototype of the modern synthesizer. This collaboration with the German musician prompted Moog to extend his range of modules and to combine them into entire systems. It wasn't until 1967, however, that Moog actually called his diverse mix-and-match system an electronic synthesiser.

Electrical voltage controlled the variables of the sound wave, namely its amplitude (volume) and frequency (pitch), while each waveform generator was built to produce and combine simple waves, thus creating new timbres.

In 1968, Wendy (then Walter) Carlos's LP *Switched-On Bach* was responsible for a breakthrough into the public domain of Moog's instruments. The vinyl recording featured Moog's modular synthesizers and was one of the earliest successful commercial multitrack recordings.

I am almost at the foot of a slope and the bottom of a field when I briefly lose the path as I try to cross a couple of rivulets. Then I realise my error as I discover the bridges I need, that were made some years ago by Royal Engineers who were keen to do a training exercise in bridge-building.

The rest of the descent leads to a farm at Lower Spoad. The farmyard is on the dyke and its farmhouse is medieval, apparently boasting a treasured Elizabethan carved hunting scene over a fireplace.

Applied science in the twentieth century enabled high quality sound systems. These can recreate original sound recordings and amplify sound energy for public performance at any place or time. Two components in the chain of sound reproduction involve a combination of electrical, mechanical and acoustical properties and these are the microphone and the loudspeaker.

Both work in the same way, but in opposite directions. The microphone converts sound pressure waves into an electrical signal;

the loudspeaker converts an electrical signal into sound. There is another device used for converting sound waves and that is the ear, so a little consideration of our mechanical devices is appropriate here before considering the way the ear and the brain work together.

The input to a loudspeaker is an electrical signal which varies in a way that follows the outline of the original acoustic wave pattern. A graph of the electrical signal should look exactly the same as a graph of the equivalent sound that it is reproducing, the electrical graph's vertical component being a measure of current or voltage.

The electric signal is transformed back into sound by coiling the wiring around a magnet. An electric current passed through the coils will cause the magnet to vibrate in sympathy with the current. The vibrating magnet is attached to the familiar loudspeaker cone which pushes against the surrounding air creating pressure waves and, bingo, you have recreated the original sound.

In 1874, Ernst W. Siemens was the first to describe the dynamic or moving-coil transducer. It has a circular coil of wire in a magnetic field and supported so that it could move axially. A transducer, by the way, is simply a device for converting one form of energy into another, in this case acoustic into electrical energy, or vice versa. However, on an historical note, Siemens did not use his device for audible transmission, as did Alexander Graham Bell who patented the telephone in 1876.

The loudspeaker originally took the form of an exponentially shaped horn. Some of these constructions were massive, others not quite so, but all were somewhat unwieldy and prone to add their own acoustic characteristics to the sound reproduction quality.

In 1898, Oliver Lodge filed for British patent No. 9712 for an improved loudspeaker with nonmagnetic spacers to maintain the air gap between the inner and outer poles of a moving coil transducer. Even then, ideas about sound reproduction were becoming sophisticated.

By 1925, the research paper of Chester W. Rice and Edward W. Kellogg at General Electric was important in establishing the basic principle of the direct-radiator loudspeaker with a small coil-driven mass-controlled diaphragm mounted in a baffle (a box!) with a broad mid-frequency range of uniform response. This was the

About Music

creation of the loudspeaker as we know it today, the 'baffle' being made by mounting the loudspeaker unit in one face of a sealed box.

At this point the making of the loudspeaker boxes becomes more complex as the air behind the speaker unit in the box will have a cushioning effect on its vibrating motion. This cushioning was cleverly used to control the vibration of the cone to give it a smooth response through the whole range of audible frequencies, about 20 Hz to 20 kHz.

There have followed numerous innovations, including separating different bands of the frequency spectrum for reproduction in speaker units matched to these bands: tweeters and woofers to you and me. Others included the use of electrical feedback to increase efficiency, and what are called 'reflex' loudspeaker cabinets which involve channelling the acoustic properties of the cabinets themselves to improve sound quality.

In 1982, 'Return of the Jedi' was the first movie exhibited using the THX sound system designed by George Lucas and Tomlinson Holman; THX "is comprised of customized acoustical design work for each auditorium, a Benwin 1998 flat panels special screen speaker installation method, a proprietary electronic crossover network, and rigorous audio equipment specifications and performance standards." The force was at work in sound reproduction.

♟ A little further on, I discover another half-timbered farmhouse at Bryndrinog and stop to take a photograph. At this point, I decide to divert westward along a minor road into sleepy Newcastle-on-Clun, only about a mile distant. Twenty minutes or so later, in the late afternoon, the temperature is peaking and although tired, I stay in Newcastle only long enough to decide there is nothing here for me, finish off the day's supplies, empty my water bottle then retrace my steps along the road, this time going east and, in about three miles, into Clun where I will rest for the night. On arriving in Clun, I have walked about eleven miles, but the enervating heat has made it feel more like twenty.

About Music

Drawing waves and graphs is not the only way of visualising sound. There is another approach which is called cymatics, the 'study of sound and vibration made visible'. Typically, a visible pattern can be formed by vibrating a metal plate on which a thin layer of particles like sand or salt are allowed to jump and bump to form areas of maximum and minimum displacement. The resulting patterns are aesthetically pleasing and geometrically complex. Similar evocative forms can be created by vibrating liquids.

The plates are called Chladni plates after their inventor, or perhaps more accurately, after the man who made the phenomenon public. In 1787, the musician and physicist Ernst Chladni published *Discoveries Concerning the Theory of Music*. In this and other pioneering works, Chladni, who was born in 1756, the same year as Mozart, and died in 1829, the same year as Beethoven, laid the foundations for a science of sound. Among Chladni's successes was finding a way to make sound waves visible.

With the help of a violin bow which he drew perpendicularly across the edge of flat plates covered with sand, he produced those patterns and shapes which today go by the term Chladni figures.

A Chladni plate can be made by attaching a loudspeaker to the underneath of the plate and sprinkling the granules on top. Similarly, if a liquid is to be used, the loudspeaker can again be employed as the source of acoustic vibration. The shapes and patterns of motion that appeared to Chladni proved to be primarily a function of the material used but also of the frequency and amplitude of vibration, making a direct relationship with the original mechanical vibration.

In 1967, the late Hans Jenny, a Swiss researcher, published *The Structure and Dynamics of Waves and Vibrations*. In this, Jenny, like Chladni two hundred years earlier, showed what happens when one takes various materials like sand, spores, iron filings, water, and viscous substances, and places them on vibrating metal plates and membranes. What then appears are shapes and motion patterns which vary from the nearly perfectly ordered and stationary to those that are turbulently developing, organic, and constantly in motion.

An interesting phenomenon apparently appeared when Jenny took a vibrating plate covered with liquid and tilted it. The liquid did not yield to gravitational influence and run off the vibrating plate but stayed on and went on constructing new shapes as though nothing had happened. If, however, the oscillation was then turned off, the liquid began to run, but if he was really fast and got the vibrations going again, he could get the liquid back in place on the plate. According to Jenny, this was an example of an anti-gravitational effect created by vibrations.

A practical application of cymatics is in understanding the acoustic response of stringed instrument backs and bellies, useful for skilled makers of stringed instruments. Indeed, the principles can be used in any situation that needs a visual representation of vibration patterns in a membrane or surface.

The appeal of the trigonometrical approach in making sound visible is that it is completely objective and therefore not dependent on the interpretations of any observer's perspective. Cymatics has an empirical side to it but also has been coloured by the need for subjective interpretation. This can be compelling and off putting in equal measures.

Some of its recent work has been focused on the behaviour of liquids, particularly in attempting to demonstrate that liquids have memory, leading on to the idea that they may have a form of consciousness, too. It is easy to regard this type of conclusion as over-imaginative, an unfortunate reaction in our prosaic world of defined demarcations of what is real and what is not, of which 'box' a phenomenon should be consigned to. A significant advantage that these ramblings have is in the ability to walk a borderline from which we can look down at will on each side of these opposites of imaginative art and objective science.

I muse at the end of today's journey that there is nothing wrong with seeing more in these patterns than exists, as long as awareness is maintained that there is a form of psychological projection at work. If this awareness can be maintained, those patterns can be explored at will and will reveal in them, like gazing into an astrological map of the heavens and seeing unconscious forces at work, a true image of sound that has come from within. These granular and liquid patterns may even represent the music of the spheres anew.

About Music

I sit gratefully resting in the shade of a tree by a five-arched bridge over the River Clun where some ducks are asleep on the bank and where my guide book tells me that this is where the playwright John Osborne died and is buried. There is another literary reference to be made here in that Clun is described in A.E. Housman's *A Shropshire Lad* as one of the quietest places under the sun.

That evening, I am booked in at the White Horse Inn. I have a meal and a pint in the bar and make notes about the day's walk. At about 10:00 p.m. I go to my room and climb into bed. My room is above the bar area where a rock band starts to play. The music is loud. There must be some pretty hefty loudspeaker kit down there. Most guests will have been somewhat disgruntled by the noise. For my part, I could tell the group were going to be good – not at first; it took the drummer a while to warm up, but once up and running they produced some inspired covers, from Nirvana to Queens of the Stone Age. So much for A.E. Housman.

I was too physically tired to get up again, but not so tired that I couldn't enjoy their music. That's the first time that I've laid in a comfortable, white-sheeted bed in an olde-worlde B&B, played to sleep by live rock music. The band continued until just before midnight and then, cloaked in the return of Clun's silence, I went to sleep.

Bill, dreaming about pendulums and guitars

About Music

CHAPTER 7

Myth and Music

In which music moves mountains and revives the dead

In the morning, I stroll through Clun and make my way back towards Newcastle. I pick up the dyke's path where I left it yesterday by the half-timbered farmhouse at Bryndrinog. From there, heading north, is a steep climb out of the Clun valley and this marks the beginning of the notorious dyke path's switchback. It is going to be another hot day.

I've been climbing for a while and come across a signpost indicating that walkers on the Offa's Dyke Path at this particular spot are exactly half way along their route, with 88½ miles in either direction to Chepstow and Prestatyn, at the beginning, or end of the walk, depending on which direction you are travelling. It's an occasion of some personal moment to arrive at this place and I celebrate with a photo and by phoning my wife to give her the good news. I've made it a rule that my mobile phone be switched off while I walk, but deem the occasion important enough to break it just this once. Any other time will be for emergencies only.

Today's stretch along the dyke, as yesterday, is not a long one, but it will be hot and hilly. The evening's destination is a farmhouse in Cwm and then tomorrow morning a walk into the town of Montgomery, which will mark the end of this chapter.

I will have plenty of time to enjoy the atmosphere and the views today. Much of the previous walks has been characterised by keeping up a steady pace while navigating, meaning that there is always something to do to occupy walking time. Today is different in that the walk is a relatively short distance. This means that there will be plenty of time for mythological musical meditations, the topic for this section of the route.

The first point of navigational note is the Hergan hilltop at about 409 metres above sea level. The views are spectacular from here with the familiar roll of the dyke stretching away into the distance. At this particular juncture there is an anomaly in the dyke's progress as if two construction teams approaching each other from opposite directions had miscalculated and missed the join. Someone took their eye off the ball, and I bet there were some quaint medieval expletives flying around in the air at the moment of discovery.

Why is myth relevant to music? One significant constituent of music making is inventive creativity and this human ability feeds from the imagination. The imagination is the stuff of mythological folk lore which comes to us from our ancient histories, the stories that have become embedded in our psychological makeup, stories that we tell ourselves about how the world is.

We may not believe the myths of old any more but we have certainly created new ones that describe the way we live. Modern myths influence our beliefs and the way we express them through our cultural activities. Myth – and the imagination - is, despite a modern, rational culture, a fundamental component of our makeup as human beings.

The word myth has come to mean something that is not true, a story, akin to a fairy tale, which is purported to represent reality. It is usually applied to a story about something which is larger than life, that represents life beyond the boundaries of our normal experience of everyday reality.

Every ancient culture had its own set of myths which represented its unique characteristics – stories about where it came from, how it began, how it was built, how it survived its great battles, how it achieved greatness or fell from grace.

Cultural myths were the basis of religious beliefs about the nature of gods and goddesses and the existence of heavens and hells, of life before birth and after death, and how humans and gods move from each of these states to the other.

From a psychological perspective, myths encompass the stories of human development, of how self-consciousness arose out of the primeval unconscious realms of the animal, plant and mineral. So, fictional they might be, but they hold the keys to understanding our psychological history and its roots.

The most sophisticated myths are those from ancient Greece with its creation myths and a plethora of stories about the behaviour

About Music

of the gods of Mount Olympus. How these gods behaved towards each other is a revealing description of our own patterns of behaviour, how we instinctively react in certain situations and what we can expect their outcomes to be. How Aphrodite the goddess of love behaves, informs the way we conduct our intimate relationships; how Ares the god of war behaves suggests the aggressive qualities of our natures and where his type of behaviour will lead.

Some of the Greek gods are specifically associated with music, but first I want to describe those that were linked particularly with the planets of our solar system. These gods are enmeshed with the Greek's view of the universe and hence with the harmony and music of the spheres.

The path descends towards Churchtown and on the way down I pass some buildings at Middle Knuck, an ex-farmyard now an institution offering safe crisis care for children, notable for its remoteness from any other buildings or habitation. This place clearly wishes to retain an anonymous nature and must surely hide behind its façade stories of personal turmoil that would contrast vividly with the stillness of the solid earth and summer air out here where I stand.

It was in ancient Babylon that a priestly cast first made detailed observations of the movements of the stars and planets. They observed that certain lights in the sky were fixed while others moved. If these cosmic objects moved, they could only do so, those observers concluded, because they were alive, were living beings who were imbued with supernatural qualities.

The two largest stellar bodies which moved were the sun and the moon and these, clearly, therefore, had the most influence upon life on earth. The moon also demonstrated another living quality by passing through its phases once every 28 days appearing to die at the New Moon and be reborn a few days later.

The sun's height in the sky heralded the seasons and brought warmth and the ripening of fruit and crops. Clearly when the sun god was displeased, great anguish would be felt on earth, so much effort was put into appeasing the gods and pleasing their whims and desires.

The role of the priests was to observe and record the movements and behaviour of the gods and interpret this as the correct way for the people to behave. Rituals were devised which copied the patterns of the planetary movements and paid homage to the planetary gods. The priests were powerful for they held the knowledge of how to work with and receive cosmic good will.

The king and queen of the heavens were the sun and moon, their courtiers were Mercury, Venus, Mars, Jupiter and Saturn. Their movements were not straightforward, for at certain times of the year, the planets would appear to become stationary in the night sky and then begin to track backwards, to go retrograde. We know the reason that this phenomenon occurs is because our viewpoint is from one of the orbiting planets, namely the earth, but the original assumption was that the gods were circling the earth, whose position was at the centre of the universe.

The behaviour of the moving planets against the fixed background of the constellations and the interpretation of these movements became the basis for astrology. The early astrologer-priests devised rituals based on their astrological observations and interpretations and left a record of their work for later cultures.

We know little about the civilisation of the early Sumerians, although it is likely that not only were they obsessed by divination of all kinds but their mathematics was of an equivalent standard to that in 17th century Europe. All that was needed was to combine observational astronomy, mathematics and divination and the result was astrology. It is probable that this process started sometime around 2,000 BC, for the earliest known astrological text we have is dated before 1,600 BC.

This is the *Venus Tablet of Amisadqa*, written during the reign of King Amisaduqa of Babylon: "In month XI, 15th day, Venus disappeared in the west. Three days it stayed away, then on the 18th day it became visible in the east. Springs will open and Adad will bring his rain and Ea his floods. Messages of reconciliation will be sent from King to King."

About Music

Ahead of me is Churchtown, a hamlet with only one significant building, its church. Located in a narrow valley, this too has the air of secrecy about it, tucked well into the narrow gap between the folds of the surrounding hills and woodland. 'Town' is a considerable exaggeration for there is little else here except the church dedicated to St John the Baptist and one house within its sight. The church building and its grounds are well kept and it clearly must serve a wide rural area.

In the porch is a note about the valuable flora that grows in the church's grounds. Nearly half of its area is wooded steep slopes while the more level grassland has a plethora of species to discover. Here is the note, a list of this church's flora, made in 1998 by J.A. Thompson. It is worth including his record to make the point that the value of historical churches is not only in their fabric but is in their immediate vicinity, too. It is an impressive list and reading this roll call is to articulate the poetry of plants.

> Trees, shrubs and climbers: sycamore, hawthorn, ash, ivy, holly, Norway spruce, scots pine, blackthorn, gooseberry, dog rose, bramble, raspberry, elder, yew and box; Grasses, sedges, rushes and ferns: common male fern, soft rush, field wood rush, meadow foxtail, sweet vernal grass, cocks foot, red fescue, Yorkshire fog, wood millet, smooth meadow grass, bracken; Wildflowers: yarrow, moschatel, ground-elder, lady's mantle, garlic mustard, cow parsley, lesser burdock, lords-and-ladies, daisy, hairy bitter-cress, cuckoo flower, common knapweed, common mouse-ear, rosebay willowherb, meadowsweet, snowdrop, common hemp-nettle, cleavers, heath bedstraw, herb-robert, ground ivy, hogwood, bluebell, perforate st john's-wort, cat's ear, meadow vetchling, common bird's-foot trefoil, honeysuckle, dog's mercury, field forget-me-not, mouse-ear-hawkwood, ribwort plantain, tormentil, barren strawberry, primrose, selfheal, meadow buttercup, bulbous buttercup, lesser celandine, creeping buttercup, common sorrel, common figwort, groundsel, red campion, betony, hedge woundwort, lesser stitchwort, greater stitchwort, dandelion, wood sage, red

About Music

clover, common nettle, germander speedwell, bush vetch and, last but not least, common dog-violet.

Betony and lady's mantle are two examples of particular interest because they were, like others, once commonly found in traditional meadows but are now rare. They illustrate the vital role that churchyards can now play in the preservation of our flora.

After a rest on a bench in the churchyard under the shade of a cool yew, there is a steep climb out of Churchtown but still with the dyke for company.

I've been impressed by how pervasive the common thistle is here and the thistle nectar clearly attracts numerous insects. There are several butterflies that feed on it but I see one in particular which I identify later as Milbert's tortoiseshell. These flying flowers are an almost constant companion as I walk.

Soon after 600 BC, the Greeks began to study astronomy and the Hellenistic and Mesopotamian worlds started the gradual process of cultural mixing which was to reach its climax with the conquests of Alexander the Great some 300 years later. Somewhere between 569 and 510 BC, Pythagoras studied at Babylon and it is possible that his example was followed by other Greek scholars.

A remnant of Babylonian culture is their sexagesimal number system which became widespread and, as applied to the recording of time, gave birth to the twelve-hour day, the division of the hour into 60 minutes and the minute into 60 seconds. We are on Babylonian time.

Three hundred years or so BC, the powerful mystery cult of Mithra developed in the Near East. The Babylonian rituals had by then become complex and sophisticated. The Mysteries of Mythra developed such that during the Roman period this cult was the most formidable rival to Christianity both in Asia and in Europe, reaching as far north as the south of Scotland.

In its mystery rituals, the neophyte, who was to undergo an initiation into the secrets of the universe, was known as 'Raven' and in the rites, the celebrants wore masks representing animals of the zodiac. This had come to represent the outermost limit within which the realm of space, time and causality operated. Outside that limit,

About Music

beyond the zodiac, there were different laws at work. Within it were the gods and man.

The orbits of the seven visible spheres were conceived as envelopes around the earth down through which the soul descended when travelling to be born on earth. As the soul descended, it acquired from each sphere a particular quality of character which was a burden, a cloak, to be borne throughout life.

The neophyte would also experience in the planetary ritual his symbolic death and the return passage back through the planetary spheres. This culminated in enlightenment about the natural condition of the soul, existing beyond the planetary spheres in its true state of freedom.

As described in *The Masks of God* by the mythologist, Joseph Campbell, in the first initiation, the mystic was identified with the Raven, the black bird of death. The bird carried him, symbolically, beyond the sphere of the Moon, the waxing and waning sign of the endless round of birth and death. Identified with the Raven, the initiate left the physical body to decay and flew through the lunar gateway to the second sphere. This is the sphere of Mercury (Greek Hermes; Egyptian Thoth; Germanic Woden, or Odin), the sphere of occult powers and the wisdom of rebirth. In completing the first rite, the initiate became known as 'The Hidden Master'.

In a second rite, he moves from Mercury to Venus's sphere of desire and delusion which must be overcome through the disciplines of the initiation. Now assuming the role of 'Soldier', he travels to the Sun's circle, the realm of arrogant power. Offered a crown and sword, the mystic rejects this, declaring that, "Mithra alone shall be my crown."

He becomes now the 'Lion', partakes in a sacramental meal of bread and water mixed with wine and then passes through the solar gateway to the fifth, Mars, zone of daring and audacity. He is now robed in the Phrygian cap and loose Iranian garb of the saviour, Mithra, and receives the title, 'Persian'.

Two further initiations followed. The first was the mystic's transfer to Jupiter's sphere, becoming known as 'Runner of the Sun' and finally, from Jupiter to Saturn, when he was sanctified as 'Father'.

About Music

The series of rites was performed in a grotto representing the world cave in which the rites celebrated the mythological theme of the unity of macrocosm (the universe), mesocosm (the ritual itself) and microcosm (the individual's soul). The mystic was led by degrees to experience the transcendental reality of his own being.

The ancient Greeks in full awareness of this transcendental reality set to work to map out the realm of the planetary spheres and used musical theory as a basis for achieving this. Pythagoras's exploration of the world of numbers and his single-stringed monochord instrument were created for just this purpose.

Simple divisions of the monochord created notes and intervals with simple mathematical relationships. Each tone's qualities were defined according to the principle of microcosm corresponding with macrocosm – as above, so below. Thus, all the planetary spheres became associated with, had correspondences with, their own musical notes.

I reach the River Unk which has run completely dry, cross it by a low bridge and further on reach the Kerry Ridgeway. This is a road with a long, long history, which runs from west to east. It has been called Wales's oldest road and follows the crest of the hills above the Vale of Kerry for more than fifteen miles, from Cider House a few miles south of Newtown to Bishops Castle. The route has been in use for at least 4,000 years. Bronze Age traders came this way and for 800 years the drovers brought their cattle and sheep from Wales to the markets in England. My route after crossing the ridge descends into Cwm - from the Welsh 'Y Cwm', meaning '(the) valley' - and I find a resting place for the night.

Cwm is no more than a few cottages nestling in richly productive surrounding farmland. The cottage where I have my bed for the night is comfortable, kept with pride and has an air of unchanging peaceful calm about it. I feel at home.

It is the job of the traveller to recount tales of adventure and great things. Here are some stories that I have heard about music and which occupied my thoughts that evening.

About Music

The progeny of the head of all the Greek gods, Zeus (Jupiter to the Romans), represent psychological complexes and compulsive personality traits. Often the stories tell how these children of Zeus were raised in secrecy, to hide them from malevolent forces that would seek to harm or kill them. When new facets of personality come into being, they don't emerge into the ego straight away but grow in secrecy. Two such children, Amphion and Zethos, the sons of Zeus and Antiope, grew up in secrecy among the herdsmen on Mount Cithaeron.

Amphion, favoured by the winged god, Hermes (Mercury), was presented by him with the gift of a lyre and he devoted much of his time to learning how to play it. His brother, Zethos, a much more pragmatic type, taunted and teased his brother for wasting so much time on such a useless impractical pursuit. Zethos suggests the personality that is capable and practical, a person who gets things done, while Amphion is the intuitive artistic type who daydreams and is not bound by convention.

To be patronised by Hermes was an honour indeed and it was the intuitive Amphion, rather than the practical Zethos who found this favour. "What use is music," asks Zethos, "When it comes to the practical tasks of life?"

Sometime later, having conquered Thebes, Amphion and Zethos were in the process of fortifying the city. While Zethos toiled and sweated to move great stones with nothing but his own strength to rely on, Amphion smiled, played his golden lyre and the stones slid effortlessly into place, seemingly of their own volition. Brute strength will work, but there is an easier way to harness natural forces. There is something in music that makes these helpful energies available to mind and body.

In the 1970s, the Dragon Project investigated the then unexplained phenomena that occurred in and around ancient standing stones, in particular for the Dragon Project at the Rollright Stones in Oxfordshire.

Their research revealed that the stones emitted ultrasonic vibrations of considerable strength which varied in a regular pattern according to the time of year, time of day and phase of the moon. Dan Robins, a professional chemist and director of the project,

About Music

concluded that the stones were acting as transducers and amplifiers of microwave energy coming from the sun.

The project created its own version of a stone circle and found that the ultrasonic energy they were able to generate was so high that it damaged their instruments. It is clear that this type of radiation can be emitted by matter and, conversely, can be used to affect it, for example, in dissolving kidney stones and to levitate and isolate cancerous cells. That is fact, not mythology.

The ancient Greeks were not inferior to us in their mental and physical capacities as their learning and feats were considerable. Perhaps the matter of the world then was different from today, less dense, less formed, more susceptible to manipulation by ultrasound and even sound waves, more akin to the modern, equally strange quantum mechanical world.

Hermes, mentioned in my story, has many facets including that of healing. His attributes include the caduceus, a stick around which two snakes coil, and which to this day is used as the symbol of the healing profession. He is also, astrologically, the god of communication and in psychology is recognised as the 'trickster' archetype, a character not to be trusted, who disrupts the *status quo* and is patron of thieves.

Without the trickster in us our personalities would be rigid, static, mechanical, so he brings the gift of new possibilities and growth – of thinking outside the box. Hermes is one of the central influences in the alchemical process, who stirs things up and makes things happen. His corresponding metal is the liquid quicksilver, mercury.

In classical Greek mythology, it is Apollo (Helios), the sun god, who is the god of music. He is head of the nine Muses, daughters of Zeus. The words 'muse' and 'music' have the same etymological root. Hermes, the thief, is said to have stolen Apollo's sacred herd of cattle and, to appease the god when found out, made him the gift of a lyre. This, Hermes had invented and made from a slaughtered cow from Apollo's herd, using the intestines for strings. The lyre was strummed with a plectrum rather than plucked and was used to accompany the recitations of poets and performers.

Orpheus was the chief among the poets and musicians. He was presented by Apollo with the gift of a lyre which he played with unsurpassed, exquisite beauty. It was said that Orpheus could coax the trees and the rocks to dance.

Apollo and Orpheus are the classical patrons of music. Orpheus, although not a chief amongst the gods, is associated with the underworld and is founder of the orphic cults of Ancient Greece. Apollo was leader of the nine Muses, daughters of Zeus and Mnemosyne (Memory). Orpheus was the son of Apollo and Calliope, the muse of epic poetry. Orpheus was wedded to Euridice and on her unfortunate death by snake poison resolved to rescue her from the underworld. Through the art of his music this would have been achieved had Orpheus not disobeyed the bidding of Hades (Pluto), the god of the underworld. Orpheus looked back to see his wife following behind as they journeyed out of Hades to the land of the living. With this act, Euridice was lost forever. Orpheus resolved never to have relations with any other woman and the infuriated Thracian maidens tore him to bits in their frustration.

This truncated version of the story contains some interesting elements: the power of music to charm even the god of the underworld and the association of music with dismemberment and re-membering, the meaning of the muse, Mnemosyne.

The same mythological theme can be found in the myths of all cultures in one form or another. It alludes to the means by which things change, grow and develop, to achieve an increase in consciousness. It suggests that the process is not one of steady progress but first of loss or symbolic death and then regeneration or rebirth. In the myths we can find a description of a psychological basis for music as a healing force. Music is a wonderful stimulant for the mind and for memory and therefore particularly helpful for the elderly or mentally disabled. A fragmented consciousness in the state of dementia can be re-membered through the power of music.

Here is another story. A composer wished to voyage across the sea to a foreign land and took with him a rich cargo of jewels and trinkets earned by the practice of his art. Arion of Lesbos by name found a ship and a seemingly friendly crew but the beauty and great value of his cargo was too great a temptation. Once at sea, the crew overpowered him and determined to throw him overboard.

Arion told them to spare his life or terrible misfortune would follow their foul deed. Even with this threat and the offer of his treasure as a ransom, the crew refused to compromise. Arion in his grief asked for a final request that he might play for one last time on his wooden lyre and so doing jump into the waters. His wish was granted. The crew realised that the music would enchant them and inflict remorse for their sin, so they plugged their ears against the sound.

Arion finished his song and with magic lyre in hand flung himself into the depths of the ocean.

A composer carries a great treasure with him as he explores his world, a realm that is filled with potential dangers. The treasure is hard earned and easily lost. However, all he can do is take the journey, rely on the support of others and trust his talent to see him through. It may be no consolation to him that the forces of destruction are themselves destroyed by their own covetous greed.

No sooner had Arion hit the water than the broad back of a dolphin rose beneath him and carried him to the island's shore where he had wished to go. While mournfully he sang of the loss of his treasures, the sea creature once more played a part. The crew had fought amongst themselves over the spoils and the ship sank with loss of treasure and shattered the crew who went down with it. Arion's sea friend witnessed this catastrophe, rescued the treasure and brought it back to the delighted and amazed composer.

♩ The next day, refreshed, there are just a few miles to Montgomery where I will spare a couple of hours to explore, then continue towards Welshpool. My previous overnight stay was a couple of miles short of the Brompton crossroads and on the way to Brompton the path crosses over the estate of Mellington Hall with its, to me, somewhat grotesque stationary caravan park of uniform holiday dwellings. The holiday park is built on an industrial scale close to the Hall, itself the creation of a Victorian industrialist in a Gothic style. The original ethos still rules the way this enterprise is run.

The rest of my way is through the arable flatlands of the Montgomery plain and I can see behind me rising in the distance Corndon Hill and the Kerry Hill Ridge where I was walking only a short while before.

About Music

Every culture develops its own musical forms and styles and it is fascinating to consider some of the mythologies that they have attached to music. In China, for example, according to legends, the founder of music was Ling Lun, at the time of the Yellow Emperor (2698-2598 BCE), who made bamboo pipes tuned to the sounds of birds, including the phoenix. A twelve-tone musical system was created based on the pitches of the bamboo pipes, and the first of these pipes produced the 'yellow bell' pitch. A set of tuned bells were then created from the pipes.

Before the 7th century BC, a system of pitch generation appeared in China based on a ratio 2:3 symbolising Heaven and Earth and the pentatonic scale was derived from a cycle-of-fifths theory.

Chinese philosophers took varying approaches to music. To Confucius, like Plato, a correct form of music is important for the cultivation and refinement of the individual. The Confucian system considers the formal music *yayue* to be morally uplifting and the symbol of a good ruler and stable government. Literally translating as 'elegant music', *yayue* incorporates elements of early Chinese folk music and religious traditions. It was originally played as imperial court music and went on to influence other East Asian traditional styles, such as *Gagaku* from Japan and *Nhã Nhạc* from Vietnam.

Proponent of universal love, the Chinese thinker Mozi, known as 'Master Mo', condemned music and argued in *Against Music* that music is an extravagance and indulgence that serves no useful purpose and may be harmful.

A powerful ruler once asked the Chinese Confucian philosopher, Mencius, whether it was moral if he preferred popular music to the classics. The answer was that it only mattered that the ruler loved his subjects.

(The path is running through more patches of bristling thistle and I am pleased to see how the flowers are turning into the softest thistledown as they seed, the gossamer down an antedote to the angry spiky defences of the leaves.)

The mythology of the Indian subcontinent in its relationship with music was complex and sophisticated. Sound played a major role in the creation of the universe, helping it to come into being. The

About Music

OM in eastern yoga teachings is an expression of the highest form of consciousness. It is represented by the three letters A-U-M. When intoned slowly, each letter is different in terms of the acoustic vibrations it creates and the physical requirement for making it. Each represents a degree of that supreme consciousness: A is waking consciousness; U is dream consciousness; M is the consciousness of deep sleep.

Culturally, this may seem a long way from home, but consider in our western history that many Gregorian chants end with an elaborate, several-minute-long AMEN. There are also medieval chants, such as those of Hildegard von Bingen (1098-1179) which conclude an antiphon, a sung religious text, with a kind of Christian mantra consisting of vowel sounds.

A mantra is a sound object that is used in meditation to focus the mind. It is deliberately employed as an object of contemplation so that the mind can free itself from all its usual distractions and inner chatter, supposedly enabling it to focus on the true nature of reality. There is an equivalent visual object used in meditation called a yantra, which may be a picture with symbolic value to help focus the mind in the same way and for the same end.

The OM mantra is the one most commonly known in the west. Its meaning is held in the sound that it makes, hence its value as a meditative object, suggestive of the oneness and connectedness of the universe. A mantra may be chanted but the effectiveness of it, according to yoga teachings, is when the sound is imagined silently, inwardly. It is an imaginative, mental process that creates the desired effect. Clearly sound can affect our inner being and in the form of music serves up an endlessly variable feast of delights to savour.

Ravi Shankar's (1920-2012) sitar music opened the door to Indian microtonal music for many people, including myself. It was a revelation for me to learn that an Indian classical raga could last for hours.

What also interested me was learning that you listen in a completely different way than to western music. Indian pundit Pandit Patekar includes in a description of how to listen, the aim of leaving aside all inner preconceptions, immersing yourself in a mood of meditation, establishing a link with the supernatural aspects of reality and placing the universal in the forefront of your musical contemplation.

The sitar has two playing strings and a whole collection of strings resonating in sympathy which have to be tuned to the scale of the raga. If a given note is played, the corresponding sympathetic string vibrates with it, producing the characteristic sitar sound.

It is not easy to describe Indian traditional music for it in no way progresses in the way that our western classics do. Rather is it played to evoke the qualities of different times and the circumstances of life that go with them. There are ragas for different times of the year, different times of the day. There is nothing definite or tangible to focus on when listening to a raga and at its most effective it is like listening to one's own self...

Indian music did not have the Pythagorean and later the tempered system of tuning which divides the octave into twelve notes, but instead developed a system of twenty-two *shrutis* which provide the subtlety of half- and whole-tone intervals of a variety of sizes. The basic scale of a raga consists of a selection of seven notes and five modified ones. In many ragas it is permissible to introduce further intervals to add richness. The transition from one note to another is often a sliding one.

Each note of a raga is heard in relation to a keynote which is constantly audible throughout a performance, often in the form of a chord comprising bass note, octave and fifth, played on a particular accompanying instrument. Every raga has its special affiliation: the time of year and the various festivals are taken as much into account as the hours of the day or night, as too are the various gods and the moods of the human psyche.

Despite an apparent harmonic simplicity, the raga is designed as a function not merely of a single note but of the whole harmonic series that each note possesses. The character of a raga is determined essentially by the type of feeling to which it is assigned. Traditional Hindu culture has distinguished a certain number of moods. Each of these nine 'rasas' has a particular psychological temperament and associated speed or tempo. They are:

1. A romantic and erotic sentiment. This represents the universal creative force.

About Music

    2.   Comic and humorous.
    3.   The third is pathetic, tearful and sad, expressing extreme loneliness and longing for either god or lover.
    4.   Then there is fury or excited anger which may portray violence in nature as in a great storm.
    5.   Heroism, bravery, majesty, glory and grandeur can be expressed, too.
    6.   Then there is fright and fear.
    7.   The seventh is the feeling of disgust but as this is difficult to express through music it is used more for Indian classical drama.
    8.   Wonderment tinged by a little fear may be expressed through extreme speed or some technical marvel that provokes amazement in the listener.
    9.   The last is peace, tranquillity and relaxation.

Another important aspect of Indian music is its rhythm, the *tala*. This derives from two basic elements, a double beat and a triple beat, which represent the beating of the heart and the rhythm of breathing respectively. Every given beat, whether drummed with the fingers or the heel of the palm, has its identifying syllable and thus the percussionist learns all the important forms and rhythmic variations as a language which is spoken by the instrument.

♣   I detour as planned into the substantial town of Montgomery and do what every self-respecting professional walker would do, head for the nearest coffee and cake. Thereafter, suitably refreshed, I walk up the hill behind the town to its castle and wander around the ruins overlooking the modern buildings below.

The town and former county owe their English name to a Norman, Roger de Montgomery, a kinsman of William the Conqueror of Normandy. Roger actively encouraged the invasion of Britain in the 11th century, providing a fleet of 60 ships and playing an important role in the French victory at Hastings in 1066.

The current castle is the third to be built at this strategic defensive location and was built at the behest of Henry III in 1223. Today's town then grew under its protective shadow.

About Music

Leaning over the ramparts I can see in the far distance the Long Mountain and know that at its western end is the Beacon Ring prehistoric hill fort where I will be headed tomorrow before descending into the substantial town of Welshpool.

A young Japanese man sporting a large fully kitted rucksack approaches and begins to talk in broken English. He too is walking the dyke. We chat for a few minutes, neither of us knowing how much the other understands of what we have been saying. I then wish him well and take my leave, make my way back, through and out of the town and rediscover the Offa's Dyke path at a track that is as straight as an arrow and which takes me unerringly towards the Long Mountain.

While walking along this track, I think about mantras and the power of sound. Then, I see with my mind's eye and discover what the spirit of music is. The perception comes to me not as a thought or an image, or even a feeling, but as a knowing. This is what I embarked on my journey to discover.

Bill, climbing up Mount Olympus

About Music

CHAPTER 8

The Musical Cosmos

*In which mind, matter and music interweave, while
we do battle in a wheat field and, like a trip down Alice's rabbit hole,
the truth of this chapter is open to question*

The route is now through a mix of field paths, quiet lanes and woodland with views over the valley of the River Severn. The dyke along the stretch north of Montgomery forms the modern boundary between England and Wales. The path opens out beyond a metal gateway, then meets and crosses a stream called the Camlad. This is the only river to rise in England and flow into Wales, flowing on eventually to contribute its waters to the River Severn.

The dyke goes under Pound House, which was built on it in 1820. This is a remote location and it is not inappropriate to assume that a nearby enclosure from which the house took its name was used as an overnight stop or collection point by the drovers.

Tiny scarlet pimpernels are dotted at my feet and I walk carefully to avoid trampling on them. I pass through the village of Forden where oak trees are like soldiers guarding the dyke. Soon, I walk into Kingswood at the northerly end of the village to find my bed and breakfast stop at Heath Cottage, conveniently located right on the dyke path. I had not intended to stop here but the logistics of this section of the dyke have conspired to leave me with an eight-mile walk in the morning into Welshpool. From there I'll catch the 11:00 a.m. train to Hereford via Shrewsbury so that I can return home before embarking on the next section later in August. This will mean an early start tomorrow morning and a walk at some pace if I am not to miss the train.

In the evening, I relax in the pub nearby and while I am making my customary notes about the day's events and enjoying a pint and some food, the Japanese traveller I met at Montgomery castle is at the bar negotiating for his own refreshment. He comes to join me and we greet each other like long lost friends.

About Music

Our conversation is much as it was earlier, that is, neither he nor I quite sure what the other is talking about. However, I did discover that he was a baker in Japan, dissatisfied with his lot and had taken to the road to improve his understanding of the world and himself, to learn and to grow. He was making his way around the world and reeled off an impressive list of the countries that he had passed through thus far. On arriving in the UK, he had decided that the best way to travel in this particular land was on foot.

His personal story was worth the effort of a stilted conversation but even more valuable was his diary. He proudly showed me a tiny book, opening out to about the size of a beer mat, crammed with jottings and sketches, a miniature record in Japanese of a trip around the world. He may well have realised it but I tried to impress on him what a valuable little work this would prove to be.

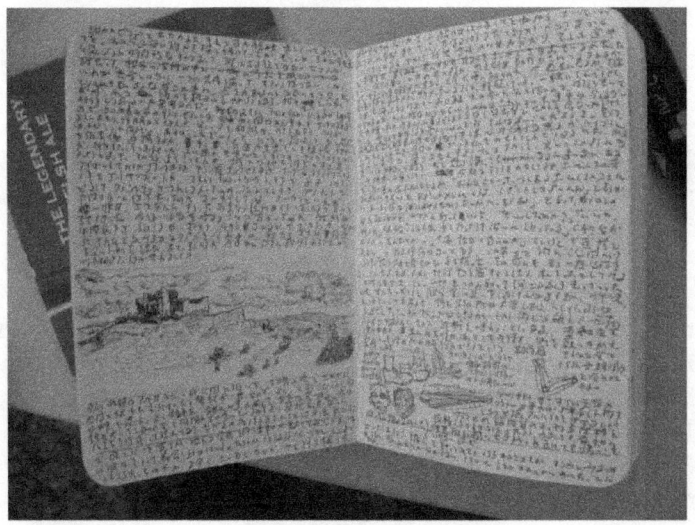

As with any form of meditative exercise, walking inevitably brings you thoughts about and an encounter with the oceanic vastness of space and the infinite nature of our universe. I hope this doesn't sound pompous as it is intended as a fact arising as a consequence of the stretching distances, the views, and the long times of silent contemplation available. Your role as a walker in this vastness is, in comparison, infinitesimally small – and yet we each have our own point of existence from which we can look out on the world. Long-distance walking can, some might suggest, drive you mad; to me and other walkers, it is a road to appreciating the clear, bright realities of life.

Such philosophical thoughts have occupied humankind since someone first noticed the sky, the stars, the sun, moon and planets. From this experience came the desire to understand it all and to work out what our place, our role, was to be. Hence, the astrologer priests of Babylon drew up their charts and devised their rituals; the gods of mythology came to life; the ancient Greeks thought long and hard and built in their minds, models of the universe. The model that held most powerful sway until so recently was based on a musical theme.

After an early morning breakfast of strawberries laced with rhubarb, washed down with homemade apple juice - yes, that combination works well, especially complemented by the more calorific and stimulating regular breakfast fare of toast and coffee - I packed my bag and took to the track again.

Today there was no time to waste and I began walking in earnest, first along the dyke running behind the houses of Kingswood and then up a steep lane into woodland and an estate forest. At the beginning of this woodland, I pause briefly to read a sign warning of 'ash die back' and asking travellers to keep to the footpaths.

This fungus, found in England in 2012, after being blown over the English Channel, or imported via nurseries, causes the crowns of ash trees to blacken and wither and can kill young trees. Its spread in the UK could affect up to three-quarters of the species in the worst-hit areas within just four years, according to government scientists.

The spread cannot be stopped, so conservationists are resigned to mitigating the distribution and impact of the organism on the UK's estimated 80 million ash trees. The sign in front of me is a consequence of that campaign.

Before continuing with my cosmic musical theme along this part of the path, I reflect on the theories of Pythagoras that were represented by the monochord, described in Chapter 3. By the Middle Ages, its construction had incorporated the symbolism that describes the relationship of sound vibration with the functioning of the universe. This was an expression of the doctrine that all things heavenly have a correspondence on earth – as above, so below. This mystical construct was continued by astronomers, culminating in the work of Johannes Kepler (1571-1630) and inspiring his laws of planetary motion.

Kepler was the bridge between the science of the Enlightenment and the mysticism of an ancient wisdom. The theories of harmony were combined, in his work, with the hermetic arts of alchemy to reveal the universe to function on the same laws of musical harmony that the monochord demonstrated. Harmony was a planetary phenomenon and from this were deduced the laws of planetary motion.

Much of the alchemical philosophy, 'hermeticism', and its practice, the transmutation of base metals into gold, may seem to be misguided gobbledegook to our modern way of understanding, but this is not the case when considered from a psychological perspective. This provides the key to interpreting and understanding what those medieval minds were getting at.

Early philosophers, practising their magical arts with such passion, were dealing with, for them, external physical and spiritual realities. Shift the perspective to view their work as an exploration of the unconscious psyche projected out into their chemical experiments, rather like gazing into the flames of a fire and seeing pictures therein, and it begins to make sense. Theirs was a journey into the depths of their own minds.

We know about the misguided folly of alchemy's attempts to create gold and find the elixir of life, the philosopher's stone. We know this, but can simultaneously acknowledge the debt that modern chemistry owes to those early pioneers of the chemical reaction. But wait; hold now the thought that this has little to do with physics and chemistry and much to do with imagination and psychology. It was C.G. Jung's realisation that the descriptions written and drawn by the alchemists were a representation of the workings of their own unconscious minds, employing the language of myth and archetypal symbol, the stuff of dreams and, subsequently, for Jung, the stuff of dream interpretation and psychological analysis.

About Music

The birth of alchemy took place about the same time as the birth of Christ. It then flourished in Greece for about two centuries, followed by a gradual decline up to the tenth century. The main texts were translated into Arabic and in the seventh and eighth centuries developed in the Arabian countries, after which alchemy evolved into the early history of chemistry. In about the tenth century it arrived back in Western Europe, became united with scholastic philosophy and thus developed further.

Greek thought was one of the main instigators. The Greek philosophers initiated rational thought about the nature of matter, space and time, but made almost no practical experiments. Maybe it didn't even occur to them to do this. However, the Egyptians were the opposite and in general gave less thought to the subject but experimented and created chemical recipes that had some practical application, in embalming, for example, a preparation for the soul's after-death journey.

When these two approaches came together, alchemy was born. From the Greek philosophers we still make use of the basic concepts to do with matter and space and the properties of time. When this alchemical birth happened, it coincided in Greece with a switch from a religious and mythological outlook to a philosophical one, but practically everything in Egyptian culture at that time was geared to the religious, mythological view of the world. Their practical alchemy was geared to the afterlife and eternity.

The most influential early text was *The Emerald Tablet of Hermes Trismegistus*, which became the alchemist's creed. The author lends his name to the Hermetic philosophy, and the word 'hermetic', as used in 'hermetically sealed', suggests a total and complete seal, a requirement for the alchemical experiment to work. The text of Hermes Thrice Born is surrounded by legend and it probably originated from the early centuries of the Christian era. The text begins:

> True it is, without falsehood, certain and most true.
> That which is above is like to that which is below
> and that which is below is like to that which is above,
> to accomplish the miracles of the one thing.

About Music

An essential part of alchemy was its connection with astrology. Nothing could be done until the right moment arrived, otherwise it would not work. Each of the base metals of alchemy, tin, iron, mercury, copper, etc., has its correspondence with a planet: Mars with iron, Venus with copper, Jupiter with tin and so forth. A metal would not take part in a successful alchemical operation unless its corresponding planet was in a favourable position. Timing was all important and astrological charts were drawn up to make sure this was calculated correctly. Later, the right moment for the chemical experiment was interpreted in a more mystical fashion as the right inner moment. This means that it is not when the planets were ready that mattered but when the alchemist himself was truly ready.

Instead of examining and experimenting with materials, alchemists following this particular route believed that one could just look inside the psyche and discover information that way. We are all part of the mystery of existence, so you can take part in its workings directly by inner observations. Even more than this, you can treat materials as if they are not inanimate but possess a living spirit. You can communicate with them, converse with them and thus learn their secrets. Imagine asking a lump of iron how it felt when it was melted!

All the alchemical materials are within us. Through prayer and meditation, the true alchemists contacted what we would now call the unconscious. They were evoking alchemical archetypes, the foundations of conscious life. Mercury might appear to the alchemist as a person or some extra-terrestrial being, offer assistance and tell him or her what to do next to make the process work. The relevant and significant alchemical fact was that what we would normally regard as separate is considered to be one, specifically mind and matter.

There are some historical reasons for the incomprehensible nature of the language that cloaks alchemical descriptions. First, in the earliest days when little was known about the chemical properties of the elements and how they might combine, there were opposing views and conflicting descriptions. Then there was the subjective approach where, rather like describing a piece of music, the description was dependent on the sensibility of the alchemist, their likes and dislikes, even their mood.

Another factor is that in the Middle Ages the alchemist might take himself off to hide in the woods and practise his art secretly. Imagine someone getting hold of the idea that you could make gold. You would be forever under the threat of lunatics beating down your door to obtain your secrets. To combat this, they couched their descriptions in a language that was hard, if not impossible to interpret and understand.

The alchemists also created a religious problem for themselves. Not only were they asking probing questions about the nature of reality and the nature of God, but they were experimenting with this nature and hence fell fowl of the religious authorities. They believed that when God created the world, he had not completed the task and that their Great Work was to make perfect what God had left incomplete and imperfect. They had an immanent view of nature and believed that they could form a direct relationship with God and had no need of a priestly intermediary. The heresy of these beliefs did not go unnoticed.

Not only did the alchemist hide away his discoveries in texts that could not easily be translated into understandable instructions but he hid himself away, too. Then having hidden away, the rumour would spread that he was conducting some form of black magic and the confusion increased.

Last but not least came the greedy overlord who wanted to have the secret for himself. Alchemy was rife with deception and intrigue. The true alchemist says, "I am not looking for ordinary gold but am seeking a higher gold, I am seeking something else." Alchemy was underground work. Today, we know it is possible to make gold and the dream has come true. It is too expensive to be practical but we do know that it is possible.

One final point worth emphasising here is that the library of Isaac Newton, the eponymous rational scientist, contained more books about alchemy than about any other subject.

♪ It is still early morning. There has been rainfall overnight although the ground is only damp and should soon dry out. The air is misty and the trees full of intermittent birdsong. Amongst the trees, I'm impressed by how loud are their calls. I would have expected the sound to be readily absorbed and attenuated by all the surrounding foliage. Their warning calls to each other are clear and penetrating.

🎻 Much of the hermetic philosophy, the *Corpus Hermeticum* of Hermes Trismegistus, was debunked in the 17th century. The protestant humanist, Isaac Casaubon, proved that the *Corpus Hermeticum* was nowhere near as old as had been supposed and 'age' was, in those days, a prerequisite for authority. It was, therefore, a fraud.

Nevertheless, the cause of hermeticism continued to be championed and foremost among its proponents was Robert Fludd, an English doctor and philosopher, one of the last examples of Renaissance Man, born ten years after the death of Michelangelo, in 1574.

Drawing liberally on the authority of Hermes Trismegistus, Fludd asserts an underlying harmony and congruity between the universe, which he calls the macrocosm, and man, the microcosm. In an illustration in the first volume of *The History of the Macrocosm*, Fludd summarises his cosmology in a figure he calls the Divine Monochord. Fludd's aim was to describe every aspect of the universe, visible and invisible, in a system that was an expansion of the concepts of *musica mundane,* cosmic music, and *musica humana,* the continuous but unheard music of the human organism. The Divine Monochord held all this within a single image.

What did the monochord and the corresponding symbols, represented by the notes of the instrument look like? It is a single string creation tuned by a peg in the same way that any of the violin family might be. A description of Fludd's Divine or World Monochord by F. Stege (*Musik, Magie, Mystik*, Remagan, 1961) does justice to it.

The instrument is anchored at its foot to the Earth (Terra) and this corresponds to the bottom note of the medieval note system (Gamma Graecum). Above it, at intervals of the second, are the other elements, Aqua, Aer, Ignis (Water, Air and Fire, the latter being the lightest element and therefore the highest). Above this we ascend into the cosmic realm from Moon to Jupiter via the planetary signs. Their centre (meso) is inhabited by the Sun.

About Music

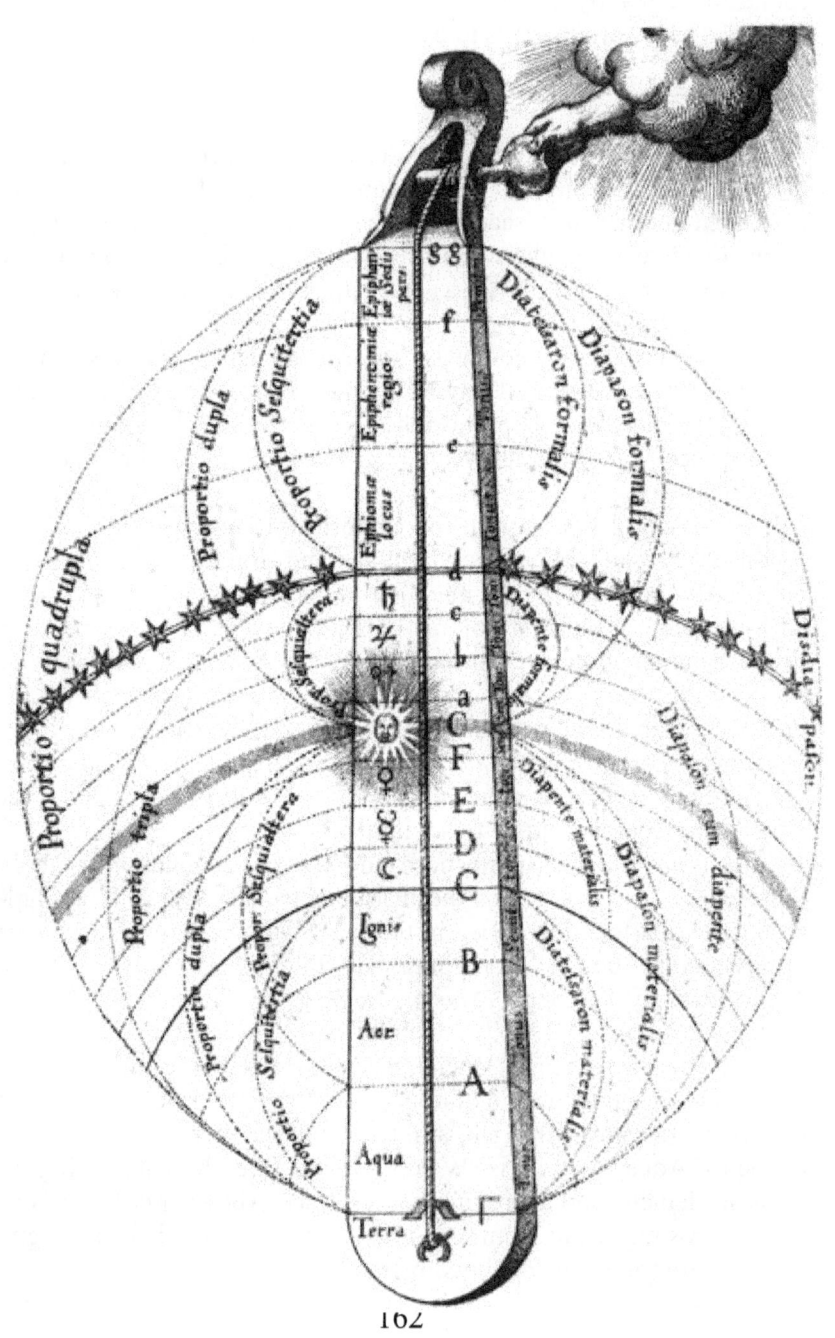

About Music

The arcs cutting the strings refer to the note spacings. On the right are the intervals, on the left the mathematical proportions. The interval between the Sun and the Earth is an octave, called by the Greeks a *diapason materialis*. This corresponds, on the left, to the proportion 1:2, or a *proportio dupla*. Other intervals configured are the fourth (*diatesseron*) and the fifth (*diapason cum diapente*). The whole universe is divided into a double octave, with the Sun at its centre.

Close examination reveals the absence of the third or *tierce*, for the octave and fifth ruled the universe as the basis of all their music. It was only later that the third took its place.

The 'interval experience' has largely gone from our awareness, even more so the experience of a single note. In relatively recent times, Anton von Webern in his orchestral pieces and Carl Orff in his opera, 'Antigonae', attributed special significance to single notes. In doing so, these two composers were merely reviving the practice of the ancient mysteries in which each single sustained note, intoned by all present, signified the invocation of a particular deity.

Antiquity's descriptions of the universe were heavily dependent on the nature of sound and music. Although they are clearly out of date as descriptions of the material universe, they may have provided us with images depicting an inner world, the non-material psyche. Those seemingly bizarre descriptions were unconscious projections onto the outside world and they might now be reclaimed as descriptions of what lies within. This will become increasingly significant when we consider on a later walk the brain and its relationship with music.

🦶 I reach a point where the path appears to curve round to the right and as there is a fallen tree across the route directly ahead, I follow the curve. After about five minutes, I become uncertain. My compass tells me I am veering to the south when I should be on a north-easterly track. I trust the compass, retrace my steps to the fallen tree, scramble over it and find the obscured but true path on its other side. A few minutes later I can confirm the correct route as I pass by a large pool known as Offa's Pool, shown on my map.

About Music

Navigating in a forest is much harder than in open country for there are no distant landmarks on which to fix a line of sight so that straying along the wrong track, of which there is often more than one to choose, is easily done. I have not used my compass much so far but on the odd occasion such as this it is an invaluable tool. North east is the direction I need and north east is what my compass arrow is now showing me.

The final piece to put into place in this musical description of the universe is that of the planetary spheres themselves. I have described the priestly rituals of the mystery cults that related the life of the planets and stars to everyday life on earth. Then I have described the Pythagorean notion of representing the planetary universe by the notes and intervals of the world monochord. These combine and result in the idea that the planetary bodies emit their cosmic notes. I marvel as I walk at how a single vibrating string became the means for representing and describing the entire universe.

A commonly shown illustration of the planetary spheres is by Gafurius, a music master of the 15th century who has provided us with a diagram (1496) containing all the relevant correspondences. He shows which significant musical symbols related to each of the planetary spheres. These include the nine muses, the notes of the A-minor scale, the music modes and also to each planet a corresponding metal, for example, silver with the Moon and gold with the Sun. The diagram is centred on a long serpent with its tail at the top and its head (in fact, three heads) at the foot. Its tail is in the heavenly sphere while the head is at the foot beneath the earth. Its three-fold nature suggests the dimensions of time: past, present and future.

To the right of the serpent ascend the symbols of the planetary spheres, the corresponding metals and the musical modes; to the left, the muses and the corresponding notes of the scale. Gafurius's idea was already known to the Stoics in ancient Greece and is developed in Cicero's, *The Dream of Scipio*, where the spheres are named in this same order and said to produce a loud agreeable sound by virtue of their revolutions. The earth, stationary at the

About Music

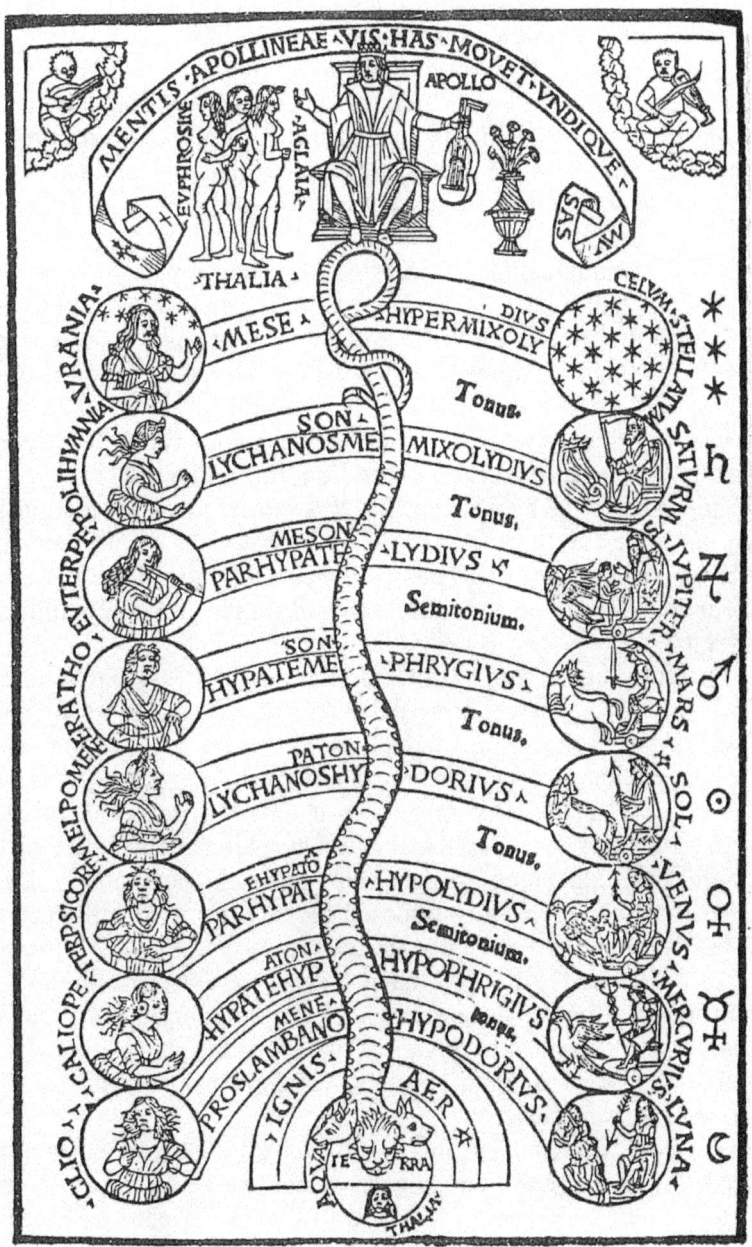

centre of the universe, surrounded by these revolving musical spheres, therefore produces no cosmic sound of its own.

At death, the soul undertakes the return journey, as experienced in the Mithraic ritual, casting off the cosmic weights that it took on at birth until it finally returns, fully naked to its original home. To learn about the music of the spheres is to discover the route of this cosmic adventure of descent to earth and subsequent return to heaven.

To contextualise how this bizarre model was accepted and could be applied, consider the space that we perceive around us. We experience this in the way of extended dimensions, up, down, left, right, behind and in front. In other words, we are living in a three-dimensional universe - plus the dimension of time. The three dimensions are up/down, left/right, backwards/forwards. It all seems perfectly normal and natural, beyond question. This is the world we live in. However, why assume that this dimensional perception has been the same for all time? Is it possible that, over the millennia, as the brain and consciousness evolved, the experience of the space that surrounds us has shifted and changed rather than remaining a constant?

Our modern mode of perception may have developed partly as a result of the perceptions that were impressed on us by early priestly cults, from their sacred wisdom. Of prime importance - taking one example from the cannon of Pythagorean numerical symbols - is the number four: four elements (fire, earth, air and water); four seasons; four temperaments (melancholic, phlegmatic, choleric, sanguine); four Gospels; four spatial directions, N, S, E and W. Perhaps this universally imposed division came to influence the way we perceive, to experience space.

Space and time may have been experienced differently in distant times. Our perception of space and time, ingrained though it is, natural and immutable though it may seem, is only one of many possible ways for our brains to have developed an interpretation of the reality we experience.

Three dimensions plus time is not as absolute as we may think and that is a good enough reason for giving some credence to the, to us, strange world views held in the past. Keep that in mind while I describe the planetary spheres and their music. We know that

About Music

the planets do not emit musical notes, let alone combine in a cosmic harmony, but is this planetary music somehow inside us, as music of the inner unconscious universe?

Writing in 1434, at the height of the polyphonic era, Giorgio Anselmi of Parma was able to envision the planets no longer tied to dreary monotones but each singing its own song in counterpoint with the others. The full realisation of this idea erupted from Johannes Kepler, whose first law solved the problem describing the planetary distances, his second law, their velocities and the third, their distances from the sun. His solution for the first was geometric, for the second it was a musical solution. His third law provided the link between these two.

I am continuing to walk uphill and when the path finally skirts the westerly rim of the trees the view opens up. I find myself above misty clouds. Through and below them I can see the conurbation of Welshpool.

The continuing uphill climb ahead is to the Beacon Ring. This egg-shaped 'ring', obscured by dense woodland is an ancient hill fort on the 408-metre summit of the Long Mountain. I head directly to it and pass by a radio transmitter mast at the hill's highest point. The path then leads down the opposite side and I march quickly on.

I have reached a gate taking the route into a wheat field of large proportions. Unusually, the path does not skirt the field but leads straight through the crop and a sign has been positioned indicating to walkers that it is fine to do this, to walk through and not round the field. There are two problems. The first is that the waist-high crop is wet and as I walk my summer clothing, socks, shorts and vest, sponges up the moisture. The second is that several narrow tracks through the crop intersect half way through the field and there is, apparently, no indication which branch to take. I spend the next valuable fifteen minutes aimlessly ploughing my own futile furrow through this endless field. Eventually, almost hidden by the tall and ripening crop I discover another way marker and, with a sigh of relief after the delay, find my way, now able to resume a north-westerly direction out of the field and onto the slopes below it.

About Music

The route is downhill from here on. In some ways, I prefer walking uphill, enjoy pushing against gravity. Walking downhill means keeping the brakes on and using different, less-practised muscles. In addition, gravity pushes your toes into the tips of your boots and if your feet are beginning to tire and react to constant punishment, as mine were, the effect is uncomfortable. Add to this soaking-wet socks and the experience is, well, a little challenging. Still, I'm a glutton for punishment and keep up my quick pace.

Copernicus (1473-1543) demonstrated that the earth revolved around the sun; Galileo (1564-1642) saw this to be true through his telescope; Kepler and, later, Newton (1642-1727), with his passionate interest in hermetic philosophy, formulated the laws of physics which described what Galileo saw. Kepler's works provided one of the foundations for Isaac Newton's theory of universal gravitation.

Kepler, who came to realise that the planetary orbits were ellipses rather than circles formulated laws of planetary motion that knock on the head the classical notion of the planetary spheres, however, they are inspired by, greatly indebted to, dependent on, theories of musical harmony. How did he arrive at his conclusions to which we are so indebted and where does this 'harmony' now lie?

There were many limiting factors and beliefs that held the medieval mind in their stultifying grip. These influences formed the context within which Kepler undertook his own great work. Three are particularly influential in Kepler's story. The first is that whatever new was discovered had to conform to ancient wisdom. If it did not, then it would face an uphill struggle for general acceptance. This led Kepler to try hard to make his theories fit in with classical beliefs.

The second cannot be divorced from the first and is the influence that Pythagoras and Plato and their scheme of a universe ruled by perfect mathematical music had on the medieval mind. The idea that the universe should be described by simple and therefore beautiful laws held sway.

About Music

The third was alchemy. A study of Kepler reveals that he was a believer in the *Corpus Hermeticum* and the authenticity of the revelations of Hermes Trismegistus.

Kepler accepted the Copernican model of a heliocentric universe. He then tried to make sense of the planets, their distances and velocities, yet the underlying pattern in the planetary system eluded him. His revelation came from drawing a triangle, then inscribing a circle within it and another around the triangle, thus:

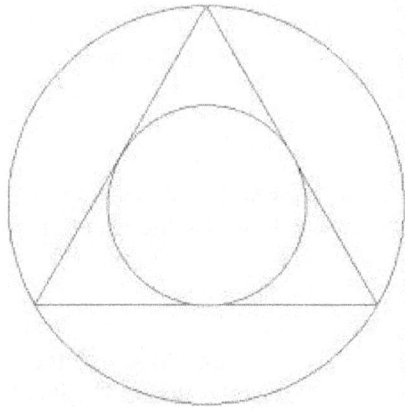

Kepler's mental thunderbolt was that the ratio between the two circles was the ratio between the orbits of Saturn and Jupiter. One more step took him into three dimensions to determine the orbital relationships of the other planets. The three-dimensional forms that described these, he discovered, are the Platonic solids.

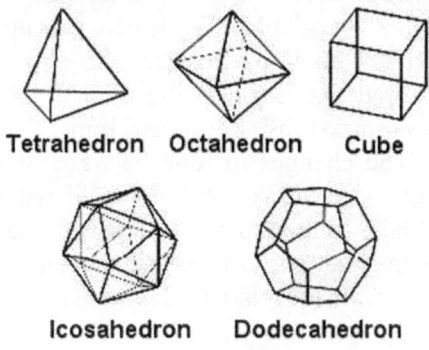

About Music

The geometric figures in this collection are all perfectly symmetrical; their faces are all regular polygons of the same shape and size. It is a fact of Euclidian geometry that only five solids will fit this requirement. Like Kepler's figure of the circles and triangle, each of the perfect solids may have a sphere circumscribed around them, touching at every vertex, and a sphere may likewise be inscribed within them. Each relationship between the spheres described a planetary orbital relationship. Bingo!

Placing these five perfect solids one within another resulted in a single, three-dimensional model that represented the intervals between the celestial spheres. The harmony of the universe was maintained and now, unlike that symbolised by the monochord, it was a polyphonic harmony, with all the planets singing in a wonderful combination. Kepler wrote, "The movements of the heavens are nothing except a certain everlasting polyphony, perceived by the intellect, not by the ear." The motions of the planets are more complicated, as Kepler himself was to discover when he formulated his laws of planetary motion.

Here is how Kepler's ratios were determined. Saturn, for example, moves quickest when closest to the Sun and slowest when at its greatest distance from the Sun along its elliptical orbit; the Sun, note, is positioned 'off centre' at a focal point of the orbit. A comparison of the two extremes results in a ratio of 5:4, that of the major third; Jupiter's ratio was 6:5, a minor third; that of Mars, 3:2, a fifth; that of the earth 16:15, a semitone; that of Venus, 24:25 (a Pythagorian comma?) and that of Mercury, 12:5, an octave and a minor third.

Small discrepancies did not perturb Kepler. Yet another revelation came when he calculated ratios by pairing off the planets. By doing this he was able to construct the entire musical scale. Further, he discovered that each of the planets has its own scale, which is also determined by its speed limits at maximum and minimum values. The changes in tone between these limits would not be divided into steps, however, but would rather be an eternal note that rises and falls continuously, a cosmic glissando.

Finally, Kepler set out to construct a celestial motet, a chord to unite the songs of all the planets. His great synthesis, the most

About Music

ambitious and comprehensive description of the music of the spheres ever attempted was completed on 27th May, 1618.

Despite his strict mathematical approach to astronomy, Kepler was, as we have recorded, a believer in the hermetic philosophy. However, he had done his science well, and after him scientific thinking became ever more rigorous. Correspondingly, the music of the spheres divorced from science and grew to nothing more than a suspect branch of backward-looking esotericism.

♪ I can see my destination clearly below in the distance. The Buttington Bridge is a couple of miles from the town of Welshpool and I push on confident of my direction, walking as quickly as I can. Again, hurrying a little too quickly, I stray from the path, this time simply by walking along the wrong side of a field's hedge, but am soon back on track. I arrive in Buttington at its iron bridge over the River Severn and even have a little time to spare, so I stop to mark the end of this section with a photo of the bridge and of myself, smiling broadly, relieved to be there.

As I stoop to fasten the straps on my rucksack, a horse rider comes towards me and stops to ask me the way.

"I am lost and wonder if your kindness will direct me to my destination." The rider was wearing a long greying beard, knee-length leather boots and a swathe of black cape. I told him I was a stranger too but would help if I could. The rider dismounted to chat with me.

"It is to the home of Tycho Brahe that I travel."

"Then I can't help, I replied, "For you are in the wrong century as well as the wrong place." He cursed then smiled.

"Then either you or I is a dreamer. For my part, I hope it is I for my troubles are great and I could well awake from them. Still, some things are not so bad. My mother was released from her trial as a witch but, believe me, not before the threats of torture she endured left her scarred deeply. During her trial I worked ceaselessly on my harmonic theory and it is those writings I carry now in this saddle." He gestured to the paniers.

I knew of this man's troubled life, of the death of his first wife and their two children in their infancy, of his work for the

About Music

Austrian emperors and their refusal to pay him his due; of the trouble that his mother caused with her potions and cures. All this and yet he became one of the greatest men of all time. I wished him well and watched as he rode away along the path by the river shouting a farewell and more obscenities into the air as he went.

At Buttington, the Montgomery canal passes through the village and in 893 a combined Welsh and Mercian army under Æthelred, Lord of the Mercians, defeated here a Danish army which had marched from Essex. This was the decisive battle in the war against the Viking invasion of the 890s and was known as the Battle of Buttington. It took place about 100 years after the beginnings of the dyke's construction.

It's another half hour of roadside walking before I finally arrive at Welshpool's railway station where I sit in hot sunshine on the platform, remove my boots and wring the water out of my socks. While doing this, I recall what it felt like to be lost in that field of wheat and determined to think of this last stretch as my own Buttington Battle. Was I in heaven, or was I in hell? At least I saw some pimpernel.

Bill, glad to have made it

About Music

CHAPTER NINE

Philosophers on Music

In which we find out what some of the top brains have said about music and encounter a ghostly owl

As this journey progresses, I am appreciating increasingly the idea of living in the moment. What has brought this on? It is the realisation that in only a few walks time the journey will be over. This focuses my mind on what lies before my eyes, here and now, so that I can savour the experience to the full.

Then, I suppose, I'll be able to reflect on the journey and pour over the memories but that won't be as real and intense an experience as every moment of doing it. There will come a time for reflection and that will be fine, but the experience here and now is vivid, alive and heartfelt with every step I walk.

It will be over before too long. Make the most of it while it lasts. Never mind the journey's end; it is every step of the way that contains the real value, the true significance. There is a Zen-like flavour creeping in here and I don't mind. It helps to focus and appreciate the experience. So, the metaphor might apply to life, but what of music?

Much of classical music involves the sense of a journey and that is a ubiquitous requirement for orienting the listener and keeping them on track. But what is it that music contains in its every moment, its every step, which can be of such compelling significance?

At this stage of our exploration, we are about to move on from antiquity's grip on the medieval mind into a land that is more familiar. There is around this transition a 'before and after' that can be identified. 'Before', music's significance was little to do with individual expression and much to do with that of the spiritual, the cosmic, the religious and, touching on its science, a means for understanding the very operation of the universe, both heavenly and earthly.

'After' – and if you need a specific moment in time as the boundary between the two it would be with the philosopher, René

About Music

Descartes – the art and science of music separate, like mind and matter, one is not the other. The term Modern Philosophy is usually used to highlight the difference between Ancient and Medieval philosophy. This means that it refers to philosophy since the Reformation.

Descartes is regarded as the inaugurator of modern philosophy. He was born in France in 1596 and died of pneumonia in 1650. His aim was to put all knowledge on a firm foundation, to find a method that would put knowledge beyond doubt. His method involved stripping away everything that was not certain. Descartes and his contemporaries knew that historical authority was not the same as fact and wanted to find out how to be certain about knowledge. The principle on which to build was his starting point that, "I am consciously aware, therefore, I know that I must exist." The fact of existence was the certain foundation.

Developing from this was his proposal that the world is comprised of two distinct types of entity, the self and the external world. The external world only has the property of extension in three dimensions, all else, all information gleaned by the senses, is in the mind which is dimensionless. This has become the tyranny of the mind/body schism. It is embedded in our way of experiencing the world with its philosophical basis in the 'Cartesian Dualism' of Descartes.

We can consider these as separate entities, as did Descartes, but here with an awareness of the significance and influence that music, which comes from within, has had on our view of the universe. This is exciting, for there is still a route to the cosmic open to us, despite the destruction of the bridge between mind and matter by Cartesian Dualism.

This bridge is now encapsulated in the study of music and the brain. Here is where the art and the science may come together, where mind and matter, rational thought and imagination reside in one alchemical container. This may well be where the most fruitful path of our journeying leads. However, we are not quite ready yet and before considering the role that the brain plays in making music, it would be helpful to learn a little of what the great philosophers have had to say about our subject since the Cartesian hiatus.

About Music

Today's section of Offa's Dyke is easy walking, with visits to the quiet towpath of the Montgomery Canal and two passages along the upper reaches of the River Severn, a quiet, contemplative stretch, appropriate for the associated musical topic. Scenically, the interest is focused on Breidden Hill and its neighbours, which rise sharply from the valley near Criggion. From Montgomery to Llanymynech, today's destination, is about twelve miles and, uniquely, this section of the dyke path is almost entirely level walking.

It begins in the centre of Montgomery through which the Montgomery canal passes and I head east along its towpath towards Buttington and the bridge that marked the end of the previous section. Immediately, the atmosphere is set for the day by this gentle canal, with its sleepy ducks, overhanging trees and the presence of one or two strolling folk taking in the morning sunshine. As long as the path continues to be well marked and I can be unconcerned with navigation, this will clearly be a walk for meditation and contemplation on philosophers and music.

Wildlife thrives along the Montgomery Canal. It is one of the most important canals in the country for providing natural habitats. Much of it is a Site of Special Scientific Interest and the Welsh section is of international importance. The canal is alive with rare aquatic plants. Otters and water voles have been seen. Several nature reserves filled with wildflowers and insects, border the canal. Both damsel flies and dragonflies are often seen. Walking along the towpath is a way to experience the peace and tranquillity of this rural waterway and to encounter the lush flora and prolific fauna it supports.

The canal was closed to boats for many years but it is being reborn as a cruiseway through the picturesque Welsh Marches. There are two restored sections. One is by my path out of Montgomery; the other will join the dyke path at the end of today as I approach Llanymynech. There are plans to unite the two stretches. The canal walk continues uneventfully for a couple of miles. Then I leave it to rejoin the Offa's Dyke Path at Buttington Bridge over the River Severn.

About Music

There are two philosophers in particular to represent here, both of whom had much to say on the subject of music and included it in the context of their outlooks on life. These are Arthur Schopenhauer (1788-1860) and Friedrich Nietzsche (1844-1900). Two great composers, Wagner and Mahler, have recorded their indebtedness to them.

Schopenhauer believed that human beings were made in such a way that it was impossible for us to know the inner nature of things but only to know what is presented to us via our senses of touch, sight, hearing, etc. We can never know 'the thing in itself'. We can only study its appearance which is presented to our senses. The senses are limited by their physical properties and function within certain boundaries. Even by inventing instruments or special techniques that can extend the range of our senses, we will never be able to employ them to obtain a complete picture of reality.

Schopenhauer postulated that the underlying reality of external appearances is a unity which is beyond our human categories of space, time and causality, and beyond the Cartesian division of mental and physical, mind and matter. However, he suggested that we can access this super reality and the way to do this is from inside our own bodies and through the unconscious mind. There exists within us a sort of subterranean tunnel that can give access to this unified reality.

There are ways to access this route and Schopenhauer believed that the purest, most effective way was through music. Music is a direct expression of the numinous reality that lies behind and beyond the external appearance of things. That reality is the source of our life force and is what we call upon to animate our lives. He called this source the Will.

Schopenhauer's Will is the same as the unconscious mind. This, according to one definition, is everything that we do not regard as belonging to the conscious self, is outside consciousness. It therefore includes the physical body and beyond this, the external world of appearances. By tunnelling inwards and taking this inner route, the opposites become one and the unity of mind and matter realised. The alchemist would describe it as squaring the circle.

About Music

According to Schopenhauer, any form of creative expression that sought to copy, interpret or present to us only facets of external reality was not being true to the highest purpose of art. Only music can represent to us in its purest form the experience of a super-sensory reality, can speak directly from that region to us.

From here on for several miles is a flatland mixture of canal and river walking, with long stretches along the Severn's flood defences. The flood bank and dyke combine along the Tirymynach Embankment and I soon fall into a rhythmic step which I estimate would be marked at about 90 beats per minutes on my metronome back home. A rhythmic step, the calm river and the open views soon evoke the experience of a walking meditation, a sense of clarity and awareness of ones being, breathing, heartbeat, leg muscles at work. There is no need to think; thoughts disappear leaving only awareness.

I wonder if this state of being has any power other than as a personal experience. I imagine my state of being radiating outwards, being transmitted like a radio signal to be received by others tuned in to the same wavelength. I remember my encounter in Montgomery with my Japanese friend and wonder if he too, at this very moment, is aware of me. We are part of a network of rambling philosophers, all doing nothing more and nothing less than walking. I have a brief stop and sit on the river bank for refreshment and open my rucksack.

Modern walking equipment and clothing is characterised by multiple pockets. This can be helpful in that they are used to compartmentalise particular items – first-aid in one, valuables in another, maps another, and so on. The rucksack should be packed methodically in layers, with most-needed items – food, waterproofs, etc. – near the top. Naturally, this system is not fool-proof. I forget which pocket an item is in and have to search through all of them. An item at the top of the rucksack slips down inside and rummaging disturbs the entire load.

Rucksack etiquette means constant attention to its contents, constant adjustment, rearrangement and checking. An efficient rucksack is the key to a successful long trek. I'm getting better at this now and know, for example, that my water bottle is in the right-hand

About Music

side rucksack pocket when the bag is viewed from the front. I drink, eat and return to my thoughts.

Like Schopenhauer, Nietzsche believed that music has life-enhancing properties. The significant difference between the two philosophers is that the pessimist Schopenhauer regarded music as a means for escaping from the torments of existence in the material world, whereas Nietzsche was much more positive and optimistic. His attitude was that music is a means for engaging fully with life, even to the extent that music can imbue it with meaning and purpose. He was presenting the possibility that the arts and music in particular can become a substitute in our psychological makeup for religious faith.

To achieve meaning and purpose in life is a process of personal self-realisation, of becoming more truly and fully oneself – akin to C.G. Jung's psychological maturing which he called 'individuation'. This process has a kinship with the alchemists' Great Work and is a creative one. It means regarding one's self as a work of art, gradually coming fully into being. It requires freeing oneself from the conventions and prejudices of upbringing and from social and religious constraints. The aim is to be fully and truly one's self.

Nietzsche describes in *The Birth of Tragedy* a dichotomy, two opposing principles which are associated with the gods Apollo and Dionysus. Apollo, the deity of light, is the god of order, measure, number, control and the subjugation of the beastly instinct. Dionysus, in contrast, is the god of liberation, intoxication and orgiastic celebration. He particularly manifests himself in music. These two correspond to the King and Queen of alchemy. The Apollonian King is inward looking and contemplates the dream world of mysticism and the music of the spheres. The Dionysian Queen is extravert and represents participation in the external world of feeling and sensation. The former is of the mind, the latter of the body.

According to Nietzsche, the aim is the union of these two. He sees art as something that can achieve this and bring us to a full participation in life, as opposed to Schopenhauer's attitude that it is a means for detaching and escaping from it. Nietzsche opened the way for an appreciation of music not just as something to be enjoyed but to be engaged with as ecstatic and painful as well as joyful. This is

About Music

not the Christian way of the soul's mastery over the body but encourages a marriage of the two on equal terms. Music is as much rooted in the body as it is governed by the mind.

The musical rhythm of my walking continues and I notice two hills over to my right, noteworthy because there are no other visible geographical features in any direction. Breidden Hill, rising sharply from the valley near Criggion, is volcanic in origin and much quarried. It was long occupied by a hill fort dating from at least 750 BC and there are traces of farming activities from an even more distant time. From the Offa's Dyke Path, I see a tall column, Rodney's Pillar, erected to commemorate this admiral's victory over the French off Dominica in 1782. The isolated group of hills provides a landmark visible from all points of the compass.

The path approaches and passes Old Mill Hill and the sound of quarrying begins to fill the air as Criggs Quarry, distant at first, emerges into the view. This is an alarming sound in the context of the peaceful river plain and soon becomes pervasive. It is a rude nudging to be aware that today's, and tomorrow's walks are through an area that although once rural and again rural today, has a history of industry and commerce. The canal network is the result of this.

Criggs Quarry is a source of basalt, a dark-coloured, fine-grained, igneous rock. Basalt underlies more of the Earth's surface than any other rock type and underlies most areas within the Earth's ocean basins. Crushed basalt is used for road foundations, concrete and asphalt pavement aggregates, rail-track ballast, filter stone in field drainage and many other inglorious purposes. In other words, it is so commonplace and ubiquitous that it goes completely unsung. Thin slabs of basalt are cut and sometimes polished for use as floor tiles, building veneer, monuments and other stone objects.

The wisdom of the ages had been the source of knowledge, but from Descartes on the source is more rational, more measured. Once mind and matter had been defined as separate entities, with no bridge between the two, the problem arose of how we could know anything at all! Hence came the subsequent endless arguments about whether or not the physical senses were to be trusted; whether or not reality was all in the mind. Opinions about music, like the universe, were becoming a matter for the individual, his taste, his proclivities, the way he or she experienced it. Balancing this subjectivity and preventing the spread of philosophical anarchy, the scientific method proved invincibly powerful as the way to build an edifice of knowledge on secure foundations.

In this context, I'll now make a brief survey of modern philosophers and their takes on music. This is by necessity a rather random approach but with the simple aim of adding a flavour of how our contemporary musical culture may have been influenced. Work on reconciling this mix of views is needed, but here at least is a start.

What this brief survey does reveal quite clearly is the dramatic shift that took place from dependence on antiquity as the source of authority on matters of truth, to a questioning of everything anew. The process has reached its extreme today with an similar reverence for the new, for the latest thing, for progress. Schopenhauer and Nietzsche are the two philosophers whose views are most often quoted on music. There are many others who contributed.

Georg Wilhelm Friedrich Hegel (1770-1831) was a German philosopher, and a major figure in Idealism, the philosophy that proposes everything we would normally call the external world, including music, is somehow created by the mind. His account of reality revolutionised European philosophy and was an important precursor to Marxism.

A question that stems from Hegel is, "Does musical thinking exist?" 'Musical thinking' is defined not as the same as thinking about music, or the thinking that might accompany music, but is something that is inherent in the music itself. This is difficult but it does suggest the possibility that music can be a medium of communication in the same way that language is.

If this is true and if 'musical understanding' can consequently arise as a result of 'musical thinking', then there must be a symbiosis between music and the brain's response to it. In the same way that 'musical thinking' is not ordinary thinking, then 'musical understanding' may arise that is not a simple, rational understanding. The main element to grip onto in this little thesis is

About Music

that in Hegel's philosophy, there is a relationship between language, music and thinking.

It is interesting to note that plain speech contains a musical element, expressed through its rhythm, meter and intonation, the latter having elements of melody about it called its 'prosody'. Without this, speech's ability to carry information would be much reduced.

Immanuel Kant (1724 – 1804) was a German philosopher who, as Schopenhauer affirmed a few years later, believed that the speculative claims of metaphysics are useless; nothing can be known about reality other than the surface appearances, so to speculate on the nature of, for example, life after death is a waste of time and effort. With such as he wielding a powerful influence over the thinking of the 18th century, it is easily understood how the mysticism of the previous 2,000 years could be swept aside. What is perhaps surprising is how religion survived in its wake.

The senses are deceivers and Kant held that the ability to reason, not sensory information, is the key to all our understanding. He also reserved a respect for music which he called 'the quickening art'. By this, he suggests that music holds within it, perhaps the brain's 'musical understanding' of Hegel, something that can bring life and vitality to the listener. This has certainly been shown quite dramatically in modern times to be true.

Oliver Sacks, a contemporary physician, describes how in the 1960s he found himself at a hospital in the Bronx seeing frozen post-encephalitic patients. These were people with profound Parkinsonism, so profound that sometimes they would stay absolutely motionless for hours on end and could not initiate any movement or speech, or indeed thought. He reports that it was originally the nurses and people who knew these patients well who said they could be transformed by music.

By listening to music, these people could dance, they could sing, they could talk, they could do things, they could think, they could become almost normal while music was there. This is what Kant meant by quickening. The effects of music can be seen in others and experienced in ourselves; there is no need for metaphysical speculation about the music of the spheres. Indeed, it is another waste of time. What is in music that can achieve this quickening? Its action on the brain, as demonstrated in the effect on Parkinsonism, is a real alchemical elixir.

Richard Wagner (1813-83) is best known for his total art opera and he had a lot to say about music, too, especially in relation to Schopenhauer and Nietzsche. In his youth, Wagner was a left-wing radical and, at the age of 35, had played an active part in the Dresden uprising of 1849. The brand of left-wing philosophy he espoused was Anarchism: the theory was that all government, being based on force, is corrupt. For his part in the revolution, he had to flee to Switzerland, and while there, he read another left-wing philosopher, Ludwig Feuerbach.

Feuerbach also condemned relationships based on power: they should instead be based on love. One of Wagner's earliest operas, Das Liebesverbot (The Ban on Love, 1836) had already extolled a love which burst through the bounds of the conventional institutions that tried to trammel it. In his later operas, Wagner proclaims that love should recognise no barriers, not even those surrounding adultery or incest.

Feuerbach said that all religions are man-made: they convey no theological truths but, when we create our own myths about the gods, we express the deepest truths about ourselves. This idea was to influence Wagner for the rest of his life and shapes the ideas in his operas. In this harnessing of mythology, we touch the psychological power contained in Wagner's operas, a power that resonates with the very foundations of the unconscious mind.

Hermann Ludwig Ferdinand von Helmholtz (1821-94) was a German physician and physicist who made significant contributions to several areas of modern science. His contribution to the perception of sound and his thoughts about music are highly original. After graduating from the gymnasium, Helmholtz in 1838 entered the Friedrich Wilhelm Medical Institute in Berlin, where he received a free medical education on the condition that he then serve eight years as an army doctor. At the institute, he did research under the greatest German physiologist of the day, Johannes Müller. He attended physics lectures, worked his way through the standard textbooks of higher mathematics and learned to play the piano with a skill that later helped him in his work on the sensation of tone.

The general theme that runs through most, if not all, of Helmholtz' work may be traced to his rejection of Natural philosophy, and the violence of his rejection of this seductive view of the world may well indicate the early attraction it had for him.

Natural philosophy, or the philosophy of nature, was the philosophical study of the physical universe that was dominant before the development of modern science. It is considered to be the precursor of the natural sciences, such as physics. The Oxford English Dictionary dates the origin of the word 'science' to 1834. Before then, the word meant any kind of well-established knowledge and the label of scientist did not exist.

Nature philosophy derived from Kant, who in the 1780s had suggested that the concepts of time, space, and causation were not products of sense experience but mental attributes by which it was possible to perceive the world. Therefore, the mind did not merely record order in nature, as the Empiricists insisted; rather, the mind organised the world of perceptions so that, reflecting the divine reason, it could deduce the system of the world from a few basic principles.

Helmholtz opposed this view by insisting that all knowledge came through the senses. Furthermore, all science could and should be reduced to the laws of classical mechanics, which, in his view, encompassed matter, force, and, later, energy, as the whole of reality.

Helmholtz' researches on the eye were incorporated in his *Handbook of Physiological Optics*, the first volume of which appeared in 1856. In the second volume (1867), Helmholtz further investigated optical appearances and, more importantly, came to grips with a philosophical problem that was to occupy him for some years - Kant's insistence that such basic concepts as time and space were not learned by sensory experience but were provided by the mind to make sense of what the mind perceived.

The problem had been greatly complicated by Müller's statement of what he called the law of specific nerve energies. Müller discovered that sensory organs always report their own sense no matter how they are stimulated. Thus, for example, a blow to the eye, which has nothing whatsoever to do with optical phenomena, causes

About Music

the recipient to 'see stars'. Obviously, the eye is not reporting accurately on the external world, for the reality is the blow, not the stars. How, then, is it possible to have confidence in what the senses report about the external world?

Helmholtz examined this question exhaustively in both his work on optics and in his masterly *On the Sensation of Tone As a Physiological Basis for the Theory of Music* (1863). What he tried to do, without complete success, was to trace sensations through the sensory nerves and anatomical structures, such as the inner ear, to the brain, in the hope of laying bare the complete mechanism of sensation. This task has not been completed and physiologists are still engaged in solving the mystery of how the mind knows anything about the outside world. However, this is the very area impinging on the forefront of current research into the relationship of music and the brain.

♩ I'll soon be in Pool Quay and in favourable conditions the River Severn was once navigable right up to this point. Cargoes were brought upstream in shallow-draught boats, the Severn 'trows', hauled by teams of men. When the first towpaths were introduced further downstream and horsepower came into play, there was much discontent at the threatened loss of livelihood on the river.

The shallow nature of the river bed and the low-lying surrounds clearly mean persistent flooding in times of inclement weather and I encounter an imposing battery of sluice gates at New Cut that will no doubt be in use again before too long. As if to emphasise the point, I am stung by drops of rain striking my skin, and reluctantly dig out waterproofs from my rucksack for the first time since Monmouth. The rain is more threatening than anything but then becomes more persistent as I approach the town of Four Crosses.

This makes map reading harder and I slow my pace in the hope that the rain will soon pass. The way leads me through some trees which form a sheltered but darkened, gloomy tunnel, surrounded outside its semicircle by a sheath of grey sky. I can hear rain dripping all around. Something skims quickly and silently over my head. An owl arrows its way down the tunnel in front of me and about 50 yards on disappears up into the trees. I heard nothing but

About Music

saw this eerie phantom shape glide speedily as if air resistance was nil.

Just before I reach the spot where the ghost disappeared, it reappears and performs the same action, noiselessly gliding at speed ahead of me then vanishing up into the darkened foliage. This time I am not taken unawares and glimpse barred markings on feathers in flight. It is a tawny owl, a night creature that I must have disturbed from its slumber. The owl does not reappear and I am left with a feeling of foreboding, a summation of grey wet weather, a dark tunnel of trees and a bird of ill omen.

I come by a small sewage works and am funnelled onto the platform of the former Four Crosses Railway Station of the Cambrian Railway, now a factory. I pass through the yard of the business with its parked lorries and cabins feeling, completely unnecessarily, as if I am trespassing, into Four Crosses. Where has the world of the dyke gone? I have walked into another realm, of houses, footpaths, metalled roads, street lighting, of cars hissing by as if I didn't exist, as if I have no right to be here. Like an owl in unfamiliar daytime, I cannot find my way out and walk up and down a featureless street until I find the unobtrusive acorn marker that shows the way.

Even after this, all is not well. I reach a busy main road and realise that I have missed the way again. Then as if a mischievous spirit that has cast its cloak over me decided to move on, the rain stops. For the first time today, I encounter two more walkers who are able to put me on the right path again. I pass by the Golden Lion pub and break into a smile. I remember reading a report from two walkers complaining about their stay here but all my guide tells me from its perspective is to "Note the fine ironwork of the Golden Lion."

Edmund Gustav Albrecht Husserl (1859-1938) was a German philosopher who established the school of phenomenology, a method of enquiry which places an emphasis on the role of the mind in determining reality. He broke with the positivist orientation of his day. 'Positivism' is the philosophy that information derived from logical and mathematical reports of sensory experience is the exclusive source of all authoritative knowledge. To the contrary,

About Music

Husserl believed that the mind could not be removed from this process.

It is Husserl's work on cognitive psychology that has relevance to music and throws some light on what is happening in our consciousness when we listen to music. Husserl's analysis of 'inner time consciousness' takes music as an example of a temporal experience. A piece of music being played is a kind of temporal object, an object of experience that has temporal extension.

The natural experience of a musical piece is that it consists of a sequence of notes. First, we hear one note, then the next, and so on until the piece of music is completed. At any given moment we seem to have immediate awareness of only one note. If these notes are separated in time as disconnected moments, though, how can we perceive melody or the musical piece as a whole? What is it that makes the individual note events into a musical entity?

One answer might be that, through memory, our mind somehow collects all the notes together into a unity at one moment. But Husserl observes that this is not our experience of music at all. We do not recall all the notes together all at once in a single temporally comprehensive act. If we were aware of all the notes at once, it would be a cacophony and not music.

Anthony Storr points out in *Music and the Mind* that when we listen to music, what we perceive as a tune is simply a succession of separate tones; it is we who make it into a continuous melody. Science can analyse the music in terms of loudness, timbre, pitch, waveform and so on but it cannot reveal the relation between tones which constitutes music.

It is through a combination of individual notes and their context that the mind magically creates music. Incompatibles in combination seem to create music. This work based on phenomenology and cognitive psychology may seem academic but it opens up the whole field of what music is, which is where we came in at the beginning of this journey.

Another eminent commentator on music, Philip Ball, describes how contemporary music is less about sequences of notes or beats and more about sculpting sounds which we hear as discrete almost material entities occupying space. Such music does not have the narrative flow of Mozart or Beethoven but exists in a kind of timeless present.

Much of modern music is made on this principle and exists not in terms of its sequence of notes and beats but in its timbre and texture. Without reference to these there would be little appreciation of such genres as, for example, rock music. Discussing rock music without reference to timbre and texture would be like discussing African music without reference to rhythm.

The best guitar riff of all time was voted as the opening of Led Zeppelin's 'Whole Lotta Love'. It is the sound texture that makes it work, with the note values secondary. Play the same riff on a violin and the effect would be unremarkable. In comparison, many of J.S. Bach's works, for example, are easily transposable for different instruments which retain the original musical message.

Charles Rosen (1927-2012) was an American pianist and writer on music. He is remembered for his career as a concert pianist, for his recordings and for his many writings, notably the book *The Classical Style*, a standard reference for the study of Mozart, Beethoven and Haydn. He went on to write books about Schoenberg and Elliott Carter and several about the romantic era that describe writers and thinkers as well as music and musicians.

On contemporary music, Rosen said, "There is still a question about how long the modernism of the 1950s is going to last. The problem is that in order to absorb any difficult style you have to hear the pieces several times. That was true of Mozart, most of whose work was considered difficult at the time. It was even worse for Beethoven, then worse again for Wagner. Strauss was in a still more difficult position than Wagner, and then Schoenberg and so on.

"You really have to hear them played well several times, and there are very few music lovers who've heard a piece by Boulez more than once. That's the fact of it. So, will it last? I don't know. Some music doesn't. Monteverdi was completely forgotten for a time. Vivaldi totally wiped out. In the case of Carter, the fact that James Levine and Daniel Barenboim have taken up the music gives it a chance. But we'll see."

Rosen writes entirely from the musician's perspective and as such is direct and clear about what is going on in a music experience.

About Music

For example, he delves into the exposition of a Mozart piano concerto, showing how each new idea fulfils various needs raised by the last, while leaving others still open: a continuous game of symmetry and asymmetry, expectation and fulfilment, "hiding beneath the innocent surface".

For me, this gives a clue about how music seeks to communicate. It seems that it is the *process* that we, our brains, respond so positively to and not any message the process might or might not carry. There is in the modern appreciation of music an existential element in that there is no end purpose or aimed-for result, no reason to be; rather it is in the moment and not in the destination that the true art and value is to be discovered, rather like the idea with which I began this chapter. The journey cannot be stilled for it would no longer be a journey but each moment, each note, has its value, appreciated only when referenced to the whole.

From here on, the way ahead re-joins the Montgomery Canal for what must be the most beautiful tow-path walk in the country. It has been a tiring route march and my legs are suffering a little. However, there is more than enough here to distract my attention from any minor sufferings and I sink into this realm of peace and tranquillity.

I encounter two swans and their cygnet gliding along, a heron, coots and a moorhen, dragon flies and lush vegetation. My progress is punctuated by lovingly restored bridges carrying minor roads over the canal and at one point an aqueduct takes the canal over the River Vernwy, a flowing juxtaposition with the stillness of the canal waters. The ironwork of the bridge is scarred by the taught tow-ropes of horse-drawn barges. The canal curves towards the cottages on each side of the bridge at Carreghofa Locks, where a tollhouse marks the junction of the Montgomery Canal and the Llanymynech branch of the Ellesmere Canal.

This brief survey of music's philosophers with all its possible routes opening up has demonstrated that the way we perceive music and what we perceive as music is open to question and that accepted views have not remained constant. What we like to listen to and what we hold in highest esteem have changed and will continue to change as musical styles evolve, come to prominence then fade away again, to be replaced by the next musical fashion. What is tuneful and harmonious now has not always been so. Charles Rosen again: "Thirds and sixths have been consonances since the fourteenth century; before that they were considered unequivocally dissonant. Fourths, on the other hand used to be as consonant as fifths: in music from the Renaissance until the 20th century, they are dissonances… It is not, therefore, the human ear or nervous system that decides what is a dissonance, unless we are to assume a physiological change between the thirteenth and fifteenth century."

There is nothing fixed or universal in music, despite the physics of the natural harmonic series that seems to form the basis of our western tonal system. What we hear when listening to music is always coloured by history, by culture and on an individual level by experience, mood and personal makeup, by which I mean our physiology. The problems faced by philosophers in determining how it is possible to perceive the true nature of reality is just the same problem when applied to music. Will we ever, as Kant denied, be able to perceive the nature of music beyond its surface appearance, if music can be said to have a 'surface'? Is there a bridge over which we can go to the inner spirit of music, as Schopenhauer suggested?

At the next stone-built bridge, I leave the canal, walk up a few steps and find myself in the small town of Llanymynech. It's just a few yards to the Dolphin Inn where I am met with a friendly reception, food and rest for the night.

I'll give the last word of the day to Martin Luther. Music, for the Lutherans, was to accompany praises to God in native tongues, not Latin, so the Word could be understood and appreciated by all. Amen to that.

> *Next to the Word of God, music deserves the highest praise. The gift of language combined with the gift of song was given to man that he should proclaim the Word of God through Music.*

Bill, supping the perfect pint

About Music

CHAPTER TEN

Between the Ears

In which we follow a sound wave into the brain and arrive in Oswestry.

Some breakfasts are worth a mention. Frying an egg and making a piece of toast are not difficult but just that little bit of extra care and attention turns something ordinary into a culinary delight. Cooking, though is not just a science, an element of luck is involved and some would say art. This morning everything was perfect for me.

A small gesture but one which made all the difference: my coffee milk had been warmed. Not only did this suggest the extra bit of care and forethought, but somehow, mysteriously, it made my coffee taste twice as good. While I was eating, my host came for a brief chat and told me about four other walkers who, the previous week, had enjoyed their breakfast too much and had asked for a taxi to take them to their destination for the day.

I didn't indulge quite that much but I certainly felt that my energy tanks were fully stocked by the time I started on the next stage, today from Llanymynech to Tyn-Y-Coed and Candy Woods, a stroll of about eight miles. The aim was to arrive mid-afternoon and explore off the dyke path for a while then rest, ready for the longer trek to Llangollen in the morning. Today's path follows undulating and much quarried countryside, using field and woodland paths and quiet lanes.

Quarrying has destroyed sections of the dyke and the path along this section diverts to the west of its line. The first stretch heads north to Llanymynech Hill. I stop to read a notice that describes how Charles Darwin was here to learn his trade. In July 1831, he visited to use his new clinometer or inclinometer, a geologist's tool for measuring angles of slope, the inclination of an object with respect to the horizontal. Soon after, Darwin had developed enough geological knowledge to be appointed naturalist advisor on the HMS Beagle in December of the same year.

About Music

Turn back the clock 100 years from today and the scene greeting the walker was very different. A great plume of smoke curls high into the sky from the quarry's chimney while gangs of men perspire as they load coal to fire a long brick kiln. The sound of shot-blasting echoing off the hillside sends birds whirring into the air followed by a great cloud of dust, settling to leave its white residue everywhere. Engines whine, bump and thump as barges moored in the little docks are loaded with the plundered stone. Country sounds then were not as they are today.

All sound is, before it reaches the eardrum, a physical vibration of unconcerned molecules in the air. The outer ear, the pinna, collects vibrating sound waves and directs them along the ear canal where they encounter the drum, a thin, cone-shaped piece of skin about 1 cm wide.

The middle ear beyond is connected to the throat via the eustachian tube. This connection allows the air pressure on both sides of the vibrating skin to remain equal. The pressure balance lets your eardrum vibrate freely.

The job of the cochlea in the inner ear is to take the physical vibrations and translate them into electrical information that the brain recognises as sound. It conducts sound through a fluid instead of

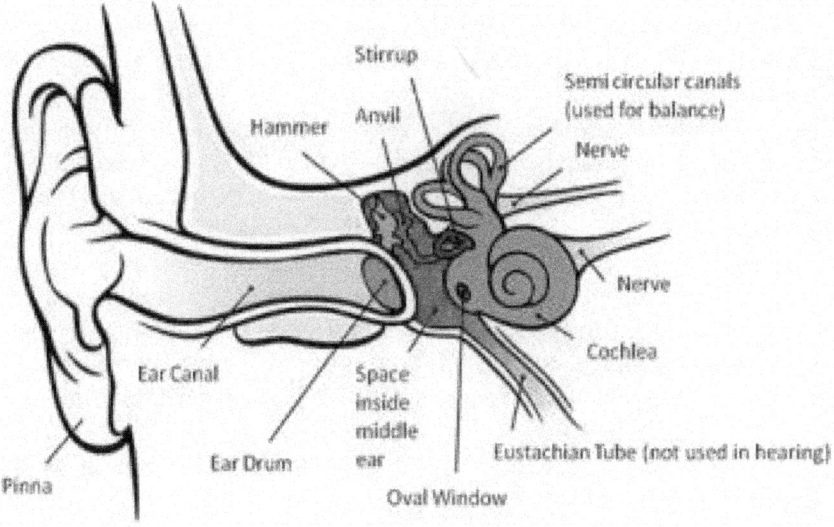

through air. The small force felt at the eardrum is not strong enough to move this fluid, so before the sound passes on to the cochlea it must be amplified. This is the job of the ossicles, a group of miniature bones in the middle ear. The ossicles are the smallest bones in your body.

The organ of corti is a structure containing thousands of tiny hair cells extending across the length of the cochlea. When these hair cells are moved, they generate an electrical current and send it through the cochlea nerve which is connected to the cochlea and on from there to enter the brain itself.

♩ The sensitive eardrum membranes of the local inhabitants around the Llanymynech quarry were well and truly blasted when, in the 1850s, a few years after Darwin's visit, a local business developer, Thomas Savin, tried using four times the normal quantity of explosive in one enormous explosion to extract a month's worth of stone in a day. The money he saved had to be spent on repairs to the houses of local residents.

The hill has at least twelve types of limestone formed in strata of rock. Local quarrymen's names for them include Gingerbread Red, Blood Vein Red and Devil's Skin. The discarded heaps of blast rubble were later found to contain useful magnesium elements. Times have changed and funding has enabled restoration work for the historic quarry works and the creation of a nature reserve.

Llanymynech began its mining history well before the industrial revolution when the Romans extracted copper from a mine close to where I am walking today. Mining was one of the most prosperous activities in Roman Britain. The country was rich in resources such as copper, gold, iron, lead, salt, silver and tin, materials in high demand in the Roman Empire. The abundance of mineral resources in the British Isles was one of the reasons for the Roman conquest. They were able to use their technology to find and extract valuable minerals on a scale unequalled until the Middle Ages.

The two ramblers who set me on the right path in Four Crosses are just ahead of me again and when I catch up, we pause

About Music

together to read the information display about the reserve and compare notes about our overnight stay in Llanymynech.

I press on and leave them behind. Everywhere there is evidence of an industrial past being inexorably reclaimed by nature. The route works its way past Porth-y-waen, but there are no real signs of Offa's Dyke in this area. Perhaps all the quarrying in these parts led to its disappearance along this particular section.

I stumble across a disused railway line with its original time-warped level-crossing gates interrupting the road. Not only was the level crossing intact, but an old truck was abandoned on the track. It was an eerie sight. The line must at one time have been used for carrying vast quantities of rocks and minerals. Now the track is rusting and tentacles of weeds are giving it an atmosphere of sombre, subdued stillness. I half expect a ghostly goods train to appear around a bend in the track, the driver returning for the truck he has left behind. I imagine the train trundling by as I lean over the level-crossing gate to watch it hitch up to the abandoned wagon then vanish up the line. I pick my way gingerly over the track and continue along the way-marked path ahead.

It is ironic that the defunct and decaying remnants of a past age of frantic economic activity are providing the means for an economic revival. It is in the resources of the meadows that my path runs through, in the canals and in the old railways, that this countryside can survive and even thrive. Restoration of the waterways, rail transport lines and the footpaths bring more people along to enjoy them, appreciate them and provide some disposable income for their continuing life. The more effort and investment that are put in, the more will they attract people to use them. Carefully managed, they are the nouveau resources that can be mined for their wealth again.

Mapping the countryside means that you and I can find our way around, moving from one place to a distant location with confidence. On the way we can read the map and discover what features we will encounter. In recent times another type of map, the map of the brain, is becoming much more detailed and accurate using such devilishly high-tech equipment as the magnetic resonance scanner. It reveals the relationships between the anatomy of the brain and our consciousness, as the mechanisms of thinking and feeling are plotted and made visible.

So far, we've followed a sound wave as far as the cochlea. The job now is to use the brain map to find out what then happens. It's a startling fact that the brain has evolved such that we carry within us the evolved primitive brain as well as our additional, new, up-to-date one. Evolution has not meant discarding the old in favour of the new and more advanced but has opted for evolving the old while adding further layers.

Evolution's approach is helpful when making an image to represent the passage of time. Instead of regarding the past as something gone, it can be viewed as a presence at the centre of a new model surrounded by time as it passes in ever increasing circles. The image of time becomes more akin to a spiral than a straight line. Old music is not something that has been left behind and discarded each time a new and more sophisticated development has taken place. It is always there, is at music's heart, surrounded by layers of its evolving form.

The most ancient part of the brain lies deepest and rises out of the spine. This is the brain stem an evolution of the reptile brain tucked deep in our own skulls, deep in our unconscious. This controls the basic functions that are essential for maintaining life, including breathing, body temperature, heart rate and blood pressure. It also controls eye movements and swallowing. It's a sensitive and important part of the brain and connects the cerebral hemispheres to the spinal cord.

Above and around the brain stem is wrapped the limbic system which evolved in mammals. This is a set of evolutionarily primitive brain structures located on top of the brain stem. Limbic system structures are involved in many of our emotions and motivations, particularly those that are related to survival. Such flight-or-fight emotions include fear and anger. The limbic system is also involved in feelings of pleasure that are related to our survival, such as those experienced from eating and sex.

The cerebellum, which is Latin for 'little brain', is the back part of the brain and is concerned with balance and coordination. These activities are carried out subconsciously by this area of the

About Music

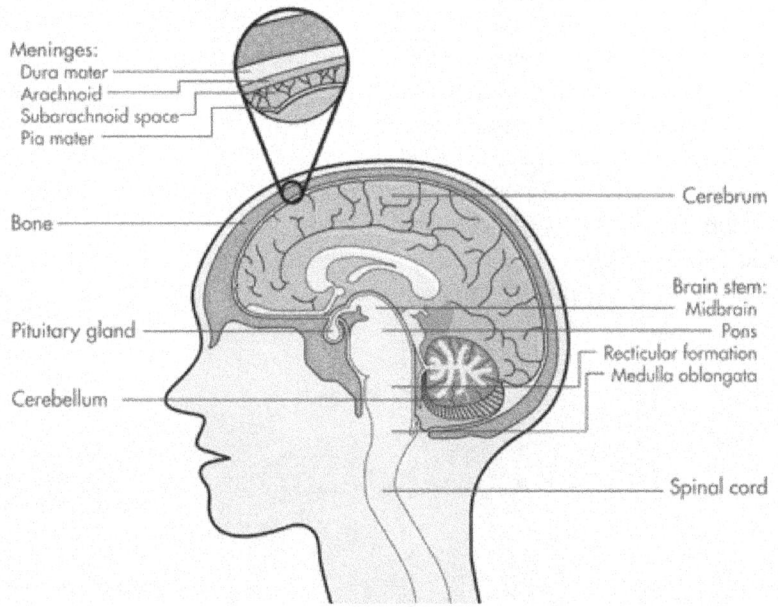

brain and are therefore not under the individual's control. The cerebellum is only 10 per cent of brain volume but holds over 50 per cent of the brain's total information-transmitting cells. Whatever the cerebellum is doing, it's doing a lot of it.

Above the cerebellum and the limbic system is the cerebrum or cerebral cortex, the sausage-like structure that everyone recognises as 'the brain'. The vertebrate cerebrum is formed by two hemispheres that are separated by a groove, the medial longitudinal fissure. The brain can thus be described as being divided into left and right cerebral hemispheres. Each of these hemispheres has an outer layer of grey matter, the cerebral cortex, that is supported by an inner layer of white matter. The hemispheres are linked by the corpus callosum, a large bundle of nerve fibres. Smaller 'commissures' also join the hemispheres. These commissures transfer information between the two hemispheres to coordinate localised functions.

This most recent evolution of the human brain allows us to think and is the seat of some distinctly human characteristics. The cerebral cortex controls the awareness and movement functions that are responsible for speech, our ability to be philosophers and musicians and to be self-aware.

The cerebral cortex is nearly symmetrical with left and right hemispheres that are approximate mirror images of each other. Each hemisphere is conventionally divided into four 'lobes', the frontal lobe, parietal lobe, occipital lobe, and temporal lobe.

Because of the arbitrary way most of the borders between lobes are drawn, the lobes have little specific functional significance, with the exception of the occipital lobe, a small area that is entirely dedicated to vision. The parietal lobe contains, for example, areas involved in hearing, language, attention, spatial cognition and somatosensation, your sixth sense.

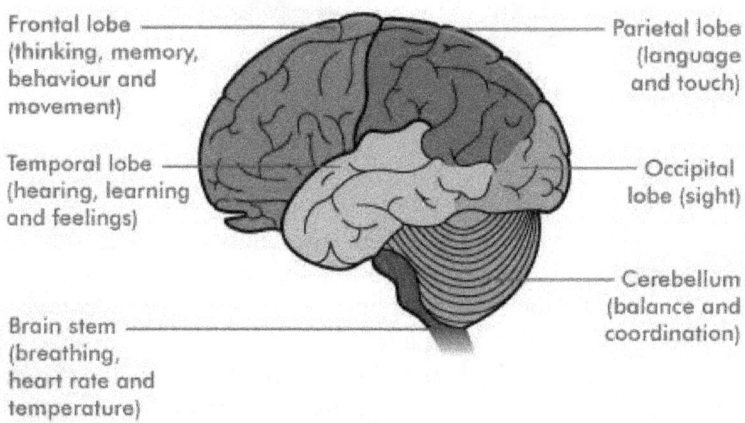

The somatosensory system detects, relays and processes sensations like touch, vibration, pressure, itch, temperature, information about painful stimuli, about the position and movement of our joints and muscles and about internal organs. It has been linked to the sense of self-awareness as it provides an internal representation of the body. In pathologies affecting the somatosensory system, such as the phantom limb syndrome, this awareness of the body is challenged.

In spite of the heterogeneity of the lobes, their division is convenient for reference. The main functions of the frontal lobe are to control attention, abstract thinking, behaviour, problem solving tasks, physical reactions and personality. The occipital lobe is the smallest lobe; its main functions are visual reception, visual-spatial processing, movement, and colour recognition. The temporal lobe controls auditory and visual memories, language, and some hearing and speech.

Prompted by the heterogeneity of the lobes, an optimistic word of caution is appropriate here. This is to be careful not to take the brain map too literally. For example, the primitive brain has connotations that it is somehow inferior and that it is similar to that of a lizard or other reptile. The primitive brain has been evolving, too, as have all areas of the brain in all creatures. Human brains have evolved differently. Secondly, it is tempting to divide the functions of the brain up into neat compartments – the left cerebral hemisphere does this; the right hemisphere does that – however, this too can be misleading.

This compartmentalising is not supported by current experimental results. Both hemispheres contribute to each hemisphere's dominant process and evidence provides little support for correlating any structural differences between the hemispheres with broadly-defined functions. Functions can't be pinned down to single areas of the brain and this is particularly true of music. This complicates the picture but it turns out to be a great boon for it means that music's role is integrated with many brain areas and functions and this only increases recognition of its importance as a human necessity. This is why I described my caution as optimistic.

With caution in mind, I do like making lists and compartmentalising as an aide memoir. It can be said that the right brain dominates rhythm; spatial awareness; Gestalt (whole picture awareness); imagination; daydreaming; colour and dimension. Left brain dominates words; logic; numbers; sequence; linearity; analysis and lists. I guess my left-brain neurons have just been firing off in all directions.

A consequence of a cautious understanding here is that it is incorrect to say that one lacks a particular ability, say a sense of rhythm. In such a person, brain research reveals that it is correct to say that it has not yet been developed in that individual.

About Music

Magnetic resonance imaging (MRI) is enabling neuroscientists to see exactly what the brain is up to when it processes music. Many cognitive tasks, such as vision or language, have fairly-well localised centres of brain activation but music does not. Just about all the brain will become active when we listen to music: the centres that govern movement, the emotion centres, the centres that process syntax and semantics, the lot.

When we hear music, information is sent from the cochlea via the brain stem to the primary auditory cortex, the part of the cerebral cortex that processes auditory information in humans and other vertebrates. This immediately activates the primitive brain, the cerebellum. The ear and the primitive brain are known collectively as the low-level processing units. They perform the main features of extraction which allow the brain to start analysing the sounds. The limbic system and the cerebral cortex are the high-level processing units.

Philip Ball (*The Music Instinct*, Bodley Head) describes how,

> *The cerebellum's timing circuits fire up to pick out the pulse and rhythm, and the thalamus takes a 'quick look' at the signal, apparently to check for danger signals that require any immediate action before more complex processing occurs. The thalamus then communicates with the amygdala to produce an emotional response – which if danger is detected, might be fear. Only after this primeval scan to warn of hazards does the detailed dissection of the sound signal begin.*

The information from the cerebellum is conducted through neurons, cells specialising in transmitting information. The output of these neurons connects to the high-level processing units located in the frontal lobe of the brain.

Historical information is stored in configurations of neurons. When a stimulus activates a certain configuration, historical information is retrieved. The high-level processing units construct musical features by constantly referencing historical information coupled with additional stimulus passed on by the low-level processing units. To understand how our brains make music researchers examine these neural configurations.

The activation of neurons (nerve cells) is called 'firing'. Firing is an electrical signal that releases chemical substances called neurotransmitters. It is because music triggers these neurotransmitters that it has such a powerful influence over mood states. Harmonious chords create regular neuron firing patterns, while discords produce an erratic neuron response. This is a physiological basis for the experience of and response to harmony and discord.

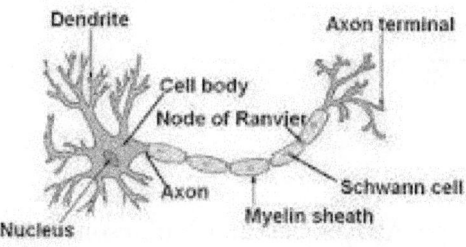

Model of a neuron, or nerve cell

A neurotransmitter is a chemical messenger that carries, boosts and modulates signals between neurons and other cells in the body. In most cases, a neurotransmitter is released from the axon terminal of a neuron after an action potential has reached the synapse, the junction between two nerve cells. The neurotransmitter then crosses the synaptic gap to reach the receptor site of the next neuron. Then, in a process known as reuptake, the neurotransmitter attaches to the receptor site and is reabsorbed by the neuron.

Neurotransmitters play a major role in everyday life and functioning. Scientists do not yet know exactly how many neurotransmitters exist, but more than 100 chemical messengers have been identified. When neurotransmitters are affected by disease or drugs, there can be a number of different adverse effects on the body.

About Music

Music on the mind

When we listen to music, it's processed in many different areas of our brain. The extent of the brain's involvement was scarcely imagined until the early nineties, when functional brain imaging became possible. The major computational centres include:

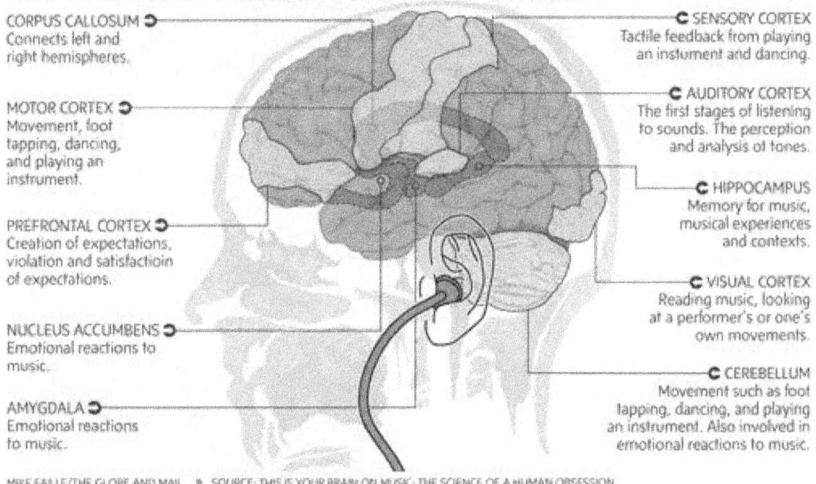

CORPUS CALLOSUM — Connects left and right hemispheres.

MOTOR CORTEX — Movement, foot tapping, dancing, and playing an instrument.

PREFRONTAL CORTEX — Creation of expectations, violation and satisfactioin of expectations.

NUCLEUS ACCUMBENS — Emotional reactions to music.

AMYGDALA — Emotional reactions to music.

SENSORY CORTEX — Tactile feedback from playing an instument and dancing.

AUDITORY CORTEX — The first stages of listening to sounds. The perception and analysis of tones.

HIPPOCAMPUS — Memory for music, musical experiences and contexts.

VISUAL CORTEX — Reading music, looking at a performer's or one's own movements.

CEREBELLUM — Movement such as foot tapping, dancing, and playing an instrument. Also involved in emotional reactions to music.

MIKE FAILLE/THE GLOBE AND MAIL SOURCE: THIS IS YOUR BRAIN ON MUSIC: THE SCIENCE OF A HUMAN OBSESSION

Diseases such as Alzheimer's and Parkinson's are associated with deficits in certain neurotransmitters.

There is no single area of the brain which processes music. Multiple regions of the brain fire upon hearing it: muscular, auditory, visual, linguistic. A consequence is that when some functions of the brain are impaired, for example, in forms of degenerative dementia, sufferers may well respond positively to musical stimuli.

It is fair to say that the brain is built around the principle of pattern recognition. This can be a pain for a musician who is sight reading a piece of music. Music is full of patterns and as soon as the brain locks onto one, the musician can easily lose focused readiness for the ending or breaking of the pattern. At that point the player may stumble and make a mistake, play the wrong note or rhythmic figure. A significant and underestimated aspect of learning to play is to instil patterns in the brain with repetitive practice so it can subsequently recognise them at will. The trick is then learning not to allow the brain to run on unchecked when the pattern changes.

About Music

Classical composers discovered what the brain likes and what it responds to. They pandered to its favoured neurone firing patterns of recognition. When listening to a piece of Mozart for the first time, it may be as if the brain knows where the music is going, knows even what the next notes are to be. Mozart and the others played on this by setting up the pattern, then perhaps suspending it or thwarting it with the unexpected, before allowing in conclusion that final, most satisfying chord to sound.

The brain seems to be hard-wired for harmony. Recall the simple relationship of the overtones in the harmonic series, which gives an instrument its characteristic timbre. If the fundamental note is, say, 100 Hz, the series consists of harmonics at 200 Hz, 400 Hz, 800 Hz, etc. There is evidence that the brain responds to the frequencies it hears in this series where each frequency is doubled from the fundamental up, with corresponding neural firings. Neurons in the auditory cortex synchronise their firing rates with the series, so there is a neural basis for the apparent coherence of these sounds.

To support this, there is a phenomenon called 'restoration of the missing fundamental'. Using our harmonic series, if the fundamental frequency (in this case 100 Hz) was omitted, but the other harmonics retained, the brain will spot the harmonic sequence and fill in the missing frequency so that the sense of pitch for the listener is not lost. For any other sequence of frequencies other than this one, the trick does not work.

♩ I arrive in the village of Nantmawr, a classic example of an old mining town now subdued and picturesque. The only sign of any activity is provided by the local pub, advertising 'food all day' and 'walkers welcome'. I resist and rest on a bench to take a little of my own refreshment before walking up the field slopes behind the village. Some of the houses of Nantmawr are set into a steep hillside making gardening, I imagine, more of an adrenalin-pumped precarious outdoor adventure activity than a relaxing pastime.

I am on a quiet lane above the village when a man with a dog comes towards me. We pass and nod an acknowledgement to each other. I am overwhelmed in this silent encounter by the good will that emanates from him. I may well have imagined this but the sensation held a strong reality. He is enjoying a walk with his dog

About Music

and sees coming towards him a fellow walker and appreciator of the country scene. I have my pack and walking stick, my dark sunglasses against the glare and a steady step that suggests I have a way yet to go. We are both caught, for an instant, in a realm of mutual appreciation which takes in and includes the scenery around us, the metalled road, the hedges, the fields, trees, birdsong, sky and clouds. It is a magic moment that comes and goes in a twinkling but which leaves a permanent imprint on my mind. The path leads on and I follow it.

Moelydd Hill is the only significant climb along the path today and I am on its southern slopes, a nature reserve known as 'Jones's Rough', looked after by the Shropshire Wildlife Trust. It is said that the area gained the name from the Jones family who had built a small cottage called 'Mount Zion' in the 19th century. They did not have permission to build the cottage, but thought they could claim it for their own under the belief that if there was smoke coming from the chimney by morning the builders could claim the dwelling as their home. However, the landowners, Powys Estates, claimed the cottage as *their* own and duly asked for rent. Maybe it was a rough deal. The family's mistaken idea may have come from Gloucestershire's Forest of Dean, where such dwellings were called 'Sun-Up' houses and ownership could at one time be claimed by their builders.

I slip easily back into my inner world and earlier musings on descriptions of how the ear works and how the brain makes music. I'm focusing on descriptions that are rational, objective and based on empirical observation. These are, by definition, untainted by speculation, imagination or religious feelings. In the early development of music history right up until the Renaissance, the opposite was the case. There were no clear guidelines when drawing conclusions about the way things work. These were often what we would now think of as imaginative, or, politely, fanciful. Only a hundred years ago, we were still finding out about the brain and our personalities by reading the bumps on the head's surface.

For many years, a neurological connection between music and language was disputed. There is now strong evidence to suggest that basic elements of syntax – words and word categories for language; notes and chords for music – seem to be encoded in separate locations in the brain but the neural circuits that combine and integrate these elements may be shared between both music and language.

It may seem in conflict with the objective approach, but for exploring the brain from the perspective not of neurons but of consciousness and self-awareness, the imagination can be a means of perception, your seventh sense. In meditation, the images and sounds that we perceive inwardly can be interpreted as symbols representing inner unconscious processes. Configurations of firing neurons are, during active imagination, thus akin to psychological functions, archetypes, the gods of ancient Greece, the weird creatures that inhabit the realm of myth and fairy tale. The imagination may be a tool to use in understanding what has been lost in the process of stark objectification.

Returning again to the fact that multiple brain functions are at work when making music, this is experienced directly when you learn to play an instrument. When learning, it is helpful to single out a particular topic or technique to focus on and with practice the brain learns to perform this action unconsciously. I've observed numerous times in my students that they will learn to play a particular ensemble part quite fluently on their own, but then, when joining and fitting it in with other players, find unsuspected difficulties. The brain is now trying to absorb and process multiple information streams and doesn't know where to focus. The player may lose their grip on what otherwise would have been a clear musical element, such as tempo, dynamic or intonation.

Overworked, not only is the brain recalling its stored memory information about hand-eye co-ordination, and information about how to perform a particular technique, say, for example, a legato smooth style of playing, but it is responding to the incoming visual and auditory information that is surrounding the player. In an orchestra, players have to respond to the conductor and will be hearing how their part fits with all the other surrounding orchestra sections and with the players on either side. There is need here for an awareness of the whole, the gestalt of a piece of music, which is a right brain function, you might recall.

About Music

So, when learning to play an instrument it is essential to separate out and study a single playing technique and focus on that. When playing a piece of music, though, this is not possible. There is so much information being absorbed and processed all the time in making music, a different attitude or awareness is required. A state of consciousness that does not have a singular focus, but contains a heightened awareness is called for. This is precisely what is learned in meditation - a condition of relaxed, open awareness. This state of being is appropriate for both playing and listening to music.

The brain's activity is characterised by electrical and chemical activity. Electrical activity can be detected with sensors and these measure the value and type of electromagnetic radiation emitted when different types of brain activity are experienced. This electrical activity is different in different states of consciousness, most notably when awake, when asleep and when dreaming. Our brainwaves change according to what we're doing and feeling. When slower brainwaves are dominant, we can feel tired, slow, sluggish, or dreamy. The higher frequencies are dominant when we feel alert.

Although there is no strict demarcation between these states, they can be identified and defined.

Delta waves (0.5 to 3 Hz) are the slowest but most energetic brainwaves. They are generated in deepest meditation and dreamless sleep. Healing and regeneration are stimulated in this state, and that is a reason why deep restorative sleep is so essential to the healing process.

Theta brainwaves (3 to 8 Hz) occur most often in sleep but are also dominant in deep meditation. In the theta state, our senses are withdrawn from the external world and focused on signals originating from within. It is that twilight state which we normally only experience fleetingly as we wake from or drift off to sleep. In theta we are in a dream world characterised by imagery and information beyond our normal conscious awareness. It is where we may encounter our taboos, fears, frustrations and unfulfilled urges.

Alpha waves (8 to 12 Hz) are present during quietly flowing thoughts, in a contemplative state but not quite meditation. Alpha is 'the power of now', being here in the present. Alpha is a resting state for the brain. Alpha waves aid overall mental coordination, calmness, alertness, mind/body cooperation and learning.

About Music

Beta brainwaves (12 to 38 Hz) dominate our normal waking state of consciousness when attention is directed towards cognitive tasks and the outside world. Beta waves are present when we are alert, attentive, engaged in problem solving, judgment, decision making, and engaged in focused mental activity. Continuous high frequency processing is not an efficient way to run the brain, as it takes a great deal of energy.

Gamma brainwaves (38 to 42 Hz) are the highest frequency brain waves and relate to simultaneous processing of information from different brain areas. In this state, information passes rapidly, and, as the most subtle of the brainwave frequencies, the mind has to be quiet to access it. Gamma was traditionally dismissed as 'spare brain noise' until researchers discovered it was highly active when in states of universal love, altruism, and the 'higher virtues'. Gamma rhythms modulate perception and consciousness, disappearing under anaesthesia. Their frequency is also above that of neuronal firing, so how it is generated remains a mystery.

Being aware in particular of what the alpha state feels like can be exceptionally helpful when playing music, for a state of mental coordination, calmness, alertness and mind/body integration is just what may be swamped when multiple areas of the brain are at work. Learning to meditate should be part of developing the music experience.

🜚 I emerge at the top of Moelydd Hill and am startled by the unexpected panoramic view for I had not realised, lost in thought about the brain and its music making, how long I had been climbing. Also, this sudden vision is a stark contrast with the general feel of today's walk through quite low-lying countryside.

I have also been surprised during the walk so far how few walkers I have encountered. Most ramblers on the dyke path walk from south to north as I am, so perhaps at any one time there are hundreds along the path all spaced out sufficiently that we can't see each other; all walking at the same speed, travelling like a train of pedestrian trucks along the same track.

Two walkers appear over the northern brow of the hill just to dispute my musings and they tell me they are on a circular walk for the day. I continue my way along the path from which they have just emerged. Now it is downhill and the walking is easy if uneventful. The path falls gently through grass, gorse and bracken to reach a clear white track. There are some early hints of the autumn to come, berries, an occasional leaf falling, fungi, a wind that has the flavour of a season's end.

Stretches of the dyke are lost to mining but it reappears as I near the houses of Trefonen. There is a brewery here dedicated to Offa's Dyke and I look forward to trying some of its beer at the end of today. As I walk along a lane past houses on my left and with a meadow on my right, my eye is caught by a child's illustration of fields and houses on a noticeboard with some yellow leaflets below: 'Housing development on Trefonen's precious green meadows! Planning applications submitted for development. Join us in objecting to the destruction of our beautiful countryside.' I take a leaflet and slip it into my pocket.

The remainder of today's walk is uneventful and I stroll into Tyn-Y-Coed where I will hopefully find my bed and breakfast for the night. The River Morda flows by this sleepy hamlet and I soak up the atmosphere while watching its waters flow through a series of culverts fashioned under the road. Ahead of me are the Candy woods that I'll clamber up and through in the morning and, right on the Offa's Dyke path, is Glan-Yr-Afon, the house where I'll stay for the night.

As soon as I've settled in and chatted with my hosts for a while, I'm up and off again to make the most of the late afternoon good weather before returning to Glan-Yr-Afon for the night. A couple of miles or so away lies the town of Oswestry. I have a choice of walking along the lanes into the town or going via open common land. I choose the latter and am soon pleased by the decision for the land rolls away on either side and into the distance, dotted with magnificent trees. The path is hard to discern but I know that if I keep heading east then I will eventually encounter the town, which, about 45 minutes later, is precisely what happens.

Oswestry is a picturesque, bustling Shropshire town with its historic features rubbing shoulder to shoulder with shops and taverns. I find my way to one called the Barley Mow, advertising its real ales and park myself inside with a pint from Trefonan's Offa's Dyke brewery. It is golden and delicious. I've noted previously the various

About Music

moods that different alcoholic beverages can create and this one is, simply, mellow and alpha-wave inducing.

In a little while I carry this feeling with me all the way back to Glan-Yr-Afon when I return there for a welcome overnight rest.

Bill, well and truly horizontal for the next few hours

About Music

CHAPTER ELEVEN

The Shape of Music

*In which we walk with the stream in the sky
and encounter an unearthly wind*

The building blocks that make up a piece of music are equivalent to the grammar of a language. Music has its full stops, commas and phrases, too. Be aware, though, that this is only helpful to a degree for nothing used in constructing music becomes musical unless given duration and shape, while the individual words of a language all retain their meaning, independent of the context in which they are used.

Take a note or even a phrase out of its musical context and it becomes meaningless, but separate a word from its sentence and it retains its particular meaning. This requirement of music, to be whole before it makes sense, that its individual component parts individually have no musical meaning, is surprising. The wholeness and shape of music, what makes music, music, is called 'form' and this is what the topic of today's ramble is about.

🌰 The next section of the Offa's Dyke path also turned out to be one of the most surprising. The walk began predictably enough at the River Morda with the trail heading up through Candy Woods, mossy and green in the soft light of early morning. I soon reach a rough bench made from the hillside's dislodged stones, thoughtfully and temptingly built into a grassy bank, but it's too early to stop so I continue on up the slope, emerging on the flat summit and an area that once hosted the Oswestry Racecourse.

The abandoned racecourse site stands on the 1000-ft hilltop of Cyrn y Bwch, Welsh for 'Horns of the Buck', and historically was considered to be the barrier between 'the Kingdom and the Principality'. It has viewpoints over England and Wales. Consisting of a patchwork of scrub, scattered trees, bracken and wildflower-rich grassland, the area supports an incredible range of birds and insects.

About Music

An information board traces the chequered history of the racecourse from the heyday of its social success to its occupation by moles, mole catchers and eventual ruin. By the eighteenth century, the area was being used for racing horses, bringing together the local landowners and gentry of Wales and England. Signs of this historic use are still evident. Much of the figure-of-eight racetrack forms the main walking route around the site and the ghostly ruins of the grandstand are still present with, I imagine, the cheers of spectators and the thunder of hooves still echoing around.

The development of the railways spelled the end of racing on the site as spectators and horses could then travel to grander racecourses. The last meeting was held in 1848, the same year that the Shrewsbury to Chester railway line opened.

The historical line that music followed has brought changes informed not only by fashion, but also by political, social and religious factors. The earliest form, essentially a single line of music accompanying recitative or poetry, included the deployment of scales, that later became the 'modes'. These were formulated in medieval times but were inspired by the music of Ancient Greece.

In a scale of eight notes, the positioning of tones and semitones relative to one another determines the mode of the music. For example, in the major scale, or Ionian mode, the sequence starting with the key note is tone, tone, semitone, tone, tone, tone, semitone. (If you start on C on a piano and play the white notes to its right up to the next C, you have played a major scale, or Ionian mode.)

The modes that have survived are mainly the major and minor forms, but others are still used today and have been employed to create new chordal harmonies particularly in folk, rock and jazz music. The jazz scale, for example, is basically the same as the medieval Dorian mode and its sequence goes tone, semitone, tone, tone, tone, semitone, tone. (If you start on D on a piano and play the white notes to its right up to the next D, you have played a Dorian scale.)

Each mode was thought to create a certain mood and have a particular influence on the listener, hence could be chosen to further the prevailing political, social or religious pressures. Start your scale

About Music

on any piano white key and you have one of the modes under your fingertips.

♪ The dyke goes over Baker's Hill but this is now private property and so the official path is compelled to skirt it to the east. North of the hill I meet a fine stretch of dyke and walk with the bank again as if it is an old friend. Stopping to admire a hawthorn tree growing out of the earthwork at an acute angle of about 30 degrees to the horizontal, I contemplate how I've grown to love the arboreal aspect of the dyke with its randomly scattered trees and bushes often growing at the most precarious angles, sometimes submissively bent by the prevailing wind.

The path skirts Selattyn Hill whose rowan trees are now covered in luminous red berries and from where the view instantaneously opens up to the north. I can see from here the distant shimmering landmark of Chirk Castle and beyond it the Clwydian mountains. There follows another long stretch of the dyke mound as Chirk gradually edges closer. I will be walking round the outskirts of the castle grounds later today but many walkers take the time to pay it a visit.

🎻 In working our way through a musical landscape, we've already skirted early forms of music such as plainchant, or plainsong, the form of medieval church music that involves chanting and which emerged around 100 A.D. Plainchant doesn't use any instrumental accompaniment. It was the only type of music allowed in Christian churches as their music's intention was to make a listener receptive to spiritual thoughts and reflections. This was why the melody was kept pure, simple and unaccompanied.

Polyphony, developing on the foundations of plainchant, is the term used to describe several lines of music which are melodically independent but which sound well together. The term is usually used to refer to music of the late Middle Ages and Renaissance. Subsequent further development resulted in fugue.

Fugue is indeed polyphonic but is usually described instead as 'contrapuntal', this term indicating that different lines of music played or sung simultaneously are melodically *and* rhythmically independent. This was characteristic of music created in the Baroque

About Music

period. A descriptive way to define fugue is as 'the art of imitation' as each voice imitates what has been sung before, while adding its own character and variation. Strict rules governed its writing so that the art of fugue became as much a problem-solving exercise for the composer as a means of creative expression.

The fugue is not strictly speaking a musical form but a method of writing. Its aim, though, is to give the music shape and coherence. It is perhaps one of the most interesting perennial types of music for audience, performer and composer alike for it is essentially dealing with pattern and this is precisely what our brains love to lock on to and respond to with delight.

The rules of fugue were designed to give the music momentum, ensuring its progression through time, imbuing it with a sense of purpose and direction. It worked like this: the fugue would be written for two, three or more parts or voices. The first voice introduces a short theme, the 'subject', lasting for, say, between four and eight bars. Then the same theme would be repeated by another of the voices but at a different pitch, usually at the interval of a fifth above or a fourth below the first subject. This is called the 'answer'. While the second voice is singing, the first voice supplies a counterpoint against it, the 'counter subject'. When the two voices have finished, a third may enter, singing the original subject then the answer in a different octave. You can see immediately how quickly the complexities build and all has to be harmonically satisfying.

Like a vocalist with his own particular line of music to follow, I stay on my track which underfoot has become level and relatively smooth. Either side there is rough moorland while sculpted dry-stone walls divide part of the lower ground into fields.

In one of these, over to my left, an alarmed flock of lapwing takes flight. These distinctive birds are much less common than they used to be. I remember their presence in the fields during my teenage years as something quite unremarkable. Nowadays, although not unseen, they are becoming uncommon are noteworthy. Sometimes known as the peewit in imitation of its display call, the lapwing's more usual common name describes a wavering flight pattern. A black-and-white appearance and rounded wing shape in flight make it distinctive, even without taking into account its splendid crest. This once familiar farmland bird has suffered significant decline in numbers and is now on the RSPB's Red List of declining species. Red is the highest conservation priority, with species in this category needing urgent care. Amber is the next most critical group, followed by green.

Walking on, Chirk Castle begins to dominate the scene ahead. Famously, the building has apparently been occupied continuously as a castle and stately home for almost 700 years. It sits on a hilltop with its best views over the Ceiriog valley to its south. The successor to two known mottes in the area, it was probably built by Roger Mortimer, of the powerful Marcher family, who was granted the area by Edward I after the Welsh defeat in 1282.

Mortimer was almost certainly given royal assistance in its design and construction. Its similarities to Beaumaris Castle, located in the town of the same name on the Isle of Anglesey in Wales and built as part of Edward I's campaign to conquer the north of Wales after 1282, suggest that work may have started as late as 1295, perhaps in response to the Welsh rising of 1294.

Chirk was besieged and taken by the Parliamentarians in 1659 as punishment for the Myddeltons' support of the Cheshire Rising. At the last moment, it sustained damage that the inhabitants had for so long sought to avoid. Most of the eastern side was demolished and much of the rest burnt. This left the family with a huge rebuilding task after the Restoration of the monarchy and the accession of Charles II in 1660.

A new stone range was eventually added on the east, in conjunction with the reconstruction of the outer defensive wall and towers. With the east range, the main structure of the castle was complete, although minor alterations continued to be made. After an abortive episode in 1762-4, when a scheme for a Gothic interior was abandoned at an early stage, the north range was extensively refurbished in neo-classical style by Joseph Turner of Chester in the later 1760s and '70s, the drawing room being completed by John Cooper of Beaumaris in about 1796.

The castle's complex and chequered history continued and in the 1820s Gothic vaulting was added, and from 1845 the interior was almost totally reworked in the Gothic manner by A.W. Pugin, architect of the Houses of Parliament. Most of these alterations have

About Music

been undone in recent years with the exception of the Cromwell Hall, where a collection of Civil War arms is displayed. The castle remained in the hands of the Myddelton family, who still owned and worked much of the estate until 1978. It is now in the care of the National Trust.

The magnificent wrought iron gate-screen at the entrance to the park was made by Robert and John Davies of Bersham between 1712 and 1719. It originally stood a little way in front of the main castle gate and was moved to its present position in 1770 during the landscaping of the park.

Offa's Dyke runs through the park. It can be seen from the air, lying submerged beneath the waters of an artificial lake and is visible as a low bank running as far as Home Farm, west of the castle. South of the castle it is better preserved, running off to the west of the official track and out into the fields beyond.

Turning from the architecture of castles to that of music, perhaps the most satisfying form of music and a ubiquitous ingredient in swathes of classical music is sonata form. However, before considering this in any detail it is worth summarising some of the other basic forms which were frequently employed and which we recognise instinctively as musically satisfying.

Binary form was at first used in short movements and in the 17th and 18th centuries was employed in the short dance movements of suites, which were collections of contrasting dance music. Quite simply a piece is in two sections, A and B, hence the name, binary. Some basic modulation takes place, that is, a change of key. The common formula would be a first part, A, of eight bars, which modulates to the dominant key, then the second part, B, of sixteen bars, works its way back to the tonic, the original key. Both sections may be repeated.

In the three sections, ABA, that comprise ternary form, the first and the third are similar with a second contrasting section between. The third section may be longer than the first and more ornamental and varied, but it does need to repeat the first section in some recognisable manner.

When ternary form was extended, the various names given to this structure were Aria form or Song form, Minuet and Trio form, and Episodical form. Many 18th-century arias are in Song form. The middle section is generally in a related key and more lightly accompanied. At the return of the first section, the singer was expected to add embellishments to the composer's written notes and to show an ability to decorate the final cadence. The equivalent extemporising for instrumental soloists became what is now known as the cadenza.

In the classical symphony, a minuet and trio almost inevitably followed the slow second movement and so common was this that the name was used to describe the structure. Each section, minuet then trio, is complete and the dance-like features of them make the music's phrasing clear cut. There are repeats in each of the sections, but the convention is that, when the first minuet is played again after the trio section, the repeats are omitted.

Episodical form is less clear cut. The middle section usually offers significant contrast with the first and instead of clear-cut divisions between the sections, they are merged one with the other. The whole tends to be more subtle than the other ternary forms.

If the ternary form, ABA, is extended by adding another 'episode', and then ends by repeating the original theme, we have ABACA and this became known as the *rondo* (Italian) or *rondeau* (French), which means a return.

Composers such as Purcell, Couperin, Corelli, Bach and Handel were known for writing suites. The suite is a group of dances, usually in the order of fast-slow-fast-slow, etc., to create contrast. Fashions in dances changed, so that new ones appeared with some regularity. For example, when the *allemande* and *courante* appeared, they replaced the pavan and the galliard.

Although in England and France the word suite was commonly used, in England the word would often be lesson and in France, *ordre*. The word *partita* was used by Bach and others and the Italian equivalent was the *sonata da camera* whose form was developed by Arcangelo Corelli (1653 – 1713), an Italian violinist and composer.

Corelli adapted the suite to the prevailing four-movement format to create a 'preludio' and three dances or connecting movements. The dance style movements were usually given names referring to the style, such as *partita*, *ordre*, *ouverture* and air. The most frequent instrumentation in *sonata da camera* was two violins and a bass. Most harmonies were completed in the bass part whilst the two treble instruments played above. This was also known as a trio sonata, as it consisted of three major parts, becoming hugely popular as a form of musical entertainment.

To demonstrate how many – and how popular – dances there were, there is a long list of names, any of which may appear in a suite of music: the *Allemande, Courante, Sarabande, Gigue, Minuet, Gavotte, Bourée, Passepied, Loure, Polonaise, Hornpipe, Rigaudon, Chaconne, Passacaglia* and *Siciliano* were the most popular. The name suite is still used by modern composers to describe a number of pieces grouped together but the dance theme may be omitted.

It is contrast and variation which play a major role in creating music and there is a particular form which quite openly panders to this, the 'Air and Variations'. Like the fugue it is not strictly speaking a form but is a variety of ways of presenting the same theme. Rather like the cadenza, which shows off an instrumentalist's capabilities, the Air and Variations will test the soloist but also give the sparkling imagination of the composer a platform, too. Variation has a long history and the repetition of a tune with some differences was one of the obvious ways to compose.

We come now to sonata form, a method for structuring a single movement of music - not to be confused with the sonata, which is a piece of music in several movements for a solo accompanied instrument.

Sonata form developed over time, reaching its fulfilment in the works of Joseph Haydn (1732-1809) who subsequently became known as the father of the symphony. Its outline is as follows: a first theme or subject in the main key is announced; a second subject is then introduced in a different key. There then follows a development section in which the themes are explored and played with, perhaps passing through several key changes and variations. After the development, the two original subjects are repeated, both now in the home key, before a tail-piece, a coda, brings the movement to a close. The effect of sonata form is to establish a home base then to take the listener on a musical adventure, finally returning home. It is the classic musical journey.

About Music

Throughout the 19th century, music became less enthralled with the established rules of harmony and more open to the employment of discordant, atonal intervals and chords. We tend to think of this as a 20th century phenomenon but even prior to the classical period Baroque composers were quite adventurous in introducing dissonant notes, but then these would always resolve into an acceptable, pleasurable harmony. This was a way of introducing tension into the music, a tension always followed by its release, propelling the musical journey ever onward. Then came Mozart and a particular string quartet now called 'The Dissonant' with some no-holds-barred strident sound effects. Chordal structures subsequently became denser and more discordant and the effect was used quite deliberately as a means for expressing anguish or emotional discomfort of some sort. The sounds themselves were physically discomforting.

Great depths of emotional expression became available to composers with this extended harmonic vocabulary but for one, Arnold Schoenberg (1874-1951), this development was too much to bear. He felt stifled by the need for ever greater dissonance, for ever heightening emotion in music. Somehow it had to be contained and this suggested that a new form for music would have to be discovered.

Schoenberg unveiled his new method for composing in 1923, which he described as the "method of composing with twelve tones which are related only with one another." Twelve consecutive notes each spaced a semitone apart make up the chromatic scale, so named as it suggests all the colours of the spectrum.

From any key on the piano, to the key an octave above there are twelve keys, black and white. The starting point of a Schoenbergian composition was to take these twelve tones and place them in any order that the composer desired. The composition using this 'tone row' progressed by working serially through the row to its end, then beginning again and continuing with the same sequence. Variation was achieved in the rhythmic content and the way that the harmonic structure was created. In addition, various technical manipulations were permitted which derived from the old art of counterpoint. For example, the row could be written in retrograde, that is, could run backwards from the last note. It could be written in

About Music

inversion. For example, if the original begins by moving up four steps, then down two, the inversion will go down four then up two. The retrograde inversion goes back to front and upside down!

His discovery released Schoenberg's creative tensions into a flurry of activity and in the early and mid-nineteen twenties he composed with a new-found fluency. Stated simply, the method frees the composer from any emotional angst and enables him to focus purely on the process of composition and to create pure music. It also frees composition from the tyranny of the musical journey, from the home key and the necessity to return to it. Needless to say, the results from a listener's point of view can be, at first, quite challenging and stark.

♣ Beyond Chirk Castle grounds, I am gradually working my way through fields and along tracks towards Froncysyllte and am quite startled to see a field speckled with black sheep. The sight defies the convention that the 'black sheep' is a one-off, a loner. It goes against nature to have so many in one place at one time. Maybe they are having a convention, glad of the chance to air their complaints about always being cast as the odd one out. I have an inkling of how they feel.

On the north side of Froncysyllte town, I reach the Llangollen canal. The canal and tow path are beautifully maintained and attract numerous visitors to enjoy their calm beauty. This is a long path that goes all the way into Llangollen, the final destination for today. However, my particular route dictates that I will be leaving the tow path to follow the dyke. Before branching off, I arrive at the dramatic Pontcysyllte aqueduct, taking the canal high over the River Dee.

I had heard about this spectacular feat of engineering but was unprepared for the experience of walking across it. The tow path and canal continue together, both narrow ways, up, onto and across the aqueduct. The path is wide enough for two people approaching in opposite directions to squeeze by without falling in the water. On my left hand is the canal; on my right is a guard against falling off the aqueduct. What I find alarming is that the canal boats have no such guard on their side and the barges' occupants can look down from this exhilarating stream in the sky, over the side of their vessel and into the huge, glorious green chasm below.

The aqueduct, built by Thomas Telford and William Jessop, is 307 m long, 3.4 m wide and 1.60 m deep. It consists of a cast iron trough supported 38 m above the river on iron arched ribs carried on nineteen hollow masonry piers. Each span is 16 m wide. Despite considerable public scepticism, Telford was confident the construction method would work: he had previously built at least one cast-iron trough aqueduct, the Longdon-on-Tern aqueduct on the Shrewsbury Canal, still visible as a surreal Victorian sculpture in the middle of a field, though the canal was abandoned years ago.

Part of what was originally called the Ellesmere Canal, the Pontcysyllte aqueduct was one of the first major feats of civil engineering undertaken by Telford, by then a leading civil engineer still supervised by Jessop, the more experienced canal engineer. It was opened on 26 November 1805, having taken around ten years to design and build at a total cost of £47,000. Adjusted for inflation this is equivalent to no more than £3,330,000 as of 2014, but bore a much larger relationship to the early 19th-century GDP of some £400 million. Such a project would cost considerably more today owing to factors that did not apply in the early 19th century, such as higher wages, safety measures, new regulations and taxes, financing fees and so on.

The trip over the aqueduct, whether by boat or on foot, will not be a pleasant experience for those who suffer from vertigo. Having traversed it, I was unaware that there would be yet another great height to experience further along and I walked away from Pontcysyllte believing it represented the peak moment of the day. There was more to come.

The way forward takes me away from the canal system and, now winding in a westerly direction, onto a steep climb up through Trevor Woods. This is lengthy but a satisfying climb through varied woodland and in today's dry conditions, although sometimes steep, it is easy walking. My legs are tiring and it seems an age before I emerge at the highest point of the woods on moorland and onto the Panorama Walk, a name that is not overstated.

About Music

A harmonious chord is created by sounding three (or more) notes simultaneously. These are the root note, the note which is the interval of a third above it and the note a third above this. This has been the basis of western harmony for centuries.

To make music move up hill and down dale the idea of chord progressions developed. It is a standing joke that pop groups only use three chords in their twelve-bar blues music, but in fact those same three chords were universally employed in classical music - with, of course, others.

One notable chord progression that has been used time and again is the 'cycle of fifths' which starts from any beginning chord, usually the key note's chord. The chord's root then moves up the interval of a fourth to become the root of a new chord, then down a fifth, up a fourth, down a fifth and so on, until the original chord comes around again.

Each note of the scale in the key of a piece of music can be represented by a number. One convention is to use Roman numerals. If the chord has a major, bright feel to it, it is designated with a capital numeral; if it is minor in feel, it is given a small numeral. The chords of a major key, formed on its scale, can be written like this: I ii iii IV V vi vii and then back to I. It was a little surprising to me to discover that some of the chords formed using the notes in a major scale or key turn out to be minor and vice versa.

The cycle of fifths looks like this and any keyboard or guitar players can try it out: I IV vii III vi ii V I. The last two chords in the sequence, V to I, form what is called a perfect cadence and give a sense of full stop and finality to a phrase or piece of music. When you have heard this sequence and know what it is, you will recognise it as something familiar and satisfying. Again, there is something about this sequence that has become embedded in the brain's physiology which recognises and responds positively to it.

The Folia was a form involving another particular chord progression that Baroque composers loved to play around with - a musical dance to the death. Its original primitive form morphed into something more stately and sophisticated. Over the course of three centuries, more than 150 composers have used it in their works.

About Music

(For the technically minded, the Folía consists of two eight-bar phrases in a minor key. The chord sequence for a Folía goes as follows: the first phrase is i V i ♭VII ♭III ♭VII i V and the second phrase is i V i ♭VII ♭III ♭VII i V i. At the end of the first sequence i V is an 'imperfect' cadence, a comma or pause, while the finality of the perfect cadence, V i, rounds off the second phrase. The ♭ symbol indicates that the root of a chord is to be flattened by a semitone.)

Because the Folía framework appeared almost at the same time in different countries with numerous variants that share similar structural features, it is not possible to establish in which country the framework originated. However, its popularity and hypnotic grip suggest that there is something in this sequence that our musical brains respond to in a most notable manner. It is, quite literally, hypnotic.

The name Folía is of Iberian origin and refers to a fertility dance in three-four time originating in the late 15th century and danced by young girls who used it to evoke a trance state in themselves. La Folía literally means madness, folly, or empty-headedness and is one of the most remarkable phenomena in the history of music. It provided a major challenge for numerous composers up to the present day ranging from part of a famous Bach Cantata to a popular film tune in the charts by Vangelis. The flexibility of the theme to incorporate and adapt features of new musical styles is not only amazing but also guaranteed its survival. Another striking feature is the variety of instruments used to play the theme in a completely natural way.

🌰 My route now takes me onto a metalled road running east to west high above the valley with the eisteddfod town of Llangollen nestling below. Along this road, about a mile ahead, I can see Castell Dinas Bran perched on top of its hill and beyond that the curve of the path and road as they head north via the steep shale cliffs of Trevor Rocks.

I'm on the last leg of today's journey and stop to rest and soak up yet another spectacular view. There are higher places in abundance, of course, but this one has an atmosphere about it, as if the real world were up here and below is a remote, other-land

About Music

existing in a different space and time. I recall a programme I had seen on TV recently about people who were frightened of heights and had been desensitised by taking them carefully to experience places such as this and the aqueduct. I feel at home here but it is not a place to live or to stay for long.

The view from the walk along the road is panoramic all the way. It is late afternoon when I reach the point where I divert off the official path to make my way up to Castell Dinas Bran and then down the other side of its hill and into Llangollen. First, I turn off along a narrow track and up the hill's steep gradient where I encounter a wrought iron gate across the path with a magnificent metal figurehead of a raven perched on it, peering over its kingdom, the valley beyond.

It is a steep climb and it is becoming windy. By the time I reach the castle, it is blowing a howling gale and the wind makes me stagger and take care against it.

The wind, by producing rival disturbances to sound waves, can alter the speed, frequency and the reach of any sound, imposing new patterns and rhythms on it, eerily bending the sound. Most wind sounds are borrowed and orchestrated in this way, but the wind certainly and clearly has a voice of its own. My wind has a cry of tempestuous anguish about it. The murmur of trees in a breeze is an evocative sound. Conifers are probably the most responsive and quite different in tone from the purring sheen of the wind in the willows. Out here, there are no trees for the wind to catch and play on.

The wind produces some of its most memorable effects once it reaches force 6, the beginning of a gale. Sailors were the first to quantify the wind with descriptive terms such as calm, breeze, gale and storm, but it was Francis Beaufort who in 1805 devised a scale that we still use today. His scale goes from 0 to 12, beginning at a wind speed too low to move a ship at all and ending with a speed too high for it to carry canvas. For a warship, this meant any wind speed greater than about 120 kilometres per hour. There are, of course, greater winds, both at sea and on land. I reckoned that my Castell-Dinas-Bran wind was about force 8 on Beaufort's scale, so between 60 and 80 kilometres per hour, described by the Met Office as one in which, 'twigs break off trees; generally impeding progress'.

About Music

The wind is an energy resource that can power industries; its energy can also be harnessed for instrumental purposes, for the primitive bull roarer and the more subtle Aeolian harp. Named after Aeolus, the ancient Greek god of the wind, the traditional Aeolian harp is a box with a sounding board and strings stretched lengthwise across two bridges. It is placed where the wind can blow across the strings to produce sounds. The strings can be made of different materials or thicknesses tuned to the same pitch, or identical strings can be tuned to different pitches. You can easily make an effective one using a cardboard box, a couple of pencils for bridges and fishing line for string.

Besides being the only strung instrument played solely by the wind, the Aeolian harp is the only stringed instrument that plays notes solely from the natural harmonic series. There is no percussive element to the sound such as that produced by a wind chime; rather, crescendos and decrescendos of harmonic frequencies are played in a synchronised rhythm with the wind. Their vibrant timbres produce an ethereal music that many find evokes a mystical experience. I like this instrument's purpose of cooperating with nature to extract music.

Henry Thoreau wrote in his poem, 'Rumours from an Aeolian Harp':

> *There is a vale which none hath seen*
> *Where foot of man has never been...*
> *And ever, if you hearken well,*
> *You still may hear its vesper bell,*
> *And tread of high-souled men go by,*
> *Their thoughts conversing with the sky.*

One of Britain's most spectacular elevated sites, 'Dinas Bran' is variously translated as 'Crow Castle', 'Crow City', 'Hill of the Crow', or 'Bran's Stronghold'. For the Celts, the crow was sacred and its name meant 'the flesh torn by fighting'. As it eats carrion, Welsh poetry uses the phrase 'the crow pierced you' to mean you have died. It was believed that crows escorted the sun during his nocturnal path, that is, as he traversed through hell.

The castle first appeared in 12th century historical documents as part of a medieval piece entitled *Fouke le Fitz Waryn*,

About Music

or The *Romance of Fulk Fitzwarine*. While this work claimed that the castle, known as 'Chastiel Bran', was in ruins as early as 1073, the remains today date to the occupation of the princes of Powys Fadog in the mid-13th century. Possibly the Chastiel Bran mentioned in the romance was a Norman timber castle, but nothing of substance supports this conjecture. However, the encompassing ditch and earthen embankments which enclose the southern and eastern portions of the stone fortress date to the Iron Age. They suggest that this hilltop had strategic value long before the princes of Powys or the Normans ventured into the region. Interestingly, the word Dinas has its origins in the Iron Age as well and is found in the names of Iron Age hill forts throughout Wales and which pepper the Clwydian Mountains that lie ahead on this inspiring journey.

Since the end of the 19th century, the idea of a piece of music as a journey has been superseded by several different approaches, each of which may create a musical landscape, rather than musical journey. Richard Strauss's tone poems, such as 'Also Sprach Zarathustra', are cited as the beginning of this musical revolution. Other landscape forms include, for example, the impressionist music of Debussy and, in more recent times, ambient New Age music which creates a particular mood, capturing and holding the listener in a meditative state.

The multifarious forms of music today mean that music has to be defined simply as organised sound. Any other definition would be too limiting. This widely encompassing definition is the result of composers moving beyond the boundaries imposed by classical music, with its focus on key centres, chordal progression and sense of musical travel. They have been able to experiment with new forms, new technologies, new sounds, new means of dissemination and this process continues.

With a broadened definition, a consequence is that what constitutes a piece of music is less clear. The borders between music and noise, music and sound, even music and silence have become blurred. Perhaps there is a physical equivalent of change and development taking place in the human brain as it become used to hearing music that simply would not have been possible to create a

About Music

century or so ago and subsequently our grey matter responds and adapts accordingly.

In recent times there has been a particular interest among composers in the role that silence and stillness play within the context of a piece of music. The most infamous experiment is John Cage's composition 4' 33" which consists entirely of silence. How can this possibly be called a piece of music as there is no sound to organise? In fact, there has never been a silent performance of this piece and Cage's intention was to alert the audience to this. There will always be shufflings, coughings, air-conditioner hum, vague traffic noises from beyond the hall and it is these ever-present vibrations that inform the music.

For music to be live, it must have not only a composer, but the collusion of a performer and an audience. Cage's composition depends on these random, unpredictable components. This music was experimental and there was, is, no possibility that it might spark off some new genre when composers would then all begin writing silent music. While walking, you can create your own 4' 33" at any time by stopping and listening.

More recently, John Tavener (1944-2013) has written a piece for double string quartet called 'Towards Silence'. This is understood as music having as its ultimate aim conclusion in silence, as we understand all music must. However, this piece's intention is to point to the oriental mystical belief that all comes out of nothing and all eventually returns to it. Some contemporary music, particularly in the second part of the twentieth century, creates in the listener the impression of a constant and ever-present silence that cradles the music, can penetrate it and interweave with the sound that we hear. Silence has become entwined in the form of music.

I spend some time battling with the far from silent and wind-torn atmosphere before beginning the descent on the hill's southern slope leading to Llangollen. The wind drops away with decreasing height for it was only interested in angrily blasting the top of the hill.

When I enter the town about half an hour later, I am returned to what I hesitate to call the real world. That evening I dine on fish and chips and drink a pint of beer in a pub with a large TV screen showing rock and pop hits from the seventies and eighties.
Bill, with a foot in two worlds

About Music

CHAPTER TWELVE

Romance and Revolution

In which all colour vanishes and magic mushrooms appear.

By the middle of the 18th century, European music reached the top of the hill. Like natural selection, it had been evolving towards its perfect form. Was it pointless to try to develop it further? Classical music was perfect. How, therefore, *could* it be improved? How *could* it develop further? This was the dilemma that composers faced and is a reason why, when they seemingly did the impossible and took music to even greater heights, it caused so much controversy. Ludwig van Beethoven (1770-1827) is not thought of as creating music that is particularly disturbing these days, but in his time he was a revolutionary.

There commenced a time of breaking down the barriers that were preventing musical evolution, barriers that had been erected by backward-looking classicism. So began a process that led to a multitude of new musical species, but before this plethora evolved, music had to become other than it was before.

🍄 Breaking the Offa's Dyke path into sections completed every couple of weeks or so means that when I began walking in May it was spring time and now, for this last stretch, returning to the Dyke again in September, it is early autumn. I have walked through spring and summer and into the autumn and have witnessed the seasonal changes in the countryside around me as I progress. At first, all was fresh and bright green. Then crops and fruits grew and ripened. Now the colour hues of green are darkening with yellows, reds and browns appearing everywhere. The fields are shorn of their crops and cattle are beginning to appear in their winter grazing territory in fields that had been left fallow over the summer to grow grasses and meadow flora, a valuable winter food source for the herd.

About Music

It has been a dry, warm summer and this is continuing in September. It is only recently though that I have noticed signs of the long dry season: grasses yellowing and streams drying up.

In history's seasons, classical as a generic term, refers to something that has stood the test of time and sets a standard of high quality but also which is uncluttered by unnecessary complexity. It is generally applied to the period of the ancient Greeks and Romans, more specifically to their architecture, art and literature.

In music, it refers to a period roughly covering the late 18th and early 19th centuries. The music then was characterised by its single melodic flowing lines supported by chordal and rhythmic progressions, contrasting with the complex polyphony of the previous era of the Baroque.

In all creative human endeavours, throughout Europe anyway, it is only in relatively recent times that reverence for the classical wisdom of the ancients was replaced by a questioning in art and science of everything that had gone before. This questioning of the old and a corresponding cult of the new is the essence of the 19th century Age of Enlightenment. Culture's face turned by 180 degrees from the past to the future.

European politics, philosophy, science and communications were radically reoriented during the course of the 'long 18th century' (1685-1815) as part of a movement referred to by its participants as the Age of Reason, or simply the Enlightenment. Enlightenment thinkers in Britain, in France and throughout Europe questioned traditional authority and embraced the notion that humanity could be improved through rational change. The American and French Revolutions were directly inspired by Enlightenment ideals and respectively marked the peak of its influence and the beginning of its decline.

In the years between 1789 and 1889, in France, a revolution was occurring. Heralded by a long and complex political and economic situation which had left the country bankrupt in both these areas, a National Assembly formed, its members took the 'Tennis Court Oath', swearing that they would not relent in their efforts until a new constitution had been agreed upon. The National Assembly's revolutionary spirit galvanised France, manifesting in a number of

About Music

different ways. In Paris, citizens stormed the city's largest prison, the Bastille, in pursuit of arms. In the countryside, peasants and farmers revolted against their feudal contracts by attacking the manors and estates of their landlords.

Dubbed the Great Fear, these rural attacks continued until the early August issuing of the August Decrees, which freed those peasants from their oppressive contracts. Shortly thereafter, the assembly released the Declaration of the Rights of Man and of the Citizen, which established a proper judicial code and the autonomy of the French people.

Though the National Assembly did succeed in drafting a constitution, the relative peace of the moment was short-lived. A rift grew between the radical and moderate assembly members, while the common labourers and workers began to feel overlooked. When Louis XVI was caught in a foiled escape plot, the assembly became especially divided. The moderate Girondins took a stance in favour of retaining the constitutional monarchy, while the radical Jacobins wanted the king completely out of the picture.

The first acts of the newly named National Convention were the abolition of the monarchy and the declaration of France as a republic. In January 1793, the convention tried and executed Louis XVI for treason. Meanwhile, and despite the creation of the Committee of Public Safety, the war with Austria and Prussia went poorly for France, and foreign forces pressed on into French territory. Enraged citizens overthrew the Girondin-led National Convention, and the Jacobins, led by Maximilien Robespierre, took control.

Backed by the newly approved Constitution of 1793, Robespierre and the Committee of Public Safety began conscripting French soldiers and implementing laws to stabilise the economy. For a time, it seemed that France's fortunes might be changing. But Robespierre, growing increasingly paranoid about counter-revolutionary influences, embarked upon a Reign of Terror in late 1793-94, during which he had more than 15,000 people executed at the guillotine. When the French army successfully removed foreign invaders and the economy finally stabilised, however, Robespierre no longer had any justification for his extreme actions, and he himself was arrested in July 1794, and executed.

About Music

The era following the ousting of Robespierre was known as the Thermidorian Reaction, and a period of governmental restructuring began, leading to the new Constitution of 1795 and a significantly more conservative National Convention. To control executive responsibilities and appointments, a group known as the Directory was formed. Though it had no legislative abilities, the Directory's abuse of power soon came to rival that of any of the tyrannous revolutionaries France had faced.

Meanwhile, the Committee of Public Safety's war effort was realising unimaginable success. French armies were making progress in nearly every direction, especially those led by the young general Napoleon Bonaparte. Napoleon's forces drove through Italy and reached as far as Egypt before facing a deflating defeat. In the face of this rout, and having received word of political upheavals in France, Napoleon returned to Paris. He arrived in time to lead a coup against the Directory in 1799, eventually stepping up and naming himself First Consul, effectively, the leader of France. With Napoleon at the helm, the Revolution ended and France entered a fifteen-year period of military rule.

It was ten years earlier, on 14th July, 1789, that the Bastille had fallen. Beethoven was then an eighteen-year-old court musician in Bonn, striving to support an intransigent family. Aware of this historic event, Beethoven subsequently matured through the period of the Terror and the temporary salvation of the French republic wrought by Napoleon Bonaparte. His musical mind was formed in this era of radical upheaval and change which was disastrous politically but proffered hope for humanity.

Beethoven's early music gave no indication of his subsequent contribution to the musical revolution which occurred a mere few years after that in Paris. So, what was the nature of this musical revolution that Beethoven forged?

Crucially, he used sonata form, not as fundamentally lyrical, as in the way of Haydn and Mozart, but as a heroic struggle. To affect this, he increased the importance of both the development section, which expounded the struggle, and the coda, which became a concluding victory celebration. Music then began to address itself to inspiring directly the individual in particular and to promoting the potential greatness of humanity in general. The individual would thus

About Music

struggle, suitably inspired, to achieve humanity's goal of freedom, equality and brotherhood: liberté, égalité, fraternité, with the promise after a heroic struggle of the final victory cadence.

For the Berlin writer-musician, Ernst Hoffman (1776-1822) Beethoven "opens up to us also the monstrous and the immeasurable". He "sets in motion the lever of fear, of awe, of horror, of suffering." Beethoven, addressing not the masses but the individual, leads us "forward into the spirit world of the infinite". Hoffman's name for this new application of music: Romanticism.

The medieval backward regard for the classicism of the ancients, expressed in classical music, became transformed in the Age of Enlightenment from an objective means of describing and celebrating the spiritual nature of the universe into a method for expressing the inner nature of man, fostered now in music by the emotional life of the composer.

Beethoven is particularly significant, not only because of his powerful works of self-expression which our musical senses can respond to quite dramatically, but because he ushers in the new age of romanticism in music. He achieves a music that comes from the depths of the composer's soul, revealing a pathway to appreciate the greatness of humanity and its universe through music. While science was banishing the subjective and striving to become completely objective in its view of reality, music, travelling a new stretch of its history, was doing the exact opposite by diving into the composer's self to find its creative source.

To begin this last stretch of the Offa's Dyke pathway, I return to Llangollen by train. This takes me first to Ruabon station and on the train, I chat with my fellow traveller. In appearance a cross between a hippy and a business man, he is sockless with sandals, a mop of black hair and a flourishing beard. On the table between us he has a high-tech laptop/tablet and mobile smartphone connected to the train's wireless signal and is efficiently tapping away. He sees my walking stick and rucksack and asks where I am going. I explain about the Dyke. I see he is wearing a sweat shirt with a Field Studies Council logo and in return ask him about this.

His interest in the countryside is professional and he tells me that today he is travelling to conduct interviews for new recruits. The

About Music

FSC believes the more we know about and take inspiration from the world around us the more we can appreciate its needs and protect its diversity and beauty for future generations. That's its remit and I'm all in favour of it. He leaves the train at the station before mine to conduct his business and I marshal my thoughts for the day ahead.

I step down from the train onto the deserted platform at rural Ruabon and soon catch a local bus that hurtles me along the road into Llangollen. It's a twenty-minute trip taken at breakneck speed along a curvy main road and when I eventually disembark and set foot on solid ground it feels as if a whirlwind had picked me up and flung me unsteadily but safely to the exact same spot on which I concluded the previous chapter.

I look around. I am invisible to the passers-by who go about their daily business, unconcerned. I turn towards Castell Dinas Bran and cannot see its top for it is shrouded in mist. I begin a walk back over this hill aiming to rejoin the Dyke's path on its other side. There then follows a slow, steep walk, up and over the summit – where has the wind gone? All is grey, still, expectant and quiet and in a while, I rejoin the Panorama Walk and am away along the final section of this whole project. It will be completed over the next four days, ending on the beach in Prestatyn after a trip through the Clwydian Mountains. Today's task is first to navigate the shale steeps of Trevor Rocks, then across moorland and woodland to the village of Llandegla where I'll find tonight's stopover.

The story of music has its own stopovers in particular forms and periods, but nevertheless always continues along an endless path. Romantic music developed over the course of a hundred years. During the 19th century, new forms emerged: the art song, (Lied) which combined Romantic poetry with voice and piano; stylised piano music such as the waltz, mazurka, polonaise, and étude (study piece); piano music in free form such as the fantasy, arabesque, rhapsody, romanza, ballade and nocturne; descriptive symphonic works such as the tone poem. Programmatic content was expressed in tone poems by Liszt and others and was found in symphonic works such as Berlioz's Symphony Fantastique and in piano music such as Mussorgsky's Pictures at an Exhibition.

About Music

The music of the Romantic period contained warm, personal melodies: expressive indications (*espressivo, dolce, con amore, con fuoco*) implied interpretive freedom (*rubato*) and new harmonic colour was heard in chords containing intervals of anguish such as the discordant ninth. Timbre was intensified by improvements in instruments, particularly the piano; performers carried the new music to emotional heights and depths with improved versions of their instruments.

The main ingredients of Romanticism are tragedy and loss with music becoming a language of the numinous and of feeling. It is music's great age of song, lyrical instrumentalism and emotional drama. Music became the new religion, a substitute for those whose certainties were being undermined by scientific enquiry; music in the home could be entertainment but also close to the act of prayer. In a universe becoming ever more complicated, the symphony offered a secure sense of a deeper knowledge, wholeness and fulfilment.

There developed the cult of the public celebrity musician who, in private, was a tortured soul able to offer showmanship and intimacy in equal measure. The idea of the musical genius was followed by the sudden arrival of a whole range of new and diverse talents, among them Chopin, Schumann, Berlioz, Rossini, Paganini, Liszt, Mendelssohn and Chopin, to name but a few.

Niccolo Paganini (1782-1840) was one of the first to benefit from public celebrity, performing stunts with his violin on stage. He would play complete works on just two strings and sometimes snap one deliberately mid-performance and still play the piece brilliantly.

Paganini earned large sums of money and indulged recklessly in gambling and on one occasion he was forced to pawn his violin. Having requested the loan of another from a wealthy French merchant so that he could fulfil an engagement, he was given a Guarnerius violin but later refused to take it back to the owner when the concert was over. The violin, Paganini's treasure, was bequeathed to the people of Genoa by the violinist and is still carefully preserved in that city. The Guarneri, often referred to in the Latinised form Guarnerius, is the family name of a group of distinguished luthiers from Cremona in Italy in the 17th and 18th centuries, whose standing is considered comparable to those of the Amati and Stradivari families. Some of the world's most famous violinists, including Paganini, have preferred Guarneris to Stradivaris.

Paganini's playing of tender passages was so beautiful that his audiences often burst into tears and yet he could perform with such force, speed and power that in Vienna one listener declared he had seen the Devil helping the violinist. His playing was so outrageously stunning that this rumour spread of how Paganini had made his pact with the Devil. When he died, the Church initially refused to allow his body to be buried in sanctified ground for this reason.

Robert Schumann (1810-56) and Clara Wieck (1819-96) are not only the ideal lovers for the audience of musical history, but their story is worthy of a high place in the romantic literature of the world. During their courtship, Schumann told his fiancé that "we will lead a life of poetry and blossom, and we will play and compose together like angels and bring gladness to mankind." That was pretty much what they did until the shadow of Schumann's mental illness fell.

Tragedy was never far away. Wieck was the leading piano professor in Leipzig and Schumann, determined to be a virtuoso of the keyboard, placed himself under Clara's tuition. While pretending to study law, he often practised at the piano for seven hours a day. Unluckily, the obstinate stiffness of that third-finger which gives trouble to all pianists set Schumann unloosening and developing the sinews with a mechanical invention of his own.

The contraption was simple enough, a cord through a pulley fastened to the ceiling of his room. By this means he could draw back his finger at will and prevent it from moving while the other fingers played. It was not only unsuccessful, it caused permanent injury to the hand such that Schumann had to abandon the idea of being a great pianist. The disappointment must have been intense and he took to composition as a remedial alternative. In the year of his marriage alone, he wrote 130 songs all characteristic, original, poetic and romantic.

The black cloak of tragedy eventually enveloped his mind until mental illness culminated in an attempt to commit suicide by throwing himself into the Rhine. He made occasional improvements but Clara was forbidden to visit him for it seemed to excite his emotions too greatly. Yet it was in her arms that he breathed his last

About Music

after two mournful years of seclusion. He was buried in Bonn, the birthplace of Beethoven and over his grave stands a monument, subscribed for by a wide circle of friends.

Composers became national heroes, heralding nationalism in music, for example, what Verdi was to Italy, Liszt became for his native Hungary. Composers became symbols of national identity and this role for them continued into the 20th century, culminating in the political propaganda music of Stalinist Russia and Nazi Germany.

♩ The walk, with a clear line dividing one national identity from another, continues along the road for a mile or so before branching off to the right and onto the scree path. I had seen pictures of this section before setting off and was prepared for an alien environment, a hillside of loose rocks with a path skirting the steep hillside. I was not disillusioned. In the mist, the scene is colourless, awash with many shades of grey and the edges of the mountainous shapes ill defined, as in a photograph whose edges have been soft focused. There is a strong sense of wilderness here, but the path although dizzying and narrow is quite safe and clear.

Occasionally I pass a stray rock plant or lonesome shrub clinging to the slope while acrobatic sheep watch me coming before hastily leaping out of the way at the last moment in disgust at the disturbance. I slow my pace to listen carefully but hear nothing except my own breathing and the scrape of my boots on the scree. Towering Craig Arthur dominates above as the path clings to its slopes, the heights inhabited no doubt by watchful kestrels and ravens keeping a secret sharp eye on my progress.

After another lengthy mile, the path descends and rejoins the narrow, metalled road at World's End in a wooded gully where a ford gushes across the road. It is a popular picnic spot and there are two walkers already resting and reviving their spirits. I cross the ford via stepping stones and emulate my two unwitting companions. Then, refreshed, I walk on past an old lime kiln up the hill, still keeping to the single-track road but now away from the trees and traversing a high wild moor, a place of unearthly, metaphysical beauty.

Music was no less metaphysical after Beethoven, but the search for transcendence turned inwards, rather than looking out into

About Music

the cosmos to perceive the music of the spheres. Composers had to search their souls while filling the role of public figure and misunderstood genius. Audiences were captivated by virtuosity. While Paganini dazzled, Darwin was sailing the Pacific on the Beagle. While Paganini fiddled, the cosmic links with the ancient world were being dismantled by scientific enquiry.

I take a sharp turn to the left to leave the road and begin to cross the moor. It has a reputation for being peaty and boggy although the long dry summer means that this is not an issue today. Stretching across this moorland, to help walkers in less friendly conditions, there is a narrow boardwalk, a snaking river of wooden planks on which to walk. These thread their way through the heather and bracken towards woodland on the horizon. As I walk, I hear the grumbling throaty sound of a red grouse. I cannot see it but it is out there somewhere.

The red grouse is a medium-sized game bird. It has a plump body, a short tail and a lightly hook-tipped bill. It is reddish-brown, with its legs and feet covered in pale feathers, ideal moorland plumage. Grouse breed in the UK in the uplands of the north and west and are resident all year round, travelling little in their lives. With an RSPB amber status, the population is declining, perhaps linked to diseases and the loss of heather moorland. Be wary, Mr Red Grouse, you are in season until 10th December. You may take cold comfort from the fact that you may not be shot between one hour after sunset and one hour before sunrise.

Moorland colours, particularly in the autumn, have always appealed to me. They are subtle, varied and blend well. I would happily wear these colours and indeed nature herself wears them as a mantle of light, not radiating from but seeming to rest upon the ground and somehow float in the air, too. Colours are pastel but permit a sudden bright dab of red or yellow to appear. The scene nature paints is wild and romantic.

Romanticism meant the cult of the artistic personality. Mozart and Haydn, while writing in their new and experimental styles, attempted to make their compositions more conventional than they themselves were; the Romantics were bent on creating the impression of being bold and original. The human scale was explicit in song form with deeply personal first-person accounts of loss and broken hearts, while instrumental music aimed to capture the emotions of the composer's struggles and sufferings.

In instrumental music, the human scale is overtly expressed through programmatic works, such as Beethoven's Pastoral and Tchaikovsky's Manfred Symphonies. In these programmatic pieces we are listening to the composer pondering, not the thing pondered.

The Pastoral Symphony has been forever linked to Beethoven's 5th Symphony thanks to the circumstances of their dual premiere. It would be unheard of today to programme both of these full-length symphonies in a single concert but that is exactly what happened back on December 22, 1808 at the Theatre an der Wein in Vienna. This historic performance included not only the 5th and 6th Symphonies but also the 4th Piano Concerto, a concert aria, excerpts from the Mass in C and the 'Choral Fantasy'. It was an under-rehearsed marathon of over four hours that had mixed results for Beethoven.

Regardless of the evening's effectiveness, the juxtaposition of the two symphonies is fascinating to consider. Though created simultaneously, they could not be more different. The 'Pastorale' is as gentle and subtle as the 5th is forceful and iconic. If the 5th opens with a clear statement of intent, the 6th whispers itself into life. The five movements of the 6th Symphony have titles that evoke specific scenes from country life and while much of the music seems descriptive, the composer cautioned that, "It is rather an expression of feeling than a pictorial representation." The disclaimer is unnecessary and, in some sections, possibly even inaccurate. The storm sequence in particular is as literal as a film score and has not been improved upon by any composer's weather music in the two centuries since. An example of the proscriptive movement notes will exemplify the need to explain to the listener what they *should* be able to hear:

> Movement I. Allegro ma non troppo. The symphony begins with a placid and cheerful movement depicting the composer's feelings as he arrives in the country. The work is in sonata form, and makes use of seven distinct motifs, each of which is extensively developed and transformed.

Movement II. Andante molto mosso. This movement, titled by Beethoven 'By the brook', is held to be one of Beethoven's most beautiful and serene compositions. At the opening, the strings play a motif that clearly imitates flowing water. The cello section is divided, with just two players playing the flowing-water notes on muted instruments, with the remaining cellos playing mostly pizzicato notes together with the double basses.

Toward the end of the movement, in the coda that begins at bar 124, there is a cadenza for three woodwind instruments that imitates bird calls at bar 130. Beethoven helpfully identified the bird species in the score: nightingale (flute), quail (oboe), and cuckoo (clarinet).

Movement III. Allegro. This is the scherzo movement of the symphony, which depicts country folk dancing and partying. It is in F major, returning to the main key of the symphony. The final return of Scherzo conveys a riotous atmosphere with a faster tempo. The movement ends abruptly when the country folk notice that raindrops are starting to fall.

Movement IV. Allegro. The fourth movement, in F minor, depicts a violent thunderstorm with painstaking realism, starting with just a few drops of rain and building to a great climax. There is, of course, thunder, as well as lightning, high winds and sheets of rain. The storm is eventually spent, with an occasional peal of thunder still heard in the distance. There is a seamless transition into the final movement, including a theme that could be interpreted as depicting a rainbow.

Movement V. Allegretto. The first eight bars form a continuation of the introduction of which the storm was the main part; the finale proper begins in the ninth bar. The movement is written in sonata rondo form which means that the main theme appears in the tonic key at the beginning of the development as well as the exposition and the recapitulation.

Like many classical finales, the final movement emphasises a symmetrical eight-bar theme, in this case representing the shepherds' song of thanksgiving. The mood throughout is unmistakably joyful. The coda starts quietly and gradually, builds to an ecstatic culmination for the full orchestra (minus "storm instruments"), with the first violins playing rapid dotted semi-quavers at the top of their range. There follows a fervent passage suggestive of prayer, marked by Beethoven *pianissimo, sotto voce*; most conductors slow the tempo for this passage. After a brief period of afterglow, the work ends with two emphatic chords.

Peter Ilich Tchaikovsky (1818-93) had an interest in religion that was largely aesthetic, but Balakirev, the Russian nationalist composer within whose orbital influence Tchaikovsky moved, had gone from being a free-thinker to a devout, if rather eccentric believer in a brand of Christianity under the influence of a soothsayer. Tchaikovsky had outgrown any need of Balakirev as a music teacher, but he was filled with a need for certainty in the face of overwhelming self-doubt and guilt at his homosexuality, so perhaps felt he had something to learn from Balakirev the mystic.

The domineering Balakirev suggested and acted as midwife to Tchaikovsky's ballet music, 'Romeo and Juliet'. At the same time, in the wake of Berlioz's second visit to Russia, the influential critic Vladimir Stasov suggested to Balakirev the idea of a symphony in the same vein as Berlioz's 'Harold in Italy' on another of Byron's works, 'Manfred'.

Tchaikovsky took a copy of Byron's poem to Switzerland and on reading it would have become aware of the subtext that is clear in Byron but absent from Stasov's programme: that Manfred's love for Astarte is almost certainly incestuous. A tortured soul wracked with guilt at forbidden passion chimed with Tchaikovsky and it was this conflation of Manfred's feelings with his own that finally provided the incentive to compose.

He found progress difficult, but by August 1885 he declared "this will perhaps be the best of my symphonic compositions." By the time of the première in March 1886, he was qualifying that "because of its difficulty, impracticability and complexity it is doomed to failure and to be ignored," and by 1888, he declared that "it is an abominable piece, and that I loathe it deeply, with the one exception of the first movement." This reflects the deep association he made between Manfred and his own troubles. It is perhaps significant that where Byron's Manfred dies refusing to submit to higher powers, Tchaikovsky's hero is granted absolution and dies peacefully, an act of forgiveness the composer was unable to grant himself. This is what the listener is being asked to discern in the music:

> Movement I. Lento lugubre - Moderato con animo. Manfred wanders in the Alps. Wearied by the fateful questions of life, tormented by the burning anguish of helplessness and by the memory of his criminal past, he feels cruel tortures to the soul. Manfred penetrates deeply into the secrets of magic and communicates imperiously with the mighty powers of hell, but neither these, nor anyone in the world can give him the oblivion which is the single thing he vainly seeks and begs for. A recollection of the lost Astarte, whom he once loved passionately, devours and gnaws at his heart and there is neither limit nor end to the boundless suffering of Manfred.
>
> Movement II. Vivace con spirit. The Alpine fairy appears to Manfred in the rainbow from the spray of the waterfall.
>
> Movement III. Andante con moto. Pastoral – a picture of the simple, poor, free life of the mountain dwellers.
>
> Movement IV. Allegro con fuoco. Underground devils of Ahriman. Infernal orgy. The appearance of Manfred amid the Bacchanal. Summoning and appearance of the shade of Astarte. He is forgiven. Death of Manfred.

About Music

As symphonies grew more and more personal, they became grander and more elaborate. Bruckner's symphonies are some of the longest and most complex ever written and in them we hear the artistic workings of the composer's psychological makeup. Bruckner's neuroses were manifold. One such was his obsession with numerology, like Pythagoras before and Schoenberg after, but in Bruckner's universe, number was something chaotic on which order had to be imposed.

There are many 19th-century composers who led 'romantic' lives but one other in particular is worthy of mention. Felix Mendelssohn (1809-47), pianist, conductor and composer, was blessed as a child prodigy and a career that brought him fame and fortune. Writing some of the most well-known programmatic music he is also credited with the revival of interest in and subsequent recognition of J.S. Bach's status in music's pantheon.

Bach's stature is so firmly established in Western culture that it is difficult to imagine that only a little over a century-and-a-half ago, his music and reputation languished in obscurity, virtually unknown to all but a few specialists. It was through Mendelssohn's recognition of Bach's genius and his efforts to make Bach's works accessible to a wider public that his works are today recognised as summits of musical expression and achievement.

Owing to the curious number of coincidences involving the crossed paths of members of both the Bach and Mendelssohn families, it was perhaps inevitable in retrospect that Felix Mendelssohn would rescue Bach's music from near oblivion. In 1823 (or possibly 1824), Felix's maternal grandmother, Bella Salomon, presented him with a gift that was to alter the course of his life: a copyist's manuscript score of Bach's St Matthew Passion. His first encounter with the full score of one of Bach's most profound works must have been nothing less than a revelation.

Despite Bach's generally unfavourable reputation at this time as little more than a musical mathematician, a putdown which would eventually become reinterpreted as his mastery of counterpoint and musical symmetry, and despite the complexity of the score and unfamiliarity of its language, Felix nevertheless conceived the idea of preparing the entire St Matthew Passion for performance.

About Music

Five years later, his dream was realised when an abridged version of the work prepared, rehearsed and conducted by Mendelssohn himself was performed at the Berlin Singakademie on March 11, 1829. For the first time in a century, the beauty of the St Matthew Passion was revealed to the German public, eliciting a response not unlike that experienced by the young Felix on seeing the work's score for the first time. He was only fifteen when he first saw the score of the Passion, and twenty when his efforts to perform the work were realised. This historic performance resulted in a full-scale revival and re-evaluation of Bach's works throughout Germany and beyond. There was a subsequent universal recognition of their genius and significance.

In May 1847, Mendelssohn's sister, Fanny, who was a life-long inspiration to him, died suddenly. Her death left him so devastated that he soon lost his own zest for life. His health, already compromised by a strenuous career, began to deteriorate rapidly. Six months later, on November 4, 1847, Felix Mendelssohn died of a ruptured blood vessel, in Leipzig, Germany. He had recently returned from a brief visit to Switzerland where he'd completed composition of his String Quartet in F Minor. Mendelssohn's romantic journey was at an end.

Music in the late 19th century become human centred, inward looking but outwardly expressive, a process fed by the demands of the paying, adoring public. Growing correspondingly was the inflated power of composers, such as Wagner and Verdi, as national figureheads. Music became dominated by an intellectual elite centred about the concert hall and the opera house, and institutions sprang up to accommodate them: "music is not for everyone, nor everyone for music" was the explanation of musicologist, Oliver Strunk. Thus, was born musical elitism and the musical snob and the suspicion with it that music might, in this context, be no more than a transient event, titillating romantic emotions while it lasted.

Unlike Mendelssohn's, my journey continues, the way ahead leading into Llandegla Woods. First, there is open sky above, then the woodland, the firs, becomes denser. The air is clear of mist but there is a permanent twilight here as I tread almost noiselessly on a thick acoustic blanket of light brown pine needles. I am startled by the sight of a brilliant red fungus... then another, then a group of them, then another patch. They are everywhere. Here be fairies and sprites, tempting the traveller to enter their world, as did Wonderland Alice, with a quick nibble on a hallucinogenic titbit.

The *amanita muscaria* or 'fly agaric' mushroom is stronger than the traditional 'liberty cap' and those who partake don't usually eat it raw as they can make their subject feel really with a risk of poisoning. They are commonly dried for making tea. The effects are to distort the senses – inanimate sounds, colours and objects take on a life of their own, and the sense of time can speed up or slow down. Perspective, both of space and time, becomes elastic, a most disturbing experience but which can be enjoyed depending on your frame of mind and attitude. I am tempted by the fairies but my intentions are elsewhere and my purpose lies along the path ahead. All I do is add to my photographic record and walk on, taking care at the forking path not to lose my way, retaining a sense of perspective and direction.

After the wood, there follows a field walk into Llandegla with signs of autumn everywhere: leaves aging, bracken dying back, grasses yellowing. As I walk into the village, I fancy I can hear Beethoven's Pastoral Symphony playing and reflect again on the passage of my route through spring, summer and now autumn, of how I have with experience eventually equipped myself properly with waterproofs – as yet untested to the full – boots, cap and stick and an efficient rucksack. The path reaches a steep bank and a metal gate with the now familiar label Llwybr Clawdd Offa wrought into its ironwork.

Llandegla derives its name from the 8th-century Saint Tegla and has a well dedicated to her. The Welsh connection is obscure as she was a nun of the Benedictine order at Wimborne in Dorset, who travelled to the continent – about the time of the Dyke's construction - to aid Boniface's missionary work.

The evening in Llandegla is worth a mention for two reasons. First, I am 'camping' in a tiny but futuristic wooden pod about the size of a largish tent, constructed next to the sparkling River Alun. The pods are in the grounds of a house that is open for guests to use the facilities, bathroom, kitchen, etc., so this offers a half-way experience between camping and B&B. The pod is equipped with a made-up camp bed, a lamp and a small heater, unnecessary in today's mild conditions. It has a veranda with a couple of chairs and a table and a river a few meters from its front door, with unseen otters and kingfishers, but – seen as I arrive – a pair of dippers plying their trade up and down the waters.

Secondly, I walk through the deserted village in the evening to seek food. I imagine to myself that round this corner, just ahead, is a burger and pizza bar, the sort that you might find in a large town or city. It has a license to serve cool lagers and has comfy seating. The service there is excellent and friendly and the price within my budget. As I walk around this corner, my fantasy becomes a complete reality. I do a double take, wonder if I had nibbled those magic mushrooms after all, enter the door of the Willow restaurant and order my burger and beer.

The beer is a light lager, chilled. It comes from the Wrexham brewery and is the oldest lager in the country. Not my particular one, you understand, but the ideal waters of the town lent themselves many years ago to creating what is still a most delicious, refreshing brew.

Bill, having had one too many

About Music

CHAPTER 13

Contemporary Sounds

In which we spend time on the bald mountain and heed nature's call.

The revolution in music that took place at the beginning of the 20th century is sending out its echoes like the remnant radiations of the big bang. This musical explosion affected everything in its path but eventually the fragmenting remains began to coalesce and reform in new ways. A diverse musical universe was created that would be unrecognisable to someone living in the previous century, let alone any era before that.

The stigma attached to experimental music, the rampant use of dissonance, the destruction of classical forms, the abandonment of tonal centres and the making of serial music, the use of sounds other than those made by violins, flutes and horns, etc., the advent of electronically synthesised sounds, recording and sound reproduction techniques, the worship of the new, the rise of nationalism in music, the lack of regard for audiences, all this meant a certain alienation, which still rubs off on the music-loving, paying public of today. Contemporary music is generally regarded as difficult if not downright unpleasant. Much of it is. Much of it is not meant to be 'nice'.

A history of 20th-century music will cite significant political and social catastrophes and their seismic influence on music. Hitler's war on the Jews, blacks and gypsies left a legacy of unrecoverable musical lives and talent and influenced a shift of music's centre of gravity from Europe to North America, but music, of course still continued to be made in Europe.

In the wake of World War II, it is sensible to separate the music of composers, such as Wagner, from the views of the man or woman, but for Wagner in particular his anti-semitism and the sponsoring of his cause by powerful Nazi cognoscenti could not be summarily dismissed. It is the plot for the opera Parsifal that most readily acquired an unfortunate racial significance. Parsifal is an opera in three acts by Richard Wagner. It is loosely based on Parsifal by Wolfram von Eschenbach, a 13th-century epic poem about the Arthurian knight Parsifal and his quest for the Holy Grail.

In the opera's story, King Amfortas, King of the Grail Knights, suffers an intractable fatal wound, which appears after he succumbs to the mysterious Kundry. She is both the devoted messenger of the Grail knights and a dangerous seductress in the power of Klingsor, a failed knight now determined to undermine the order which is charged with looking after the goblet from which Jesus drank at the Last Supper and which was then used to collect his blood as he died on the cross. Kundry has been condemned to live forever because she mocked Christ at the crucifixion and now desires only death and redemption.

Amfortas might be the modern German whose blood has mixed with inferior races. Kundry is a female version of the Wandering Jew who laughed at Christ on His way to the Cross and is now condemned to wander the earth. Only Parsifal, by remaining pure of blood, is able to regain the lance that pierced Christ's side and preside over the healing of the company of the Grail. As Parsifal holds the spear aloft, Kundry falls dead.

Wagner's personal rantings had a malicious intensity. The Jews, he once said, were "the born enemy of pure humanity and all that is noble in man." Another phrase often used by Goebbels in his speeches came from the pen of Wagner: the Jews were, he said, the "plastic demon of the ruin of mankind."

Stalin's oppressive regime (1924-53), like the Third Reich, made specific use of music as propaganda and used the Terror as the means to make internationally known composers, such as Shostakovich and Prokofiev, toe the party line and submit to its definition of what music should be. The Terror grew from Stalin's paranoia and his desire to be an absolute autocrat. It was enforced via the NKVD, the Soviet Union's police force, and public show trials that developed into a centrally-enforced cult of Stalin-worship and a terrifying system of labour camps, 'the gulag'.

When the Soviet Union fought for its survival in the early 1940s against the invading German military, it was a Shostakovich symphony around which the battle for Leningrad pivoted. Besieged Leningrad heard the symphony on 9th August, 1942. The

About Music

circumstances of its performance were intensely dramatic, unimaginable even. Only fifteen musicians turned up for the first rehearsal and as a result all competent musicians were ordered to return from the front lines. The players would break from rehearsals to return to duties which included the digging of mass graves for victims of the city's siege. Three members of the orchestra died of starvation before the symphony's premiere. The Germans planned to disrupt the performance but the Soviets made a pre-emptive bombardment of German positions. An array of loudspeakers then broadcast the *Leningrad* symphony into the silence of no-man's-land. The music was used to strike a blow against German morale.

It is worth recording that the day of Stalin's funeral in March 1953 was also that of Prokofiev who had suffered so badly at the hand of his master and whose coffin had to be moved around streets blocked by crowds and tanks. As the masses moved towards the Hall of Columns, where Stalin's body had been on view, Prokofiev's body was carried in the opposite direction down an empty street. The Soviet leadership had ordered every florist in Moscow to send all of their flowers to Stalin's funeral. Prokofiev's family had none for his funeral and had to drape his casket with paper flowers. Sadly, too, every musician in Moscow was ordered to perform at Stalin's funeral so none could be found to play at Prokofiev's. His family listened to a recording of the funeral march from his 'Romeo and Juliet.' Heroically, Shostakovich was amongst the composer's mourners.

After World War II, American occupying forces in Western Germany waged war on the censorship in music that the Third Reich had imposed. For pre-defeated Germany, it was Wagner and Richard Strauss who represented the music that was OK, while modernism had been side-lined. In response to this, the American occupiers attempted to reintroduce both the music of composers who had been deemed inappropriate (Jewish) or meaningless (Schoenberg). Concerts became laden with Mendelssohn on the one hand and somewhat unentertaining modern fare on the other.

The project of freeing the German mind went by the term 're-orientation'. Anything that could be employed to degrade the concept of Aryan cultural supremacy was promoted, from jazz to international contemporary music. One result was the emphasising of a split that still exists today between popular music (traditional, romantic, classical) and difficult music (contemporary, atonal).

There is another factor to consider here in following the path music was taking in the 20th century and that is the situation of post-World-War-II composers. Many had witnessed grave atrocities and sights that would naturally wound, in the manner of Amfortas, their inner being and the music that they subsequently wrote.

Luciano Berio, an Italian composer, noted for his experimental work and for his pioneering work in electronic music, was conscripted into the army of Mussolini's Republic of Salò and nearly blew off his right hand with a gun that he did not know how to use.

Iannis Xenakis, a Greek-French composer, music theorist and architect-engineer is commonly recognised as one of the most important post-war avant-garde composers. Xenakis joined the Greek Communist resistance and at the end of 1944 a British shell landed on a building where he was hiding; after watching a comrade's brains splatter against a wall, he passed out and awoke to find that his left eye and part of his face were gone.

Stockhausen, working in a mobile hospital behind the western front reported, "I would try to find an opening in the mouth area for a straw in order to pour some liquid into these men, whose bodies were still moving, but there was only a yellow ball-like mass where the face should have been." It is hardly surprising that the music of Stockhausen is a little weird, that Xenakis did not write tunes and that some post-war music has a reality at its core which makes it discomforting to hear.

Music from the romantic period, from today's perspective another universe and once a hot and happening cauldron of fermenting ideas and vigorous expression, is providing the innocuous light music of our world; it has become wallpaper, merged into the background. It has become so through over familiarity, through piped music in supermarkets, dental surgeries and restaurants, through advert-driven radio stations. The result is a cheapening of classical music, but it is not down and out. The endless striving for high standards and perfection continues: audiences still listen to the classical and romantic repertoires; their CDs and downloads sell, above all else because those audiences are attracted by and lulled by

About Music

a sense of knowing what to expect: soothing familiarity, stress-relieving adagios and andantes; the certainty of the final forté chord.

This is not what contemporary music can or should be providing, if it is to be an art form that has some relationship with the real world. It is a consequent fact that contemporary music suffers from lack of exposure and would naturally benefit from more. Promisingly though, for the uninitiated who may be tempted, with repeated listenings, even the angular tunes of Harrison Birtwistle become hummable. So, for music, where to from here? One way leads through the refined, academic and technological world, where newness and complexity are the key words, or there is the natural world to turn to for inspiration.

I wake and dress, thrust open the door of the wooden camping pod and listen to the river sounds coming from a few meters away. There is a chill in the air. The pod next to mine is empty; its inhabitants, two men, have left already on their long day's trek to Bodfari. I'll be following them in an hour or so, but I've split this next stage into two sections so that I'll be arriving in Bodfari tomorrow afternoon. The way will be mountainous and I know that when they arrive at their destination tonight, they will be exhausted. I want to take more time to think and enjoy. I'm hoping this will be one of the great experiences of the whole of the Offa's Dyke path and it will need savouring.

In the house, while I breakfast on toast and coffee, a TV is burbling away in the corner of the kitchen with news ticker-taping about the Scottish referendum. The result has just come in, 45/55 in favour of remaining in the UK.

Life is an endless process of setting up borders and barriers, physical and psychological, then knocking them down and redrawing them. That's a part of this project, but patrolling the borders of music, not with any intention of obliterating them, only looking to see where a barrier may be moved or opened up. When western music hit the twentieth century, revolution occurred as in all walks of life and borders were redrawn everywhere.

Previous musical eras can be neatly – and often misleadingly – compartmentalised to describe their historical development:

About Music

Ancient to Medieval to Renaissance, leading to Baroque, to Classical, to Romantic. Then, all walls crumble and any attempt to follow a straight timeline through the 20th century is doomed to failure as the evolutionary tree branches, branches and branches again in an exponentially fruiting mathematical function. My ramblings concept here comes into its own, for this approach can follow whichever branch seems fruitful, then jump to another at will. So, it is my intention over this section to consider some of the unique properties of contemporary music, what makes it characteristic of our time, and ramble on about one or two quirky representatives who influenced the course of its chequered history.

What in particular represents music of the 20th and 21st centuries? Much is clearly driven by social and political forces, but from the point of view of the individual composer, and the listener, it is more basic than this. New ways to make, record and listen to music meant that the lure of exploration and experiment was opened up first to the privileged and lucky, then, eventually, literally, to almost anyone. Experiment is the century's watch word.

The changes in music were so overwhelming and fast that it has taken until our own time before any possibility of assessing and seeing clearly what was going on. Not only were never-before-heard types of music emerging but the understanding changed of what music can be. As in the realm of the emerging quantum physics, any definition was – is – not only difficult to pin down, but turns out to be contradictory, or at least to beg further questions.

For example, the definition of music as organised sound takes a hit when you consider who or what might do the organising: a human, a machine, natural forces, an artificial intelligence? And how much chance can be allowed in before a piece of music might become random noise? These were questions that drove the experimental nature of contemporary music.

🌰 The gentle River Alyn leads me out of Llandegla and away through the fields to the north east. I meet one or two early dog-walkers but then am alone again as the path eventually works its way to the Clwydian foothills. In the distance, outlined in the grey, misty skies, the mountainous shape of Moel y Plas emerges. At the beginning of its slope the track is wide and grassy, with a wood to

About Music

my right. There is a climb towards the summit but the track skirts just short of the top then drops down to cross a minor road before the ascent up the next peak, Moel Llanfair. In the midst of this misty, moody atmosphere, my breathing becomes deeper and more rapid, there is a regular rhythm to both heart-beat and step and my mind opens to receive free-flowing thoughts about the spirit of music.

Edgard Varèse (1883-1965), my first representative today, appears before me. A French composer who spent much of his working life in the USA, Varèse is probably the first composer to talk about music in terms of organised sound. The idea germinated in his mind at the turn of the century following an encounter with the writings of the physicist, musicologist and philosopher, Hoene Wronski, who defined music as, 'the corporealisation of the intelligence that is in sounds'. Wow!

Varèse's music emphasises timbre and rhythm. His conception of music reflected his vision of "sound as living matter" and of "musical space as open rather than bounded". He conceived the elements of his music in terms of 'sound-masses', likening their organisation to the natural phenomenon of crystallisation. Varèse thought that "to stubbornly conditioned ears, anything new in music has always been called noise", and he consequently posed the question, "what is music but organised noises?"

Although his complete surviving works only last about three hours, Varèse has been recognised as an influence by several major composers of the late 20th century. He saw potential in using electronic media for sound production and his use of new instruments and electronic equipment led to him being dubbed the Father of Electronic Music, while Henry Miller described him as "The stratospheric Colossus of Sound".

Typical of Varèse's work, Poème électronique is an eight-minute piece of electronic music written for the Philips Pavilion at the 1958 Brussels World's Fair. The Philips corporation commissioned the pioneer of modern architecture, Le Corbusier, to design the pavilion, which was intended as a showcase of their engineering progress. Le Corbusier came up with the title Poème électronique, saying he wanted to create a "poem in a bottle". Varèse composed the piece with the intention of creating a liberation between sounds and as a result used noises not usually considered musical throughout the piece.

The pavilion was shaped like a stomach, with a narrow entrance and exit on either side of a large central space. As the audience entered and exited the pavilion, the electronic composition Concret PH by Iannis Xenakis, who also acted as Le Corbusier's architectural assistant for the pavilion's design, was heard. Poème électronique was synchronised to a film of black and white photographs selected by Le Corbusier which touched on themes of human existence.

This was music living on the furthest reaches of the musical cosmos. It is worth taking a step back at this juncture from the post-war modernist, experimental period to consider more of the forces at work at the beginning of the 20th century which filtered through to influence Varèse and beyond. Schoenberg is credited with bringing dissonance, chaos and difficulty into music, but in fact his music was still composed within the forms of classicism and is highly structured. He simply wanted to escape from the burden of romantic expressionism and return to the purer music that went before. He may seem entirely forward looking and destructive of the old principles but his genius was as a musical Janus in forging a new 20th-century way while keeping a firm hold on the past.

The wish to explore worlds outside the boundaries of normal experience was the force behind Schoenberg's abandonment of tonality and Stravinksky's emphasis on rhythm. This was a psychological approach to music. Sigmund Freud and Carl Jung were the leading psychoanalysts of their time delving into the hidden functioning of the human mind, into the mysterious realm of the unconscious, into dreams and the psychological forces that battle with our free wills and often hold sway. It was into the depths of the human psyche, as described by Freud and Jung, that these composers journeyed, perhaps mindful of Schopenhauer's philosophy that human salvation and enlightenment could only be found by tunnelling inwards.

The psychological exploration of the mind had a clear influence on the visual arts and this in turn corresponded with and influenced the course of music. Abstract art uses a visual language of shape, form, colour and line to create a composition which may exist

About Music

independently from visual references in the world. Music, as we have seen, is the purest form of abstract art, but there are other crossovers.

Expressionism was a modernist art movement, initially in poetry, painting and film, but then in music, too, originating in Germany at the beginning of the 20th century. Its typical trait is to present the world solely from a subjective perspective, distorting it radically for emotional effect in order to evoke moods and ideas. This is very different from romanticism and is a pure expression of the inner world of the artist/composer without the weepings and wailings of emotional expression in romanticism. Schoenberg was an expressionist.

A culmination in the visual arts of this inner exploration and psychological adventure was achieved by the school of Abstract Expressionism (The New York School of the 1950s) within which there were two broad groupings. These were the so-called action painters led by Jackson Pollock and William De Kooning, and the colour-field painters, notably Mark Rothko, Barnett Newman and Clyfford Still.

The action painters worked in a spontaneous improvisatory manner often using large brushes to make sweeping gestural marks. Pollock, 'Jack the Dripper', famously placed his canvas on the ground and danced around it, pouring paint directly from the can or trailing it from the brush or stick. In this way, the artists transferred a representation of their psyche's inner impulses onto the canvas. The paint brush was a sort of gramophone needle following the grooves of the painter's psyche, equivalent to the vinyl disc, while the end result, the painting, a visual soundscape, is a snapshot of the artist's unconscious and its psychological complexes at work.

The colour-field painters were interested in religion and myth. They created compositions with large areas of a single colour intended to produce a contemplative or meditative response in the viewer. In this respect the suicidal painter, Mark Rothko (1903-70), and his composer friend, Morton Feldman, made a holy alliance. Feldman wrote a beautiful, commemorative piece on the posthumous opening of the Rothko Chapel in 1971 in Houston Texas, the chapel containing an octagonal array of Rothko paintings. Feldman's dedication was simply called, Rothko Chapel.

About Music

Founded by Houston philanthropists John and Dominique de Menil, the chapel was dedicated as an intimate sanctuary available to people of every belief and faith and welcomes over 60,000 visitors each year. The mission of the Rothko Chapel is to inspire people to action through art and contemplation, to nurture reverence for the highest aspirations of humanity and to provide a forum for global concerns.

Not everyone can visit in person, but Feldman's music will take you there. It is one of his most accessible works, lasting around 25 minutes for chamber choir (but having no words), viola, celeste and other percussion. As a sparse, meditative piece, it might be described as minimalist, a word coined later by composer Michael Nymann to identify a new musical genre. The last part of the piece features an achingly beautiful, simple, tonal viola solo which sits on top of a background of meditative sonic dissonance.

I recall Carl Jung's description of the collective unconscious as everything that seems to be 'not us'. The consequence of this definition is that it signifies, at bottom, that the unconscious is the physical world, our bodies and the world we see around us. Far from being a mysterious intangible entity, the unconscious has a physical reality that we can touch and see.

I see a mountainous wilderness. The Clwydian Hills - 'mountains' is an exaggeration - are formed from an upstanding block of Silurian-age sandstones, mudstones and siltstones. The range's rocks are intensely faulted; the major Vale of Clwyd Fault is responsible for the impressive west-facing scarp of the Clwydian Range. It has thrown down rocks to the west and separates the younger Carboniferous and Permo-Triassic rocks of the Vale of Clwyd from those of the hills.

There is a succession of peaks along this route and each is characterised with a topping of tumulus or hillfort. The path tends to skirt the summits to avoid erosion to these precious prehistoric sites. The tumuli were burial mounds dating from the Bronze Age, about 4,000 years ago. Often, ancient sacred sites such as these will contain a burial at their centre and sometimes cremations added in later. They are located in these upland centres so that the descendants of those buried could visit and be reminded of their ancestral roots.

About Music

Somewhere in the low-lying land will be the settlement built by the farmers who used these burial mounds.

Hillforts, defended enclosures, can also date from the Bronze Age, but most in Britain were constructed during the later Iron Age. Hillfort can be a misleading term for many were neither built for fortification purposes, nor on hills. An enclosed space is a more general but accurate description. Some, however, were built on hill tops, which held a special fascination for the prehistoric mind. Being in this place, it is easy to imagine why. The sight of towering hills is humbling, while overlooking the valley from a hill top evokes a sense of how the gods might see the world from their lofty vantage point. Here, one can be both human and cosmic, can contemplate our little lives far below, then look up and beyond to the infinite.

In all pieces of music composed by the 1950s avant-garde, the initial material (for example, the tone row) and the system that produces a structure for it (for example, Neoclassicism) have to be devised by the composer. For John Cage, this was not radical enough: "The composer must give up the desire to control sound, clear his mind of music and set about discovering means to let sounds be themselves rather than the vehicle for man-made theories of expression of human sentiments." Cage was certainly continuing along the expressionist path but now not even allowing Schoenberg his backward glance. He was challenging not only how new music might be created but how it should be perceived by the listener.

Meanwhile, the recording studio was becoming an editing suite, rather than a place where music was merely played and recorded. This led to two creative techniques in particular. With the invention of magnetic tape, collage in sound became possible, a technique that had been introduced into modern art by Picasso almost 40 years earlier. This gave the listener multiple audio view-points, removing the experience of observing from a single location in space, another quantum-type effect. The technique, developed at the end of the 1940s, was to record sounds, alter them in any way desired and then edit them into a montage.

The second technique was to make music from natural sounds, a process pioneered by French composers, which became known as musique concrète. This was a way of composing by incorporating and expressing real sounds: the sounds of the street, the city, the natural sounds created by any means, including musical instruments but no longer limited to them. The original exponents were Pierre Schaeffer and Edgar Varèse, who paved the way for experimental music of all kinds.

Contrasting with the natural sounds of music concrete were the Cologne composers such as Stockhausen and Xenakis. Herbert Eimert created a studio at Cologne Radio, in 1951, a centre for a whole generation of composers specialising in electronic music whose sounds were the equivalent of the oils of a palette, rather than being like clipped up bits of newspaper or the 'found' items of music concrete.

The German composer, physicist and acoustician, Werner Meyer-Eppler (1913-60), believed that, with electronic music, the composer would be similar to the visual artist, in that he would compose directly to tape, with the results then laid before the general public, like an artist exhibiting his canvasses. In fact, all of these new techniques, found sound, montage, music concrete, electronic music, far from being in competition were all – and there were more to come - applied with the expressionist intention of portraying the human psyche. The pioneers of Paris and Cologne laid the foundations of modern music, mainstream or otherwise, pop or academic.

The hill walking begins in earnest with views over heather-covered moorland, high pastures, crystal clear streams and both broad-leaved and conifer woodland. In the distance are the mighty mountains of Snowdonia. I have a sense that this is what I was made for and where I should be, a feeling of being at the right place at the right time, dare I say, at one with the world. All I need to do is walk.

I halt on Moel Llanfair and am struck by how much noise I make when I walk: percussive footsteps, rustling clothes, the in- and out-take of breath, none of these loud in the common sense of the word, but when they cease and you can then hear the natural sounds of birds, a breeze in the heather or the wind draughting up a hill, perhaps the tinkle of a spring, the buzz of a bee, those crude personal sounds are more than enough to hide those emanating from the subtle complexity of the natural soundscape.

About Music

There is another call of nature that I must heed and at the very moment when I am in full sway another walker hoves into view and I hurriedly compose myself again. At the only moment when I need privacy, in an environment which screams out solitude in every direction of the compass, I manage somehow to conjure up the presence of a fellow human traveller. We exchange cursory greetings, both mine and his a little self-conscious, then continue along our chosen paths.

The walking is relaxed and effortless. I must be getting fit, or maybe I'm just on a high. The paths are well defined and their direction easy to discern as the view is clear for a long way ahead. For these reasons, mountain paths are, in good weather, generally more relaxing to navigate confidently than any low-lying farmland.

There is another area where experiment was taking place in music and that was in the field of improvisation. In the defining words of author David Stubbs, "... free Improv continues on its bloody-minded course to nowhere in particular, forever making something out of absolutely nothing." For many listeners, there is much in composed and prescriptive contemporary music that would also fit this description.

AMM was a British free-form jazz group which began in the 1960s. AMMusic, the title of their first 1967 album, was the result of a collective reflection on what it meant to make music. The music itself was spontaneous and unscripted: no melodies, no themes, no regular pulse, simply exploratory playing, punctuated with silences when the players gathered themselves for the next stormy outpouring. This was music responsive to its own needs, with no individual spotlighting, a true musical collective. The idealism of AMM was apolitical but eventually its sense of free improvisation created a metaphor for a way of living that had much in common with communism. This moved to the core of the music for two members, Keith Rowe and Cornelius Cardew (1936 – 1981).

Cardew was a friend and contemporary of the composer and pianist Richard Rodney Bennett at the Royal Academy of Music, where the two nineteen-year-olds had caused a stir by giving the first UK performance of Pierre Boulez's 'Structures Book 1 for Two Pianos'. While Bennett would go on to study with Boulez, Cardew would study with Stockhausen, later becoming his assistant and collaborating on his 1960 composition, 'Carré'. By then Cardew was already writing music of great originality and had begun the 'February Pieces', arguably his finest piano music.

Cardew was particularly prominent in introducing the works of American experimental composers such as Morton Feldman, La Monte Young and John Cage to an English audience during the early to late sixties onwards. In 1966, Cardew joined AMM as cellist and pianist. Performing with the group allowed him to explore music in a completely democratic environment, freely improvising without recourse to scores.

While teaching an experimental music class at London's Morley College in 1968, Cardew, along with Howard Skempton and Michael Parsons formed the Scratch Orchestra, a large experimental ensemble, initially for the purpose of interpreting Cardew's 'The Great Learning'. The Scratch Orchestra gave performances throughout Britain and elsewhere until its demise in 1972. It was during this period that the question of 'art for whom?' was hotly debated within the context of the Orchestra which Cardew came to see as elitist, despite its numerous attempts to make socially accessible music.

Through the Scratch Orchestra, Howard Skempton met numerous composers and performers, including Christopher Hobbs, John White and various Systems artists, and the pianist John Tilbury. However, tensions arose during the politicising of the Scratch Orchestra in the early 1970s when Cardew and a number of other important members pushed the ensemble in a Marxist direction. Skempton, Hobbs, Parsons, White and many others refused to be associated with this political line and the break-up of the Orchestra was accompanied by (in Parson's words), "a split between its 'political' and 'experimental' factions."

In 1974, Skempton and Michael Parsons formed a duo to perform their own works. The 1980s saw an increase of interest in Skempton's music, which led to more commissions and permitted him to compose more for larger forces. 'Lento', an orchestral work composed in late 1991, became one of his most widely recognised pieces. In the 1990s, important recordings of his works started

About Music

appearing, such as a disc of piano music recorded by his old friend and former Scratch Orchestra colleague, John Tilbury.

Cardew died on 13 December, 1981, the victim of a hit-and-run car accident near his London home in Leyton. The driver was never found. Musician John Tilbury, in his book *Cornelius Cardew – A Life Unfinished* suggests that the possibility that Cardew was killed because of his prominent Marxist-Leninist involvement, "cannot be ruled out". Tilbury quotes a friend of Cardew's, John Maharg, "MI5 are quite ruthless; people don't realise it. And they kill pre-emptively."

There follows a succession of peaks: Moel y Plas; Moel Llanfair; Moel Gyw; Moel Eithinen; Foel Fenlli. By now and rather late in the day, I have realised that 'Moel' and 'Foel' probably mean hill, but there is more to it than this. Both words can be variously translated as 'bald', 'bare' or 'stark', as well as hill. The implication is that these peaks are places empty of purpose and void of any sense of compromise towards the visitor. This is a description that could be applied to much contemporary music. They are what they are and will never be other than bald, bare and stark. Having looked only cursorily into the meaning of 'Moel' and 'Foel', I conclude that these words in this context are probably best left untranslated.

Here are some other Welsh words that the borderland walker may find helpful:

Bach, fach, small	Dyffryn, valley
Bryn, hill	Llwybr, way or path
Bwlch, pass	Llyn, lake
Caer, gaer, fort	Llys, hall or palace
Cefn, ridge	Maen, stone
Clawdd, dyke	Mawr, fawr, big
Coed, wood	Melin, mill
Du, black	Nant, stream
Dwr, water	Pont, bridge
	Ty, house

About Music

Naturally, it is the relationship of landscape to music that interests me. Brian Eno, one of the principal innovators of ambient music, once summarised minimalism as "a drift away from narrative and towards landscape, from performed event to sonic space." I can quite see that the landscape which surrounds me is a symbol of the self, the mountains, forests and rivers all a pictorial representation of the inner world of the collective unconscious, a land inhabited by archetypal forces, psychological complexes, gods and goddesses, both old and new.

The corporeal landscape has been a rich source of inspiration for composers, not least in modern times. John Luther Adams, born in 1953, is an American composer (not to be confused with the more widely known John Coolidge Adams) whose music is inspired by nature, especially the landscapes of Alaska where he has lived since 1978. His orchestral work, 'Become Ocean', was awarded a Pulitzer Prize for Music in 2014. The title clearly suggests the wholeness that can be achieved between inner and outer landscapes.

The Place Where You Go to Listen is a unique sound and light environment created by Adams in The Museum of the North, on the grounds of the University of Alaska in Fairbanks. This ever-changing musical ecosystem gives voice to the rhythms of daylight and darkness, the phases of the moon, the seismic vibrations of the earth and the dance of the aurora borealis, in real time. The title refers to Naalagiagvik, a place on the coast of the Arctic Ocean where, according to legend, a spiritually attuned Inupiaq woman went to hear the voices of birds, whales and unseen things around her.

Is it music? The Place Where You Go to Listen is an acoustic soundscape controlled by natural events occurring in real time and, having been designed and set in motion by the composer, its organisation depends on no human being. However, the events which it represents are not random, occurring within long, repeating cycles of sun, moon and seasons. The result deserves an audience who may listen with the reverence accorded by Naalagiagvik for her own sonic experience. Adams describes his music not as abstract but as corporeal, echoing Wronski's definition of music as, "the corporealisation of the the intelligence that is in sounds".

About Music

Björk (1965-), like Adams, another composer/creator from the cold northern lands, has been similarly inspired by her own Icelandic landscape to create Biophilia, her eighth studio album, a concept album with its references to the linking points between nature, music and technology. The album was announced as a multimedia project, released alongside application software that linked the themes of the songs, which deal with nature, to musicology concepts.

An electronica album, Biophilia features influences of avant-garde music, alternative dance and experimental music in most of its tracks. Bjork attracted what, superficially, was an unlikely collaboration with the naturalist and broadcaster, Sir David Attenborough.

The term 'biophilia' literally means love of life or living systems. It was first used by Erich Fromm to describe a psychological orientation of being attracted to all that is alive and vital. Edward O. Wilson popularised the hypothesis in his book, *Biophilia* (1984) where he defines biophilia as "the urge to affiliate with other forms of life". Wilson uses the term in the same sense when he suggests that biophilia describes "the connections that human beings subconsciously seek with the rest of life." He proposed the possibility that the deep affiliations humans have with nature are rooted in our biology. Unlike phobias, which are the aversions and fears that people have of things in the natural world, philias are the attractions and positive feelings that we have towards our natural surroundings.

I have been writing about some of the 20th century's most offbeat but influential composers and my final choice for an odd-ball who disproportionately influenced the course of our music is Harry Partch (1901-74), an American musical hobo who made his own version of ramblings about music. Partch took his music from as close to the earth as possible and when instruments were not available, invented them. An artist in sound, he composed with scales dividing the octave into 43 unequal tones derived from the natural harmonic series. To play his music, he built a number of unique instruments with such quirky names as the Chromelodeon, the Quadrangularis Reversum, and the Zymo-Xyl.

About Music

Like John Luther Adams, Harry Partch described his music as corporeal, and distinguished it from abstract music, which he perceived as the dominant trend in western music since the time of Bach. His earliest compositions were small-scale pieces to be intoned to instrumental backing; his later works were large-scale, integrated theatre productions in which he expected each of the performers to sing, dance, speak, and play instruments. Ancient Greek theatre and Japanese Noh and kabuki influenced his music theatre.

Partch set up a studio in late 1962 in Petaluma, California, in a former chicken hatchery. There he composed 'And on the Seventh Day, Petals Fell in Petaluma'. He left in summer 1964 and spent his remaining decade in various cities in southern California. He rarely had work during this period, surviving on sparse grants, commissions, and record sales.

His final theatre work was 'Delusion of the Fury', which incorporated music from Petaluma and was first produced at the University of California in early 1969, while his final completed work was the soundtrack to Betty Freeman's 'The Dreamer that Remains'. In 1970, the Harry Partch Foundation was founded to handle the expenses and administration of his works.

Perhaps the most remarkable aspect of Harry Partch's output is the *Bitter Music* diaries that he kept during 1935-6, of his wanderings up and down America's West Coast, chronicling his experiences with pen and ink drawings, words and music. While struggling to keep body and soul together, Partch attempted to remake western music while in and out of jail, transient shelters and odd jobs that came his way.

His premise was that new music, to be true, could only come from the people, neither from institutions nor composers beholden to any tradition from a country other than the land on which they walked:

"I heard music in the voices of all about me, and tried to notate it, and I tried to enhance the mood and drama of such little things as a quarrel in a potato patch. The nuance of inflection and thought of the lowest of our social order was a new experience in tone and I found myself at its fountainhead – a fountainhead of pure musical Americana." So, here was a true heroic folk musician.

About Music

There follows a long descent to a straight road called Bwlch Penbarra which cuts through the mountains. I pick my way carefully down a steep slope to the end point for today's ramble and when I finally reach the road, all I have to do is navigate for a further mile or so to find the Druid Inn at Llanferres where I have booked a room for the night. After the spartan pods of the previous night, this will be a luxury I'm looking forward to.

Bill, with an unerring aim for the inn

About Music

CHAPTER FOURTEEN

Reprise – What Will Music Be?

*In which we hear the music of the spheres
and eat a blueberry muffin.*

The evening's stay in Llanferres at the Druid Inn has been enjoyable and I would like to have stayed longer. However, on waking I find there is adrenalin already coursing through my veins at the prospect of another – and the final – walk through the mountains. I open my window's curtain and see that it is another grey, misty day. This is fine by me as the drab atmosphere lends an appropriate spirit to the austere hillsides. They are not meant to be bright and colourful; they are imposingly sombre, steadfast places with muted colours that swirl and blend, Turneresque style.

There is a mile and a half to go back along the route that led into Llanferres before I find the Offa's Dyke path again at the foot of Foel Fenlli, the hill fort I came over last night. The route back is uphill along a quiet lane leading to the straight Bwlch Penbarra road.

For the final two days, I have decided to make one or two brief audio recordings and as I walk uphill along the lane, breathing a little heavily, I make the first off-the-cuff recording into my little portable recorder. Here is what I said.

> I'm at the beginning of the penultimate walk and would like to express a few personal thoughts. I'm walking up a very narrow lane away from the Druid Inn, where I stayed last night and in about half an hour I'll join the spot where I left the Offa's Dyke walk yesterday evening at a point lying about half way along this mountainous part of the route.
>
> It's the 20th September, nearly the autumn equinox; it's a grey overcast day with potential for rain later on but fortunately it is reasonably clear so I'm looking forward to some spectacular views. The final two days of this journey are going to be quite a thing for me after everything that has gone before, with all the effort that I've put into organising

it, but I can say quite categorically that the experience has been absolutely fantastic in many different ways.

Musically, this particular section is to do with the future of music and I'm not sure what that means of course, not being able to predict the future. What I do know from this brief survey is that there are so many different aspects to music making available to us now, the practical, the physical and scientific, that I'm sure a lot of interesting things are going to develop. These will be in the light of our increasing understanding of how the brain works and how it responds to music in such a holistic fashion for, as we have discovered, pretty much the whole of the brain fires off when it is listening to or making music.

A consequence is that the future of music could well lie in exploiting the brain/music relationship as we become clearer about what that is. Music might well be a major boon to people who have debilitating functions such as dementia.

It's warm and it's humid and I'm expecting to take my jacket off before long and we'll just see what lies ahead, what the future brings. I started off today at the Druid Inn breakfasting with a couple of Australian walkers who are completing the Offa's Dyke Path over two weeks. Naturally, I discovered their great interest in music. Very few people haven't got some sort of involvement so it's an easy talking point with strangers.

I'm a little bit nervous about today, partly because of the potential for bad weather and also the fact that I'm always at risk of coming off the track while walking on my own. In these bleak uplands, this is not a happy prospect. I've strayed from the path once or twice as I've put on record along earlier treks, but, so far, not with any great difficulty in getting back onto it. (Audio note ends.)

When I arrive at the Offa's Dyke path, there are already a few visitors milling around the car park at the beginning of the first climb. There is a heavy mist over the hills but it is dry underfoot. Now begins a long and steady climb up to the highest point of today's route, to Moel Fammau, 'Mother of the Mountains'.

About Music

It is truly a joy to make this walk in the damp air, warm as it is for the time of the year. As I approach the summit, I can see the giant memorial that has been built there, a folly which was constructed to mark the 50th year of the reign of King George III. In 1810, it is hard to imagine that thousands of people made their way up here for the dedication of the tower. The following year, the madness of George took hold and his son became regent for the remainder of his reign.

For 50 years, this building dominated the surrounding countryside but in 1862 autumn gales brought all but the tower's base crashing to the ground. It was never rebuilt, but work in 1970 brought some order to the then chaotic structure. Its location, significance and history all lend an air of significance that attracts visitors to stare, some open-mouthed, at this mountain-top folly. I am surprised by how many are already there before me today.

From the tower the path takes a change of direction and heads northwest, soon descending quite steeply next to a magnificent dry stone wall on my right, and with the watery gleam of Pwll y Rhos ahead. This pool is seen beyond the wall before the path rises again to Moel Dywell, with a large cairn marking the route. Another hilltop that I climb is Moel Llys-y-coed and from there I can see an even more evocative sight than the Jubilee Tower.

Embedded in the greying atmosphere, Moel Arthur is a great breast of a hill with clear hillfort terraces circumscribing its summit. There is no doubt in my mind that this is a place to stop and breathe in the prehistoric atmosphere which permeates the air. It is easy to picture ancient folk about their business on the mound, fires burning, food being prepared, earth being moved, buildings built. In my mind's eye, this bald mountain is a hive of activity. Its outline even looks like a bee hive. I take out my sound recorder and begin to speak into its microphone and record my thoughts again. Breaking the magical atmosphere with the sound of my voice. With no one else here to listen it feels a little uncomfortable at first but I persist. Here are some more of those notes that I recorded.

> The form of music is the frame that holds it together. It seems to me that those forms of music that were classically developed over time are disintegrating and there is nothing

collectively recognised taking their place. Music is becoming a picture without a frame, having no clear, defining borders. That is disturbing from the listener's point of view who likes to feel a sense of limit and definition. It is almost as if the music is literally escaping from its classical framework and is seeping into the surrounding world. With its traditional forms, we knew what to expect from music; it was played, we listened, we understood and appreciated. Now, music may be without performer, it may be in the landscape, it may simply be inside our heads. Who knows where it will go. We can be certain that something significant is happening. (Audio note ends.)

How are writing, performing and listening to music escaping from their frameworks into the 21st century and where are they going? Classically, composition was limited to the select few by education and personal circumstance. When writing, the composer needed to be able to hear with their inner ear what the end result would be. Without this ability, writing music was almost impossible because the means for trying out anything but a keyboard or solo instrument part was impractical. Today, computer software enables the modern composer to hear instantly the results of their compositions in multi-part harmony and with synthesised instruments. Not only this, but correcting, updating, reproducing or editing a score is always just a click away.

The result is that anyone with the inclination and the will can now become a composer. Even a few years ago, this would not have been possible. Is this a good thing? There are pros and cons. It is, whatever your point of view, a significant factor in the changing spirit of music.

Here's a potted portrait of a modern composer, compared with the moody creature who used to sit down with a quill pen and scratch inky marks on some parchment paper, balanced precariously on the top of a piano or harpsichord (the parchment not the composer). This new being uses a digital audio work station, patches and loops, samples and special effects, ready loaded into his mixing desk. Then, on stage, in front of a shouting, jumping audience, he starts with a bass line and synthesised drums. On that the remixes are layered of prerecorded music.

This is where the composition factor kicks in, for our composer can now be as creative as he can or wants, mixing in, mixing out. The audience love it and will groove along for hours. The place is jumping and our composer is having a great time, too. Oh, and don't forget the syncronised light show, the laser beams and disco lights, the backdrop film that turns the whole set into a spaceship or a volcano, a journey through mountains or a trip to the bottom of the sea. That's a face of contemporary composition, a skilful scribbling with sound.

The customary concert environment with audience positioned facing the performer is a relatively recent innovation which coincided with music's classical and romantic eras. The performer/audience relationship was challenged considerably by contemporary music through the 20th century but has largely remained impervious to change.

Concert formality is essential in maintaining standards and providing the cash to support music, performers and composers. Without the unpredictability, visual delights and socialising that make up a live performance, the listener misses a great deal that the spirit of music seeks to convey.

However, a much more informal presenting of live classical music has much to recommend it, particularly for any younger generation, schooled now in the wild informality of their music festivals. These are not anarchic but have their own rituals, stages with audience separate from performers, commercialised ticketing and merchandising with social media used to the full in this respect.

The formality of the classical concert is a relatively recent innovation. The apparent reverence that audiences hold for performers is a veneer and beneath this lies the old ways of audiences who express themselves throughout the music, as well as at its end. The apparent reverence for the composer's score was also not always so. For example, the performer would not necessarily start at the beginning of the piece, nor conclude at its end. Nothing to do with music performance is written in stone. Classical concert venues are remarkably slow in coming into the ways of the 21st-century generations but they are coming.

About Music

The opportunity to hear classical music used to be limited to royal courts, rich families and churches. Then concert halls and the making of music at home arrived. Later came recorded music, film, TV and radio. Now we have digital broadcasting, with music streaming into every room of your house controlled by your mobile phone and we have portable devices that can hold complete libraries of recordings.

Listening to live music is a social occasion. In contrast, a bi-product of digital technology is the ease of having your music with you and available any time and any place, with the ability to listen in complete privacy, 'between the ears'. A way of listening that is a private and intimate personal experience is a characteristic of our time.

You may remember that when I was preparing for this pilgrimage along the Dyke, I visited a contemporary art gallery in Middlesbrough. There I picked up a leaflet which was a beginner's guide to looking at modern art. Its content applies equally to listening to modern music. For example, I've substituted the words 'ears' for 'eyes' and 'music' for 'art' and this is the result: open your ears; listen to the piece of music; decide what you think of it; never let anyone tell you that you are wrong; enjoy yourself.

Top of the list about how to listen is that any preconceptions about what music is and what it should be doing have to be abandoned. I recently had an argument about music with a friend who was telling me what he required a piece of art to do, whether visual or audible. It should excite him, it should be expressive of the artist's feelings and thoughts, what the artist has created should be admirable. This is fine, but an overriding factor is to listen or see with an open mind, possessing not a single preconception of what art is or should be doing.

Rather like the recorded safety announcement on a well-known national bus service, which concludes with, "And now sit back, relax and enjoy the journey", my leaflet has advice to travellers: You are entering a preconception-free zone. Please leave behind: your ideas of what music should be, your conception of a familiar musical landscape or portrait; your prejudices about cacophony, discord and noise. Bring in: an open mind and open ears; your memories your stories, your ability to associate and connect,

About Music

your understanding of the human race and our endlessly varied journeys. Modern composers are like poets with sound: their work is packed with meaning and it is up to us to peel back the layers and start unpicking and interpreting.

We are surrounded by music as never before and can pick and choose what era and what style we wish to listen to at will. A price we pay is that sometimes we can't avoid music and it is piped into our ears whether we like it or not. History can be imagined as a timeline stretching back into the past. Now, it can be a sphere that surrounds us. Placing ourselves in the centre of this, music becomes person-centred, a little like returning the earth to the centre of the universe and creating another viewpoint on the music of the spheres.

There is a fragile comma butterfly spread-eagled on the path. Ravens are circling blackly overhead, croaking in their communicative deep-throated ancient way. It is a privilege to be here and I spontaneously begin to meditate. I stand, close my eyes and feel the ground beneath my feet, drawing up earth energy through the soles of my boots into my body. Then, eyes still closed, focusing inner awareness on the sky above, I draw down a different vibration through my head, down to meet and mingle with the force that is coming up from below. The sky and the earth meet in me and unite. I can hear a music and I like to think that at that moment in this spot I hear the music of the spheres, sounding not from without but from within, from where the true spirit of music lies.

The walking continues, first downhill, then up, hard going but delightful work along clear and even pathways. The mist has lifted but not completely cleared as I reach one more hillfort. Penycloddian is unlike the others for it is half a mile long and, unusually, the path travels right along the top rather than skirting it. There then follows a long, three-mile descent into Bodfari and I have to focus on navigation again.

I arrive at a road leading into this small town. The first building I reach is a pub called the Downing Arms which I note for later use and opposite this, a steep hill, still on the official path, leading to my place for the night. My B&B has spectacular iron gates at its entrance and when I arrive the owners are out but have left me

About Music

instructions to find my room, an exceptionally large bathroom – and a complimentary blueberry muffin. I make use of all the facilities.

In the evening, I take my notebook to record the day's events and head back down the hill to the pub. 'Downing' is an interesting name, not one I've encountered for a pub, more usually represented by the King's Head or Fox and Hounds, etc. The naturalist and travel writer Thomas Pennant (1726-98) came from Downing, not so very far away, but the connection may be with the titled family of that name. The first baronet, Sir George Downing, fought for the parliamentary cause in the Civil War and later followed a diplomatic career under Cromwell and also for Charles II after the Restoration. Downing built the row of terraced houses off Whitehall in London which bears his name, with its number 10 the most famous address in the country, let alone the capital.

The pub is a honey-pot for walkers. On Sundays, when they are not serving food in the bar, I am told that the management orders up a Chinese meal and leaves the dishes out for walkers to stumble across as they, in their exhaustion, hunger and thirst, stagger happily into this veritable oasis.

For music to be music, is an audience, or at least a listener required? John Cage highlighted this with the most famously misunderstood piece of music ever created, 4' 33". The piece proscribed an audience but no sound content, other than the normal coughs, scufflings and other ambient sounds ever present in the concert hall. His point was to impose this very question.

Considering it from the opposite viewpoint, when there is sound content but no audience, like the famous Zen conundrum - does the sound of a tree falling in a forest exist if there is no one there to hear it? - does a piece of performed music exist without a listener? And, after a piece of music has been written, does it remain as only the idea of a piece of music until it is performed, converted into sound, with an audience?

These may seem wildly abstract questions, but they force us to consider music not as just an event external to us, for it is clearly possible to imagine music, to hear it inwardly. Most people can imagine tunes, sometimes a tune will get stuck in one's head and go round and round, so-called ear-worms. Gifted musicians can hear

About Music

complex music and harmony and may even have the ability then to write it down. Music is becoming appreciated as a personal experience, an inner process, a function of the brain and this situation is clear when you consider the physics of acoustics. As we discovered earlier, music exists only as mechanical vibration until it is perceived by the brain.

With these questions and whatever our definition of music may be – organised sound, say - it is a fact that our understanding of what music is, our experience of it and our appreciation of it, is fundamentally changing. This process was begun in the 20th century, became clear with contemporary music post WW II and today the perpetual revolution in music continues apace caught up and swept along by digital technology, social media and our rapidly developing understanding of how the brain works.

Imagine in the future that music will be made knowing precisely the effect that it has on our consciousness and our unconscious thought processes, emotions and psychological complexes. Imagine that music will be fed directly from its source into particular areas of the brain for pleasure or for therapy.

I'd say that these radical changes do not mean a loss of the old, simply a broadening out to encompass new and more varied forms. We'll still be appreciating classical music for many years to come and that means continuing the formality and the joy of live performance. Nevertheless, it's the hologram, the brain scanner, streaming and high-tech audio feeds that will shape the future of music.

🌰 It is worth recording here that I have been humbled by the goodwill there is towards walkers and what friendship there is amongst them. It is so easy to chat with others along the way – there is no ice to break, just a natural and easy sharing of experiences. The hostelries and resting places have without exception all gone just one step further than they needed to for commercial expediency, to welcome and encourage the walker. It is as if we walkers were carrying out a function that has value and is appreciated, but if encouraged to state exactly what that function is, I would be hard pressed to do so.

Bill, with one more day to go

About Music

CHAPTER FIFTEEN

The Spirit of Music

In which the sun rises and sets at the same time and we meet old friends.

The walk out of Bodfari leads uphill and follows the fence line with Moel y Gaer and its fort rising on the left. I find a convenient wooden bench to adjust my clothing to suit today's weather conditions and to take stock of what lies ahead. In contrast with the previous days, the sky is cloudless and blue, the air is clear and the sun is shining brightly. It almost seems pre-ordained. The previous days in the hills have been shrouded in mist, enhancing their ancient and mystical, lonely atmosphere but now to mark the final stage and a walk through quiet fields and lanes to the sea, the sun has emerged to guide me home.

As I re-shoulder my rucksack, I notice that on the bench there is a small plaque: 'Bless the weather that brought you to me.' I am unsure what this means but it carries a certain significance that resonates with my heart. Perhaps a couple of lovers met here once on a sunny day like today.

The words, I discover later, are lyrics from a song by John Martyn whose constant refrain is, 'Bless the weather that brought you to me; Curse the storm that takes you away.' For me, the line on the bench is a suggestion of how great it is to be alive and to be at this place, today, now. I begin to record my audio diary for the day. It translates roughly as the following.

At the beginning of this little adventure, I perhaps rather foolishly suggested that what might emerge is an understanding or at least an awareness of what the spirit of music might be. This was a fanciful idea. What has surprised me is that I can, as a result of everything I have considered and experienced say something about this.

About Music

To say what the essence of anything might be has to be an imaginative speculation but the idea of an essence of music has become more than imaginative through undertaking this whole exploration of walking the borderlands. The key element is that music is all pervasive. It doesn't need a framework or anything else that might limit it.

When you listen to or play music, your whole being is responding, body and mind. There is more. Music does not just happen inside, in the brain, but outside, too. It is in nature, in birdsong, in the wind, in the earth, in the unconscious mind. Imagine that music is a secret stream, always running under the surface, beneath your feet. Every now and again it emerges, like a volcano erupting or a geyser spurting up from below and what we see – or rather what we hear – is music. Pieces of music are the manifestation of something that is there all the time. Musicians don't make the music; they release it from inside – from below. So, that's the spirit of music. It's not what we hear for those few minutes of listening; it's a life force there all the time, a secret stream.

The first stage of today's walk is amongst some outliers of the Clwydians, so substantial physical effort is still needed, although my average walking speed is quicker than on previous days, reflecting the generally easier terrain. This has a down side as it means that, if not mindful, I will finish the final walk before I know it, so I determine to make slower progress and savour these concluding miles. This is not so easy, as, like most people, I have a natural walking rhythm and instinctively fall back into it.

The scenery is exceptionally varied giving me a recapitulation of the whole glorious symphonic, pastoral, mountainous experience. Then something else happens that makes me realise that events, like the approach of some music's finale, are being restated. I see ahead of me the two Australian walkers that I had met at the Druid Inn. We greet each other like long lost friends and talk about our experiences since breakfasting together two days before. I'm not surprised to learn that tonight they are staying at the same guest house as myself – of course they are. Where else? We laugh and joke before I walk on, leaving them to take their own good time.

About Music

Ahead, I can hear traffic noise as the path approaches a major road and a bridge over the A55 trunk route near Rhuallt. Beyond this is a steep path up by the side of a wood, then an easy trek along a narrow lane into the village of Marian Cwm, then up again onto the high ground of Marian Ffrith. I am shocked to find motorcyclists scrambling around the hillside here. After the care taken to divert walkers from hillfort tops to avoid erosion, this seems to be a travesty. However, they are clearly having a great time and I expect a track has been laid out for them. The noise from their exhausts stays with me for the next mile or so.

The psychological process of growing and maturing has been described as one of discovering all the different facets of oneself and then marrying them into a complete life. Nietzsche, like the hermetic, alchemical philosophers, explained this as a marriage of opposites, achievable through art and in particular music.

Music can be a path to enlightenment; one of many paths, but a valid one nevertheless. To arrive at an ultimate destination requires a long journey during which every piece of music, every style and genre can present an opportunity to respond and learn about oneself. Music is not just an entertainment and this is probably why Plato made his complaint, "Through foolishness they deceived themselves into thinking that there was no right or wrong way in music, that it was to be judged good or bad by the pleasure it gave."

The spirit of music has the ability to influence us and change us. We know this to be a physical fact when all those neurones fire off and release hormones into the brain. Music can push us to become whole, to unite mind and body, to strive for individuation.

From my elevated path I see on the horizon that the sky has taken on a different hue and contains some tiny, white rotating objects. It takes several moments before I realise I am looking at a wind farm in the ocean. This is my first glimpse of the sea and I know that I am heading towards the end of the Offa's Dyke trail with every step heralding the last. There is not far to go now. I navigate over several stone styles and begin to encounter other walkers enjoying the late summer sunshine.

About Music

The final stretch of countryside is along Prestatyn's hillside cliffs. There are juniper trees growing here, a species of only three native conifers. This is the time and place to make a final brief audio diary, for I want to put on record my feelings, which are mixed. There is joy at being privileged to have been able to experience this wonderful walk and there is sadness that it will soon be over.

Time is accelerating, the minutes and miles cruising by and I have no brake. Then I am descending, picking my way down the hillside path, the sea a constant companion on my left while I am walking east for the last stretch and before I can find a way to suspend time, I reach Prestatyn and a metalled road.

That is that. The path passes the front door of my guest house for the night so I call in, meet the hosts, leave my backpack behind and then continue to the sea front. There is just the formality now of reaching the very end of the trail. It's a straight road through the main shops, over the railway line and station, along a wide, open stretch that leads to the sea; the end – almost.

Playing and listening to music is an endless process of self-discovery. Finding out what you respond to and how you respond, finding out what your limits are, discovering what turns you on and what repulses you, communicating with others, playing with others, developing technique, learning to play in an ensemble, going to a concert, listening on your own, all these can be elements in a process of discovery, a personal journey that everyone can take and in so doing meet with others on the way. Whatever you discover in music, you will discover in yourself.

On the sea front, I find the stone that marks the end of the route and am pleased to see nearby a tall silvery metal sculpture called 'Ends and Beginnings' erected to celebrate this conclusion, or beginning of the path, with an image of the sun. For those starting from this point to head south it appears to rise against the eastern sky and for those, like myself, who are concluding their adventure, it sets in the west. There is no welcome party, no fanfare, so I purchase a celebratory coffee and sign the café's book proving to the world that I have arrived. Then I go to the beach for a paddle. It is over.

Post Script. Our journey started in Babylonia, with priestly astrologers and went via Pythagoras to the Middle Ages. Throughout

About Music

this time, the spirit of music was projected into the cosmos which reflected back down to earth the wonders of harmony.

Then our journey continued through the Renaissance and the Age of Enlightenment, when Descartes questioned everything and created a clear division, the cartesian duality, between mind and matter, between art and science, between inner and outer realms of experience, and the music of the spheres fell silent.

Arriving today, we find that composers, in their disconnect from the cosmic musical spheres, have turned to explore their inner universe. New music, like that of the old, is not an expression of the composer's feelings and beliefs but is music with a selfless and spiritual purpose, meant to make the brain respond and resonate with musical awareness. The music of the spheres is resounding again, this time inside ourselves where the spirit of music is most easily found.

The next morning, I go down to breakfast in the guest house and find my Australian friends already seated and to my surprise in conversation with the young Japanese traveller who I met in Montgomery, many miles before. They are discussing how rambling is a pastime for the old and the young alike. This coincidence of we walkers meeting together pleases me. It seems to have a neat symmetry telling me that all along there have been – and always will be – subtle forces at work just underneath the surface, bringing events into alignment, adding a dash of the unexpected, making our paths through life an adventurous wonder. The music continues.

Bill, wondering where to go now

About Music

SOME OF THE SOURCES USED

Background Noise: Perspectives on Sound Art by Brandon LaBelle (Bloomsbury)

Computer Orchestration: Tips and Tricks by Stephen Bennett (PC Publishing)

A Concise History of Western Music by Paul Griffiths (Cambridge University Press)

Emblems of Mind: The Inner Life of Music and Mathematics by Edward Rothstein (The University of Chicago Press)

Fear of Music: why people get Rothko but don't get Stockhausen by David Stubbs (Zero Books)

The Great Animal Orchestra (finding the origins of music in the world's wild places) by Bernie Krause (Profile Books/Little, Brown & Co.). Focus is entirely on sounds and 'music' within the natural world.

Harmonies of Heaven and Earth: from Antiquity to the Avant-garde by Joscelyn Godwin

How Equal Temperament Ruined Harmony: and why you should care by Ross W. Duffin (W.W. Norton and Company, NY)

The Inner Game of Music by Barry Green (Pan)

Leaving Home: A conducted tour of 20th century music by Michael Hall (Faber)

Listen to This by Alex Ross (Harper Collins, 2011)

The Music of the Spheres: Music, science and the natural order of the universe by Jamie James (Abacus)

About Music

Music and the Mind by Anthony Storr (Harper Collins). First published in 1992, still in print

Musicophilia: Tales of Music and the Brain by Oliver Sachs (Knopf Doubleday). Focused on the neuropsychology of how music can transform our cognition, behaviour and sense of self.

Music Therapy: an art beyond words by Leslie Bunt (Routledge)

The Musical Mind: the cognitive psychology of music by John A. Sloboda (OUP)

The Music Instinct (how music works and why we can't do without it) by Philip Ball (Vintage, 2011)

Of Mozart, Parrots and Cherry Blossoms in the Wind: A composer explores mysteries of the musical mind (Limelight Editions, NY)

The Rest is Noise by Alex Ross (Harper Perennial)

Silence: lectures and writings by John Cage (Marion Boyars)

The Singing Neanderthals – the Origins of Music, Language, Mind and Body by Steven Mithen (Orion Books, 2006)

This Is Your Brain On Music – Understanding a Human Obsession by Daniel Levitin (Dutton, 2007)

Through Music to the Self by Peter Michael Hamel (Scherz Verlag)

Walking Home – Travels with a Troubadour on the Pennine Way by Simon Armitage (Liveright, 2016)

About Music

Contact the author:

billanderton90@gmail.com
www.billanderton.blogspot.com
www.facebook.com/billandertonmusic

www.billanderton.uk

www.ingramcontent.com/pod-product-compliance
Lightning Source LLC
Chambersburg PA
CBHW022110040426
42450CB00006B/655